FROM A CANOE TO A CHEVY

Brazil - Ministries and Memories

Ralph J. Poulson

To Joyce
What a joy you have been
to us through the years.
We pray this will be good
reading for you.

Ralph J Poulson

(Lam 3:22-23)

INTRODUCTION

T he title for the book comes from our earlier days on the Amazon, when canoes were the main transportation. We were fortunate, however, to have a motorized craft, which made traveling much easier. When we moved to the big city, we purchased a Chevrolet, thus the name: From a Canoe to a Chevy.

Have you ever read *untold stories* of missionary life? Are you ready to hear some *unusual* but real stories from Brazil? Are you in a hurry and prefer short stories?

This book will give you what you are looking for. The stories and anecdotes here are short, to the point, and very interesting. The reader will benefit from this book because spiritual and practical lessons are given at the conclusion of each chapter.

This book was written to tell the world how we faced the day-to-day experiences on the mission field. It gives the *raw side* of missions. It tells the personal family issues and choices missionaries face on foreign soil.

Each chapter takes the usual happenings on the mission field and unfolds them the way they actually happened. In this unfolding process, you will be intrigued with what goes on.

In the first chapters you will get acquainted with our ministry. Each chapter is short, and soon you will be traveling with us down the Amazon River—our first trip on this gigantic waterway. You will not forget the gas-saving method used to get us to our destination. Thereafter, each story will catch your attention, and you will see the marvelous way God introduced us to our dear Brazilian friends. They taught us a lot, but at the same time you will discover how we were able to impact their lives.

DEDICATION

———❦———

We dedicate this book to:

- The many unnamed but precious Brazilian friends that God allowed us to evangelize, disciple and serve with, during our twenty-four years on the field.
- To the Association of Baptists for World Evangelism (ABWE), that sponsored us during our stay in Brazil.
- To our home church — First Baptist Church of Ferndale, Washington, who, along with others, made it possible for us to accomplish our ministry. Without their prayers and financial support this would not have been possible.
- To Shepherds Home in Union Grove, Wisconsin, which lovingly cared for our developmentally challenged daughter, Joy, for forty-five years. Without their help we would never have been able to remain on foreign soil to serve the Lord.

To each of these we agree with the apostle Paul who said it best. *I thank my God upon every remembrance of you.* (Philippians 1:3)

ACKNOWLEDGMENTS

───❦───

I thank my wife, Margie, for the multitude of hours spent reading our journals, carefully selecting seed-thoughts for these stories. This is a considerable task since we have fifty-nine journals; one for each year we have been married.

Our son, Rawlie, has kept insisting we write a story about our years in Brazil. His encouragement has been the main, but not the only, motivation to embark on this enjoyable journey.

We are indebted to friends who have heard us tell some of our stories repeatedly and have encouraged us to put them in book form for others to enjoy.

Our thanks go to Helen Steele, who at the last minute willingly proof-read an unedited story. As a result of this, she read the entire manuscript, giving valuable suggestions which were needed and appreciated.

It was suggested we have one more person read the final manuscript. Our friend Laurel Hicks did this, and we appreciate her help. Her work for over thirty years with A Beka Book in Pensacola, Florida gave this final editing a delightful and practical touch.

We want to thank my brothers Ernest and Harold, and our son Rawlie and wife Gina along with our friends Stephen & Victoria Adenau for their tangible and kind, generous assistance, enabling us to dedicate time to this project.

Last but not least, we thank the Lord for leading us to Brazil. His watch care over us and direction in our lives made it possible to have the wonderful experiences we share in this book.

ENDORSEMENTS

———∞∞∞———

I have known Ralph and Margie Poulson from the time I was a child and have been enriched spiritually by the testimony of their ministries. This book, written in a humble, God-honoring way, takes the reader into the heart of missions. That is a good place to be.

Laurel Hicks, Litt.D, editor, A Beka Book (retired)

I'm recommending this book to every person who is interested in learning how the Lord can work in the life of a believer, as well as the blessings one enjoys and the sacrifices one makes when choosing this path. It was hearing of bits and pieces from Ralph and Margie Poulson's life in Brazil that I had heard before, as well as their personal, humble testimony when they returned home, that encouraged me to join the mission field ten years ago.

Helen Steele, serving at the Greek Bible College in Greece.

". . . . .I'm honored to edit the work of my former BIOLA roommate!."

*". . . . .Last night and this evening I read through all the material you sent. It was all so interesting that I just kept going. **It gave me a new appreciation of your** ministry there."*

". . . . .Ralph, you have a nice writing style: personal and warm. It is a pleasure to read. "

". . . . .These stories give an interesting picture of your life in Brazil. And your chapters are well written."

". . . . .It was a pleasure to read your material. I hope the book will be a blessing to many people."

(Dr. Roy B. Zuck, senior professor emeritus of Bible Exposition and editor of Bibliotheca Sacra, Dallas Theological Seminary, editor, and long-time personal friend of the author, went to be with the Lord on the evening of Saturday, March 16, 2013. He finished editing this book before he died. This endorsement has been taken from the many emails we had exchanged.)

TIMELINE

———⊶⊷———

- Ralph Poulson: born February 26, 1931, in Miami, Florida
- Marjorie (Monroe) Poulson: born July 16, 1930 in Bellingham, Washington
- Ralph and Margie Poulson married August 20, 1954, at First Baptist Church, Ferndale Washington
- Departure for Brazil: March 1957 to serve with the Association of Baptists.
- Rawlie Poulson: born December 1, 1957, São Paulo, Brazil
- Joy Poulson: born October 31, 1959, Iquitos, Peru
- Permanent departure from Brazil after twenty-four years of service: December 1981
- Called to pastor First Baptist Church, Ferndale, Washington: October 1981

MAP OF BRAZIL

TABLE OF CONTENTS

—∞∞∞—

FIRST TRIP DOWN THE AMAZON RIVER

———— ✺ ————

The trip from the States was grueling. We circled an hour in the clouds over Colombia, trying to get clearance to land, but Bogota was socked in, so we had to take a lesser airport before continuing on to Bogota much later.

In Bogota we were met by missionary John Schlener, who accompanied us in a much smaller plane over the Andes Mountains to the jungle town of Leticia located on the bank of the mighty Amazon River where Colombia, Peru, and Brazil come together.

Going from the small airport to John's boat docked at the muddy bank of the river, was without event; soon we were on that immense river called the Amazon. We were excited. This was our first experience of traveling on such a huge body of water. John kept us entertained with all sorts of tales of his years of adventure on this river. Rubbish floated all around us, and he had to carefully dodge the bigger items in order not to get anything entwined in the propeller.

After a long time, we came alongside a huge floating tree which, if standing upright, would be several stories high. John had an idea. Why not latch onto that huge floating hunk and let its branches take us along the river, and save fuel? So with the motor turned off and the boat securely tied to the floating tree, we quietly made our way downstream. When we got closer to the Port of Two Brothers, John untied the rope, started the engine, and motored over to the bank near his home. We were mighty glad to be there, having experienced our first view of and first ride on the Amazon. In a way this was our first introduction to Brazil. We had planned, prayed, and worked hard to get to this point. How gracious it was of the Lord to allow us to spend our first night in Brazil in the home of the missionary who had introduced us to this country and to the mission agency, Association of Baptists for World Evangelism (ABWE). What a joy to keep our eyes on the Lord and ask Him to lead us! *I will instruct you and teach you in the way you should go; I will guide you with My eye.* (Psalm 32:8)

MERENDA SNACK TIME

Living in the Port of Two brothers was an experience we will never forget. We got our missionary start in this small village, which had been named for John Schlener and his brother Paul. We had already completed language school, could converse fairly well in Portuguese, and had even preached one time in the language. But this was a learning experience. Margie had the same attitude. It was a learning time for her also to get used to the routine procedures of jungle life. Away from grocery stores, pharmacies, post offices, and department stores, the everyday routines of living took on a new meaning.

Margie learned from Fran and Jessie Schlener that one of the highlights every week was the Thursday afternoon call for "Snack Time." In Portuguese it was "Merenda." Both Americans and Brazilians looked forward to that call each week. Thursday was baking day. To do any baking required much preparation. Flour was purchased in huge cloth sacks. It had to be sifted carefully to get rid of all the living things in it. Milk had to be mixed from powder form, and all ingredients had to be on hand before such a project could be completed.

No electric stoves were available for baking pastry. We used Perfection kerosene-powered stoves that looked similar to the stoves you have in your kitchens except they were not electric or gas. The kerosene had to be purchased from a river boat in 55 gallon drums, just like gasoline.

But the Thursday call for snacks had come. Let's go into the Schlener kitchen and take a look at the counter. There were loaves of beautiful freshly baked bread and cinnamon rolls. The glaze on top of caramel-like icing was so tempting! Thursday was a big day on the mission station. Every other week the ladies traded off and were the hostesses for the event. A cup of coffee and a freshly baked cinnamon roll were "out of this world." This along with all the chatter of missionaries was a delight to witness. This was an institution.

God's Word talks about fellowship with Jesus Christ and with one another: ***But if we walk in the light as He is in the light, we have fellowship with one another, and the blood of Jesus Christ His Son cleanses us from all sin.*** (I John 1:7) How great it was to have these special times of fellowship with each other, and all because of Christ, the One who had sent us to Brazil to preach the gospel.

LIKE TIN SOLDIERS

——⁂——

Some experiences leave indelible impressions on us as we review God's leading. At the Port of Two Brothers, Margie and I were soon alone, as the Schlener brothers and their wives went home on their regular furlough. We attempted to maintain the work they had started years ago. Besides the regular services in Portuguese at the Baptist church in our little village, we also conducted a special service for hundreds of Ticuna Indians who came to the station on Sundays. As they walked across the compound lawn, it sounded like a soft breeze blowing. It takes a lot of feet to make that kind of noise. They all stood for the entire service.

Before the Indians constructed their own church building (which was enormous), we met in the yard just outside our Baptist school building. Hundreds of Indians gathered at one side of the school house. Because I never learned their language, Miguel served as my interpreter. I always gave him credit for being able to listen to the Portuguese spoken by us Americans and translate it into his native Ticuna tonal language.

TICUNA INDIAN CHURCH

The Indians attended church in great numbers. Sometimes there would be as many as 1,500 standing in the hot sun listening as long as I preached. The amazing part of this service was their rapt attention to what was being said. They stood like tin soldiers, hardly moving. Adults, children, and babies – all were very quiet. The ladies wore "baby slings" over their shoulders. In each was a baby lying in its cozy hammock. Seldom did we hear the babies cry, and we never learned the mothers' secret. It was impressive how well behaved their children were.

The Schleners had a good supply of gospel recordings in the Ticuna language. It was our privilege to know Joy Riderhoff, the founder and director of the Gospel Recordings ministry. She had recorded songs and Scripture in the Ticuna dialect, and we played these before the preaching part of the service.

Now, just a word about some interesting sounds occasionally heard during a Ticuna Indian service. Besides a crying baby (which was seldom) you could hear miniature monkeys "singing their songs." These animals were less than the size of one's index finger and very cute. We called them lion-faced monkeys, but we are sure there must be a scientific name for them. The women actually use them as hairpieces, and so there were several of them in the congregation. They are ordinarily well behaved, but occasionally they let out a shrill screech like the call of a canary. Maybe because of live inhabitants in their hair, women also place a vanilla bean pod in their hair. This cuts down on the otherwise disagreeable odor that could be produced by a combination of hot weather, oily hair, and a living monkey.

A footnote to this story is fitting. After we had left this station, Paul Schlener had the singular blessed experience of witnessing a real revival among the Ticuna Indians. For a long time, scores of Indians came daily seeking the missionary, wanting to accept Jesus Christ as their Saviour. What a wonderful thing it was to hear Paul relate this inspirational story! We are so thankful for these missionaries who pioneered this ministry. Jesus said, ***Go into all the world and preach the gospel to every creature***. (Mark 16:15)

JUNGLE DEPRESSION

—∞∞∞—

The Bible clearly states in Ephesians 6:12, *For we do not wrestle against flesh and blood, but against principalities, against powers, against the rulers of the darkness of this age, against spiritual hosts of wickedness in the heavenly places*. We may not know how to explain this theologically, but suffice it to say, Christian workers experience depression sometimes while they are doing God's work.

Many times on Sunday nights before we would walk down the pathway to the little thatch-covered Baptist church, I would literally be sick. I would lie down feeling so badly that I wondered how I could stand and preach in front of the people. I prayed and committed myself to the Lord. There is one thing I knew would be true: even though I was depressed, sick, weak, and feeling completely unable to preach, I knew God would help me. He did, so every time I was able to proclaim the message He had given me for that sermon. Another thing I knew was when it was all over, I would feel perfectly well and all would seem quite normal, so I rejoiced in God's blessing during the service. I firmly believe that our faithful supporters at home who prayed for our ministry were key to our success.

I remember being alone in our boat, returning just before dark on the Amazon River after an important trip for supplies, medicine, etc., and being almost overtaken by the feeling of enemy oppression. Thankfully I would pray, plead the blood of Jesus, and sing hymns of praise to the Lord. He ALWAYS saw me through those rough times and brought me safely home. I experienced the truth of 1 John 4:4, *You are of God, little children, and have overcome them, because He who is in you is greater than he who is in the world.* Thank God for the indwelling of the Holy Spirit and His intercessory ministry for us in times like these. According to Romans 8:26, *Likewise the Spirit also helps in our weaknesses. For we do not know what we should pray for as we ought, but the Spirit Himself makes intercession for us with groanings which cannot be uttered.*

The lesson for us is this: When a name comes to your mind of someone you know, or don't know, please pray for them; you are being prompted by the Holy Spirit to minister in prayer for someone who needs it at that very moment.

OUCH!

———∞∞∞———

According to one research article, a single square mile of rainforest often houses more than 50,000 insect species. Many articles attest to the fact that this area of the Amazon has millions of insect species.

The missionaries introduced us to a fly which they called a "delta wing." Actually they did not need to introduce us, because the flies introduced themselves. They had an obnoxious bite which one did not soon forget. These insects were attracted by certain odors. One day we were having a picnic on a sandbar, enjoying the luxury of a propane powered stove. Before long, our "visitors" had detected the smell of gas and were intrigued by it. They covered the pipes and places where the odor was coming from.

Another nuisance fly was about the size of a flake of pepper and so prolific and abundant in certain seasons and areas that people had to eat their meals covered by mosquito netting. There were so many millions that they look like smoke, and they were miserable to be around. They also bite, and that's why we called them: "wings and a set of teeth." Those who live on the Amazon tributaries are plagued more than others by this species.

Another pesky fly was what we referred to as an "upright vacuum cleaner". An upright vacuum cleaner usually collects dust and dirt in a bag. Well, this is what these insects did. We would scratch our arm because it itched, and blood would appear. It was because those bugs had bitten us and were filling their bodies with our blood. We gave this annoying insect the name: a miniature vacuum cleaner.

With so many millions of insects in the Amazon, you can well imagine what a fight we had dealing with them. Someone said the most noticeable thing about missionaries on furlough in the States, was they were not scratching. How true. Little things can be such a nuisance. Christians have problems with temptations, just as we had with so many malicious insects in Brazil. We need to always be on our toes spiritually; that's why the New Testament warns us to *Watch and pray lest you enter into temptation. The spirit indeed is willing, but the flesh is weak*. (Matthew 26:41)

GASOLINE IN THE WRONG PLACE

—⁂—

A t The Port of Two Brothers, the missionary wives taught children's Bible classes, and the men usually worked with the adults. We all had a hand in teaching in the school. To help my wife teach her classes, I painted some flannel backgrounds on which she would place cutouts of Bible characters and other items as she taught the lessons to the children. I washed out my artist brushes with gasoline, the only product available for such a task. I kept a glass of gasoline in a safe place against the wall at the back of the table I used for painting.

Safe until our son somehow climbed up and over all the stuff on the table and got the gasoline and quickly drank it. In seconds we caught our tragic mistake and wondered what to do. Fran Schlener, fellow missionary, tore out a page of Dr. Spock and rushed it over to us, showing we should NOT let Rawlie vomit. That would be serious. Dilution of the stomach contents was the partial first aid. Rawlie was in my arms, turning blue and dying. The closest hospital was 100 miles upstream by motor boat, and the journey would have taken several hours. Our son adored one of John Schlener's boys, nicknamed Pito. Only by the help of God was Pito able to coax

Rawlie to ingest some very strong chocolate milk. Thanks to much prayer, it diluted the gasoline and saved his life. Thank God it did. At all times we should totally depend on God. A trip to the nearest hospital would have taken hours, and Rawlie would not have survived. It was only the Lord's mercies that saved him that day. How thankful we are! ***Through the LORD'S mercies we are not consumed, Because His compassions fail not. They are new every morning; Great is Your faithfulness.*** (Lamentations 3:22)

FISH STORIES

M y first fishing trip on the Amazon was with the Schlener
brothers. We anchored at a choice spot, and that day
I caught several large catfish and two of the prized tambaqui
fish. That was a wonderful feeling for someone who is not a
fisherman. This fish was the favorite for many meals.

There is a fascination with the famous piranha fish. These
are deadly, and fishermen have to handle them with much
care to prevent serious consequences. Remember when the
7-UP commercial was: "You like it—it likes you"? That describes
the piranha fish. They do like to attack us, and for sure they
make for good eating.

One time John and Paul Schlener had a local resident carry
a canoe to one of the many lakes on a nearby island in the
middle of the Amazon River. In this canoe we paddled around
on the lake and looked down through crystal clean water.
There were multiplied thousands of piranhas. You would not
dare dangle a finger in that water, because they are ferocious.
We were grateful the canoe stayed upright.

John Schlener, returning home in his small outboard motor
boat one day, hit a large fish, and the impact threw him out

of the boat. It may have been an Amazon pink river dolphin. He yelled loudly, and a lady and her daughter paddled out to get him and saved his life. He also was able to rescue his boat, which was going full speed in circles around them. That was a scary moment. Later, John and I returned to the spot where the accident occurred and filmed the sequences that were later made into a film. This film urged people to pray for missionaries. You never know when they are going through situations that need prayer support.

BRAZILIAN TARRAFA NET FISHING

According to reports, the Amazon River has between 2,000 and 5,000 species of fish. Truly there must be a wealth of stories that could be told about many of them. We were always entertained as we watched fisherman use their fishing nets, called tarrafas. These nets, made from strong twine, are circular and have weights at the bottom edge. As a net is thrown, the secret is making it keep its circular shape as it hits the water. The weights take it downward, and it encircles and catches the fish.

The pirarucu is the largest fish in the Amazon. Some reach 15 feet in length, but most are smaller than this. Brazilians salt the meat and hang the huge slabs of meat on racks to dry in the sun. When there is a scarcity of fish in the dry season, this delicious dried pirarucu is appreciated.

I am reminded of the true fish story in John 21:6, when Jesus told the disciples to *Cast the net on the right-hand side of the ship and you will find a catch.* They did as He said, and they caught a great number of fish.

A KNOT HOLE FOR A SUNDIAL

———⬦———

We never cease to be amazed how folks who have so little don't seem to miss a whole lot. On our visit to the little village of Santa Rita on the Amazon River, we visited a gentleman who was a member of our church. He was a kind man who made his living simply by living off the land and from the abundance of fish in the great river.

This man had been severely bitten by a very venomous snake. It took years for the hideous-looking spot to heal. The venom had eaten away a good part of the surface of his leg at the spot where the snake bit him. In spite of much medication, it certainly took its toll on this poor man's limb. As I was talking with him, I was delighted to hear of his great faith and trust in God. As we sat in his simple thatch-roofed home on a home-made chair or bench, we were intrigued to hear him tell his stories of survival in these awesome jungles that surrounded us. We visited for a long time, and when it seemed the time was getting away from us, I casually asked him what time it was. He squinted toward the wall as if doing some mathematical calculation, and said, "It's 3:30."

That answer puzzled me, and I asked how he knew. He said, "See that knothole in the wall board?" I glanced at it while he explained that the sun shining through it cast a shadow on the opposite wall. He knew from experience that when the sun was in "that" spot, the time was about 3:30. I checked my wristwatch and saw that he was right.

We learned so much from the Brazilians and will always be thankful to the Lord for that. In Bible times, the sundial was used. We read about it in **Isaiah 38:8**. The Brazilians had their own way of telling time by the sun, and we were intrigued to see how they did it.

SURVEY TRIP OUT ON A LIMB

———⊗⊗⊗———

John Schlener invited me to join him on a survey trip to find new towns and villages where we could hold gospel services. We left in the cool of the evening, and to economize fuel, we made a sea anchor. A five gallon can of water lowered into the river and tightly secured to the boat did the trick. The current took us down the main stream, thus saving much fuel. There are no gas stations along the way, so ingenuity is needed. We had to carry all the gas for the trip back home, which would be upstream.

We floated all night and eventually discovered that the wind had blown us off course and around a loop of the river. Our boat gently nudged against the bank, where the largest mosquitoes we have ever seen invaded the boat. What a mess! Finally we got back into the main stream again, and in the morning darkness we were awakened by the sound of rushing water. We were puzzled. We heard a thud and more gushing water. John checked the motor; water was just about to rush over the stern of the boat. In seconds we would be deluged with water and sink. We were on a huge tree stuck in a sand bar and literally "out on a limb." We had a prayer meeting, and I decided to check the motor again. John yelled, "Don't go out there Ralph". I was overweight and would have sunk the boat for sure. I had an idea: I shook the boat with my extra pounds helping, and soon the boat slipped off the limb. We had many other experiences on that trip. In Hebrews 13:5 we are told that the Lord *will never leave us*. What comfort this is for His children!

HOW IT ALL BEGAN

Margie and I were students at Biola Bible College in Los Angeles. We did not know each other. My brother Ernie was studying there but would soon graduate and be off to the mission field. I was interested in missions because of my brother, who planned on serving in Indonesia. A man from that country by the name of Ais Pormes studied at Biola. He headed a group called Christ for Indonesia Fellowship.

RALH & MARGIE POULSON

I noticed Margie in the school library each night and was definitely attracted to her. But she had a "friend" who sat with her each evening, so I knew that I would not be able to pursue her. One evening after several months, I noticed her by herself. That continued for some time, so I concluded that that friendship may have ended. I braved the storm and began visiting with her and eventually asked for a date. At vacation time from school I traveled to Ferndale, Washington, her home, to meet her family and visit her church. It was wonderful to do both. I had never been in such a friendly church, and her family was delightful. Margie and I became engaged. I even joined the church that summer. When I joined the church, the pastor suggested I give a testimony, because he and all the others knew why I was in Ferndale. I was pleased to tell them of my appreciation for this church family, and I was accepted into membership of First Baptist Church of Ferndale, Washington.

Margie had just graduated, but I still had two more years of college. She remained in Ferndale while I went back to finish my education at Biola. After working for a year for a doctor, Margie returned to Biola to attend the School of Missionary Medicine during my last year of studies there. We were very interested in the Christ for Indonesia Fellowship ministry, and attended their weekly prayer meetings and information times. My brother and his wife, Ernie and Verda, were also interested, and they applied for service in Indonesia with this group. In the providence of God, this field closed in those years to the gospel, so my brother was led to Singapore instead. We were still undecided about our field of service at that time. Soon graduation was history and I was once again back in Ferndale to seek employment and make plans for our marriage

August 20, 1954, was our wedding day. We honeymooned in Banff, Alberta, Canada, and on returning to Ferndale I began working at Safeway.

We desired to serve the Lord on the mission field. Margie had been called to foreign service before I was. Together we prayed and decided to attend the Summer Institute of Linguistics in Norman, Oklahoma. There we would study the science of learning a language so we would be better equipped for this skill when the Lord opened up His will for us on foreign soil. We were on our way to Oklahoma when our pastor in Ferndale phoned advising us to return, if possible, and talk with John Schlener, a pioneer missionary working in the Upper Amazonas state of Brazil. Through my godly grandmother Robbins, God wonderfully supplied the means to return to Ferndale, where we met with the missionary, and this led to our applying to ABWE (Association of Baptists for World Evangelism) for work in Brazil.

In 1957 we went to Campinas, São Paulo, Brazil to learn the Portuguese language. Our son Rawlie was born while we were in this school, and from there we went to the village of Santa Rita, also known as The Port of Two Brothers, in the Amazonas State of Brazil, to get initiated into missionary life in the jungle. Several of our stories tell the rest. What a powerful God we serve! We can only thank Him for His leading in our lives and bringing us to this great country of Brazil to begin our years of service. And that is how it all began. The Scriptures exhort us to ***Commit your way to the Lord, trust also in Him, and He will bring it to pass.*** (Psalm 37:5)

CHRISTMAS ON THE AMAZON

We were living in the Schleners' home at The Port of Two Brothers. Christmas day was upon us, and we did not have the opportunity to make the 100-mile trip by outboard motor boat to get supplies, mail, or anything—including gifts for our son. We did not consider our ministry a sacrifice, because we were serving the Lord and content to be there. But one does get a bit nostalgic around Christmas time. We wondered how we would spend this special day. We asked the Lord to make it a pleasant one in spite of having no gifts at Christmas. We knew that we did have the greatest Christmas gift possible, the gift of Jesus Christ. *Thanks be to God for His indescribable gift!* (I Corinthians 9:15)

I heard the horn of a Peruvian river boat upriver. Sounds carry very well over the water. Later the boat reached our port and stopped. I went to the launch, and to my utter surprise, the simple river launch that traveled these waters selling gasoline, diesel, kerosene, medical supplies, food, and clothing, had some toys. I looked over the limited array of gifts and chose some for our son. How amazing that on Christmas Day we were able to get a few things to make this day enjoyable.

We thanked the Lord for His provision for us. Even though this was not a necessary purchase, it was so amazing to have it happen. On this shopping tour I had another surprise. Among the canned items, I found hamburger patties in light gravy. What a nice thing to discover when meat was not always easy to find! How good God is in giving extra blessings along the way. That is a Christmas we will never forget.

A DIESEL ENGINE REPAIRED
BY AN AMATEUR

—❀❀—

Missionaries are often called on to do many things for which they are not trained. One of my favorite Scripture verses is,

The Lord preserves the simple. (Psalm 116:6)

One of our colleagues built a boat in our backyard. He had no training in building. I once wired a complete house for a fellow missionary downriver. Our senior missionary, an astute electrician, drew out the schematics; I followed directions, and it worked out well. The missionaries in Santa Rita asked me to install the timing belt on an outboard motor. With instructions in hand and hours of practice, I finally got it done. These things were intriguing to me. I worked on gasoline engines and was called on by others to come get their machines working. This was fun, but I owed it all to the Lord, who gave me the ability to do it.

Our Lister engine and generator were dandy. One day the engine stopped working. A pinpoint hole had appeared in the high pressure tubing. I am not a welder. I had one welding rod in my garage, but no clue as to how to use it. I dug a hole, placed charcoal in it, and with a blow torch was able to heat the rod and the tubing, twist the melting rod, and fill the hole. I thank the Lord for His help. Another time I fixed the fuel injector, which the manual said had to be repaired in a controlled atmosphere with no dust or impurities. So I submerged it in five gallons of kerosene and worked on it that way. It worked. Almost always one can accomplish a task, if we just ask God for wisdom on how to get it done. ***If any of you lacks wisdom, let him ask of God, who gives to all liberally and without reproach, and it will be given to him***. (James 1:5) It really does work.

THE DAY THE TAXES DIDN'T GET PAID

—— ⬿⬿ ——

O ne day I decided to travel about 30 miles downstream to the town of São Paulo de Olivença to pay taxes for the mission station. The day was beautiful as I prepared John's boat for the trip. With gasoline onboard, we had prayer and I set out downriver for my destination.

On the river one has to expect the unexpected. Things happen quickly. As I traveled smoothly in the middle of the river, I saw some small ripples on the surface of the river. They were two inches high, like miniature waves. The next second I looked, they were the size of a quart jar. I looked to the horizon and noticed a huge area of black clouds, the bottom edge of which was straight as an arrow. Strong wind caused that straight edge of the clouds. I looked down at the surface of the water, and the waves were the size of a five-gallon bucket. I was in a major storm.

The waves grew to a height of three or four feet, so I headed for the shore to find shelter. At the shore where I wanted to dock for safety, however, the trees were falling like toothpicks into the river. I had to ride out the storm in the middle of the river with those huge waves. I kept busy handling the boat and tying down the gas cans so they wouldn't turn over and spill. I didn't even have time to get sea-sick. For hours I rode the relentless waves. Finally things calmed down, and I headed back home. The taxes were not paid, but I thanked God that He got me home safely. Yes, we need to learn to thank Him in every situation. ***In everything give thanks, for this is the will of God in Christ Jesus concerning you.*** (Ephesians 5:20)

A SCENE FROM THE CLASSROOM

---⊗⊗⊗---

We taught school in Brazil even though we were foreigners; our love for the people motivated us to want to help them as much as possible. They overlooked our strange accent as we tried to speak their language. We had gone to language school and knew more or less how to use the language correctly. What a joy to teach grammar and mathematics and other subjects in the school context. Of course, we were also learning how to use the idioms of their language and all the wonderful ways they express themselves. When the people we taught learned the knack of mathematics, no longer could they be fooled at the corner store, because they understood how to make change, read bills, and all important things dealing with money. And once they learned to read, they were able to read God's Word.

MARGIE IN THE CLASSROOM

When my wife began teaching Brazilian school, she gave each student a pencil. Some had never held one of these strange things before. One student tried to write with the eraser end on the paper. It was all very new to Evandro. Oh, the delight in showing him to turn the pencil around and use the lead to write. That young man was a model student, went on to graduate, attended Bible school, and later travelled to a foreign country as a missionary to preach the gospel. This boy, we discovered, was also a gifted musician, and he learned to master any instrument placed before him. What a blessing he has been to us and all who have heard him preach and lead people to the Lord. We missionaries learned the importance of the individual, and we never knew what God was going to do with the students who trusted Jesus as their personal Savior. Today many of them are faithful servants of God.

"THAT'LL DO"

At the Port of Two Brothers, the tanks that collected rain water from our aluminum roof were an important part of the house. It was not easy to get up in the upper part of our house and check the water level. I decided it was time to make a gauge to take care of that. With pulleys, a homemade buoy, and a vertical support system, I marked the outside of the water tank with proper lines to let us know how much water was in the tanks. The arrow affixed to the small cable pointed to the water level. We were happy to have that to save us a lot of climbing.

My study in Benjamin Constant, where we went after our stay at the Port of Two Brothers, doubled as a classroom. It was practically all screen windows rather than glass, so whatever moving air there was outside could enter in. The bright sun, however, made it hot inside. I got an idea from some pulpy wood that was the main stalk of a tree. It resembled balsa wood, and who knows, that might be where they got the material to make model airplanes. I really don't know. I had our yard man find and cut some of these small trees. We shaped slats similar to those of a venetian blind, and I devised a pulley system to raise and lower the blinds. The blinds were quite long but very light. I always marveled that the termites did not invade this wood, which appeared to me wonderful food for these insects. At any rate, the students and I enjoyed the nice coolness inside the study-schoolroom.

In our first years in The Port Of Two Brothers, we had a wonderful Transoceanic Zenith short wave radio. It worked fine until the commercial battery died. There was no place to order one of these, and we had no idea how long it would take to get one from the States. Would it clear customs and get to us, anyway? I came up with the idea of a flat box, the sides of which were a little higher than the height of a battery. It took a lot of batteries, and I had to have the right polarity so it would work on the radio. With some innovations we got it working, and it was wonderful to have regular D batteries doing the job of one big battery. It was fun to make these things "work" even when we didn't have the right material to work with. As we finished each task, about all we could say was, "That'll do!" And we thanked the Lord for helping by giving us these ideas. You know the Lord is always there to give us wisdom to do what He wants us to do. James 1:5 is pretty clear on this: *If any of you lacks wisdom, let him ask of God, who gives to all liberally and without reproach, and it will be given to him.*

BLINDED BY FOG

———∞∞∞———

Before we left on any trip, we prayed, asking God to direct us on our way. This particular morning it was cool and foggy. We could see the surface of the Amazon River just fine, and quite a distance in front of us. As we traveled upstream by speedboat, the fog intensified, and then all of a sudden it rolled in like a huge wall, and we were completely blinded. What do you do when there is no orientation? You are in the middle of the river and you don't know if you are going upstream, downstream, sideways, or anywhere. It is the most helpless feeling possible. I prayed for wisdom to know what to do.

I slowed the engine down to almost a stall. Among the missionaries we had an expression: "It's the decisions that get you." I didn't know what to do. The likelihood of hitting another vessel on the river was small, but we couldn't be sure. Large ships often travel the Amazon, and we certainly didn't want to collide with one of those. We had only a certain amount of gasoline for the 100-mile trip to Leticia, Colombia, and we did not know if we were headed in the right direction. What if we ran out of gas? Well, after what seemed like hours of "nothingness" we felt a thud and a jerk, and the fog cleared just a bit. We had hit the bank of the river. We had no idea where we were, so we had to wait for the fog to clear more. It did, and we finally finished the trip to get our mail, medicine and groceries, and returned home without more incidents. I am reminded of part of a verse in Isaiah 43:2: ***When you pass through the waters, I will be with you; And through the rivers, they shall not overflow you.*** When we pray for God to lead us, we should do it with confidence.

BOYS WILL BE BOYS

In any culture, children have the ability to play and entertain themselves in many innovative ways. Brazilian boys made slingshots using rubber from the latex from rubber trees. This involved a process, and they knew how to do it. They also made whistles to call the birds. There are no rocks for slingshots, so they used nuts from the trees of a certain plant. Even crudely fashioned "birdies" from corn husks served well for hand games similar to badminton. One father carved for his daughter a rough-shaped doll from a piece of wood.

BOA CONSTRICTOR

During the drier season in the Amazon, when the river is low and the streams are almost empty, boys like to investigate. One day some boys poked a stick in a hole along the bank. As they pulled the stick out, a very large head appeared. It was a boa constrictor. In panic, they called their dad, who came and beat it until it was unconscious and then he pulled it to our mission station yard. When they called me, I went to take a look. It was the width of a normal salad plate and about 8 feet long. That's a lot of snake! The end of that story is interesting. They later dumped the snake into the main channel of the Amazon River, where we are sure it survived, revived, and found another hole in which to rest. Serpents, in the Bible, remind us of our enemy, the devil. He tempted Eve in the garden. In Revelation 20:2 we read of Christ: ***He laid hold of the dragon, that serpent of old, who is the Devil and Satan, and bound him for a thousand years.*** We always had a healthy respect for snakes in the Amazon. We should also be aware of Satan and his evil work in the world today.

SHIP FROM ENGLAND

━━━⊰⊱━━━

L iving in the little village of Santa Rita (also called the Port of Two Brothers) along the banks of the Amazon River gave us ample opportunities to see and hear a lot of things coming from the river. Occasionally a very large ship would pass by. Because the river is a great conductor of sound, many hours before this ship passed our station, the Brazilians could hear it coming. They could differentiate vessels that traveled the river by the particular sound each engine made. Those ships went up the river all the way to Iquitos, Peru. Our fellow workers would make the long trip by boat and plane to where the ship was docked. They went aboard to purchase any number of delightful things. Frozen turkeys, bread, frozen milk, all sorts of desserts, and many other things were among the items they brought back in styrofoam boxes. Sometimes this took place close to Thanksgiving, so you can imagine the wonderful meals we enjoyed.

ENGLISH SHIP

We told our Brazilian friends that the frozen food section of this ship was probably larger than their house. They would be amazed at such stories. To get the supplies from Iquitos, Peru, to our mission station took some doing, but the Schlener brothers were masters at innovation and brought these items in special boxes which kept the food from spoiling in that hot, humid Amazon climate.

One can only imagine the fun we experienced on Thanksgiving Day in the heart of the Amazon, eating delicious turkey with most of the usual trimmings. We were thankful the men had made arrangements to be in Iquitos when the ship was there so they could bring back those goodies for the others. On Thanksgiving Day we certainly agreed with the Apostle Paul when he reminded the Thessalonians, ***In every-thing give thanks; for the is the will of God in Christ Jesus concerning you.*** (I Thessalonians 5:18)

A SNAKE BITE WITH A LOT OF BEEF

———∞∞∞———

The Amazon River provides abundantly for the inhabitants along that great body of water. We were amazed at its size even at our station, 2,000 miles upstream. The jungle along the river also has wildlife which is good for food. Nevertheless, at certain times of the year fish and game are harder to catch, so when other meat was offered, we quickly responded. Some domestic cows were raised, and one day a man offered us a quarter beef, so we bought it.

We had him put it near the kitchen sink. Margie washed it, and moments later we were going to carve it up. I noticed bubbles coming out of the tendons, sinews, and other places of the newly purchased meat. I concluded that something was wrong. At this point we decided we did not want this meat, even though we could benefit by having some beef in our diet. About this time, one of the villagers came to tell us that this cow had been bitten by a snake. Now we were sure we didn't want it. It was too risky to take a chance.

How did that villager know it was bitten? You must know that in the jungles information travels FAST. We never ceased to be amazed how fast people knew things that were going on. No telephones, just word of mouth.

What would you do with this beef? We decided not to throw it into the river or bury it, because the townspeople said they would gladly take it. A lemon tree grew on our mission station. The folks who took the meat from us picked a lot of lemons and rubbed down the meat with lemon juice and divided it among themselves. No one got sick. Amazing! God gave these folks a lot of common-sense ways to handle their day-to-day problems. They had obviously had this experience before and knew what to do. It was a little too much for us foreigners, however, so we gladly passed on that piece of meat. Once the Apostle Paul gave thanks for bread on a ship that was in a storm (Acts 27:35). I don't suppose the bread was very fresh, but all aboard were glad to have the nourishment. I think the Brazilians felt the same way about this beef they received.

RIGHT TIMING

I like challenges, and one day John Schlener asked if I would like to try my hand at putting the timing belt on his Mercury outboard motor. I was not familiar with this high precision motor. In fact, I was rather ignorant of the whole concept of engines, even though I had owned a car or two before going to Brazil. For some reason, John had sort of given up on this engine. He handed me the user's manual and timing belt. I went into the workshop and started my long and laborious task of trying to install this belt.

REPAIRING OUTBOARD MOTOR

I confess I went at it completely unaware of what I was doing, even though I knew what I should be doing. After hours of tinkering with this engine, I finally discovered some revealing things about timing belts. Unseen before when I was using the trial and error method of getting the job done, I noticed there were two score marks on the timing gear, and these must line up to complete the job correctly. Finally, after many attempts, when I pulled the starting cord, the motor took off and ran like it was supposed to. I thanked the Lord that He once again, *had preserved the simple*. (Psalm 116:6)

This victory started a chain reaction. Later I was asked to work on the missionary's generator plant, which I did successfully. As is often the case, several other machines on their station were in various stages of disrepair. By degrees, I learned about motors.

I remember Lindsey Harrel contacting me about five motors on his station that needed help. I was pleased to go there and get them all working. Again I give credit to the Lord for giving me wisdom, and also to the Schlener brothers, who gave a greenhorn new missionary the opportunity to learn about motors. They initiated me on their Mercury engine timing belt project. Sometimes if you know too much about mechanics, you can't get some motors going. It helps once in a while to be ignorant (or stupid) enough to try anything. See "Miracle Sparkplug," another story in this book. My verse for work on such difficult tasks is James 1:5, *If any of you lacks wisdom, let him ask of God, who gives to all liberally and without reproach, and it will be given to him.*

POIS NÃO

———⌾⌾⌾———

I f you do not understand Portuguese, how would you ever figure out the heading of this story? Simply put, it means "yes, of course." In the village of Santa Rita, we met many delightful and interesting people. The Schleners worked there for many years, and quite a few folks were evangelized. They had received Jesus Christ as their Savior and were members of the church.

In the course of our getting acquainted with different people after we arrived, we met a man we nicknamed Pois Não. As we spoke to him, he would say many times, "Yes, of course." It became his trademark, and thus our nickname for him. He was a strong, distinguished looking man, with almost snow white hair. He was a fisherman by trade. Although faithful in church attendance, he was not a believer.

In each service at the church, I always gave those attending the opportunity to receive the gospel by inviting Jesus Christ into their lives. As I prolonged the invitation that day, I could tell that Pois Não was thinking things over rather seriously. In fact, there were some verbal comments being made by him, especially to Bernardo, who was sitting next to him. I sensed that Benardo, a new convert himself, was encouraging Pois Não to make his decision. Right in the service he said out loud to Pois Não, "I made this decision and I am glad I did. You can too, Pois Não." Well, before that service was over, Pois Não did what the Scriptures say so clearly, ***Believe on the Lord Jesus Christ and you will be saved***. (Acts 16:31) What a joy it will be to fellowship with Bernardo and Pois Não in Heaven one day.

THEY HAD NEVER SEEN IT

—∞—

W hen we went to the Port of Two Brothers right after our language training, we lived in Paul and John Schlener's toolshed. It was brand new, and we were the first occupants. After we left, they put their tools in it. It was very gracious of them to fix this new place for our living quarters.

With a Servel kerosene refrigerator we could make ice in large plastic glasses, and eventually we made ice cream with an old crank ice cream maker. One Sunday morning when we were eating our breakfast, we looked up and noticed a crowd of Ticuna Indians squeezed onto our little front porch which was the entrance to the tool shed. With their faces pressed against the screen door, they were examining the contents of this strange place that was so different from their thatch-roofed homes in the jungles. Margie was so startled by their sudden appearance that she burned her hand on the stove.

Later, after church, we took ice made in our Servel refrigerator and made hand-cranked ice cream. That was a treat beyond measure for us. I decided to have some fun with the ice left in the bucket. I threw it out on the lawn in front of our workshop home. Pretty soon the Indians came to inspect what it was on the ground. Remember, this is something they had never seen, as far as we knew. I saw an adult lean over, inspect it, and then, almost as if he were afraid, pick up a piece of the ice. As soon as he touched it, he yelled out "HOT" and threw it down.

Among themselves there was a lot of Ticuna Indian talk going on. They speak in soft, mellow tones, almost as if they were whispering. An interesting note about their language is that they talk in 5 tones. Some were laughing, others looking in wonderment at this strange stuff on the grass. Finally, one picked up a piece of ice, not fearing if it was "hot" or not, and placed it in his mouth. He liked it. Others followed his example. There was a lot of laughter, and we were witnessing the great discovery of ice by this small group of inquisitive Indians. It was great entertainment for us as well. Later we explained to them how we took water and made it "hard and cold" with the refrigerator. They seemed to be pleased with the explanation, and we are sure that this story circulated among the tribes people for a long time.

It was a privilege to be called to Brazil to preach the gospel. Jesus' command was to preach the gospel to every one (Mark 16:15) included the Ticuna Indians. Our colleagues had the privilege of seeing many scores of them come to Christ.

THE AMAZON RIVER FULL OF DEBRIS

During heavy Amazon rains, the surface of the river is often cluttered with all sorts of logs and vegetation that grows along the bank. When traveling these waters, operators of boats must take precautions. Many times large hunks of the riverbank break loose, causing "floating islands." Can you imagine the wildlife in those islands? Snakes that are uprooted and dumped into the river swim to these islands for safety. I would not like to be found on one in an emergency.

MANY CANOES ON THE RIVER

There is another site that is wonderfully amazing. Each Sunday morning we looked at the river in front of our mission station and saw the whole thing cluttered with what looked like logs. On closer inspection we discovered that each of these "logs" was a canoe filled with Indians on their way to church. What dedication this represented! Other Indians who lived on tributaries would travel by canoe to a certain spot, park their boat, and start trekking through the jungles overland. They walked on trails made on previous trips to the station. Some would have to walk for hours, heading for the Port of Two Brothers, where church was held for this wonderful tribe. The ones arriving by canoe in front of the station would tie their canoes and then start the short walk to church. As hundreds walked across the grass, it made a sound like a soft breeze blowing. You would have to hear it to appreciate it.

We often thought of the dedication of these people. How many of us would travel hours to get to church? What about the return trip? Certainly they taught us many lessons we needed to learn. We are grateful to God for them. Missionary John Schlener once told me that an Indian was asked one day where he was going, and his answer immediately was, "To see God." How humbling is this? To think we had the privilege of taking the gospel of Jesus Christ to these folks! The Schleners are the ones who ministered greatly to them. I am so glad they responded to the command of Jesus, ***And he said unto them, Go ye into all the world, and preach the gospel to every creature.*** (Mark 16:15)

RISKY PROCRASTINATION

A man named Bernardo came to our medical dispensary at the Port of Two Brothers. He had a serious sore on his shoulder blade. I can't remember how it happened, but it was probably from an accident in the woods. His condition worsened, and eventually he was taken to the hospital in Benjamin Constant, some 100 miles upstream from our station.

For a long time he was hospitalized. Then one day he decided to check out and go home. He purchased a small canoe and paddled the 100 miles. He revisited our dispensary and continued his treatments. One day he asked me, "Can you save me?" He was concerned about his spiritual life before God. I told Bernardo I could not save him but Someone else could. If he would believe in Jesus Christ, who came into this world to bring salvation to all who would confess their sins and receive Him, he would be saved. The Bible clearly states, *For God so loved the world that He gave his only begotten Son, that whoever believes in Him should not perish but have everlasting life.* (John 3:16) He said he wanted to do this. He proceeded to pray a simple prayer, and God saved him right there. Right after this, he got up and said, "Do you know why

I did this today?" I said, "No." Then he pointed to a distant point across the river and said that 25 years ago he was very sick and he told the Lord that if he would keep him alive until he was 58 years old, he would become a Christian. "Today," he said, "is my birthday." I told him he should pray again thanking God for keeping him alive all these years. It is risky business to postpone important decisions. We are told in II Corinthians 6:2, ***Behold now is the accepted time; behold now is the day of salvation***. Have YOU made this important decision?

MOVING WAVE OF DESTRUCTION

———⊸⊱⊰⊷———

Life on the Amazon River is not without its tense moments. I remember a couple of Germans who stopped at the Port of Two Brothers on their way to Manaus, 1,000 miles down river from us. We went to prayer meeting at night, and these men stayed in John's boat house, anchored close to the river bank. While we were in church, a very large boat passed by our place. As is true of every vessel that travels on water, it disturbed the water, making wakes. Sometimes the wakes are violent, and this one was. One of the fellows was actually thrown out of his bed by the huge wakes that beat against the boat house. This is not all the damage that was done. The village people whose canoes were tied up also suffered. Some canoes broke loose from their moorings and subsequently floated away. This was a terrible shock to the folks, and I guess there was nothing the boat owner could do, either. Along the river are houses, and if the boat were to reduce its speed for each house, it would take a long time to reach its destination.

The Amazon River is very wide and varies from place to place. I have seen it several miles wide with huge islands in the middle. Because of its enormity, high winds play havoc with the water. They cause huge waves that crash into the bank, causing damage to docks, canoes, boats, and stairs that lead down to the water's edge. At one point John Schlener devised a clever plan to have his houseboat and stairs on a floating ramp system. These could rise and lower with the level of the water and yet remain fairly stable. This helped greatly in controlling things, but in the case of high waves, hardly anything could survive. The winds also created situations that were hard to combat. We heard of a tornado-like storm that swept through the jungles, leaving a clean path.

James in his book mentions wind in relation to our faith. Our prayers should be with faith, not doubting. ***But let him ask in faith, with no doubting, for he who doubts is like a wave of the sea driven and tossed by the wind.*** (James 1:6)

MEAT MARKET IN A TURTLE

—⚬⚬⚬—

Before being missionaries we had always heard that turtle dishes were a delicacy in fancy restaurants. Little did we know that one day on the Amazon we would be able to eat turtle often, if desired. One time a visiting pastor and his wife were with us at the Port of Two Brothers, and the missionary wives were excited about preparing this tropical animal for our meal with them. I am sure these ladies were disappointed when the visitors actually showed no enthusiasm for what was about to be served. Oh well, maybe that's because we were in Brazil and they were from the States. Who knows?

Let's talk about turtle eggs first. I used to go to Benjamin Constant's port on the Amazon River and watch the huge canoes come in from distant places up the tributaries. There the egg gatherers had filled their vessels with hundreds of thousands of these precious, soft-shelled delicacies. At the port they would sell quickly, because they are a prize food. Boiled in salted water for a few minutes, the little oval eggs are ready to eat. You tear carefully the egg's pliable soft shell and gently pop out the yoke. There is no white, it is all yoke.

And this is not a "yoke"! (I just had to get that one in!) They are most delicious.

Now to turtle meat. To start we will just pass on what we have heard and read. Any local person will tell you that an ordinary mud turtle contains several kinds of meat — pork, beef, mutton, chicken, duck, and fish. I should say that I have not researched what kind of turtles we have in Brazil. I know that many of them up our way were LARGE. A child could take a bath in its shell.

The missionary ladies will tell you that depending on what part of the turtle meat you used, you could get the different flavors mentioned above. It is quite amazing, to say the least. So we were privileged to serve this prize food to our guests. Unfortunately, they were not as impressed as we were with this very special meat. About giving thanks to God for what is eaten, the Apostle Paul gives us a word in Acts 27:35: ***And when he had said these things, he took bread and gave thanks to God in the presence of them all; and when he had broken it he began to eat.***

I FORGOT THE MEDICINE

―⸺∞―⸺

Living about 100 miles downstream from Leticia, Colombia, at the jungle settlement of the Port of Two Brothers, meant we had to occasionally go upriver to that Colombian town for supplies and mail. It was a major undertaking, because all gasoline for the outboard motor on our boat had to be mixed with proper measurements of oil. Sometimes we took enough for the return trip, but not often, because fuel was more available near the frontier towns.

One time returning from a trip to get supplies, I stepped into the clinic next to the Schleners homes, where we tended to people's medical needs as much as possible. I looked up and there was a man standing on the porch, so I asked him how we could help him. I was shocked as I took a second look at him. He was Miguel, our Ticuna Indian interpreter for classes with the Indians on Sundays. He was so gaunt and sickly that I barely recognized him. His yellowish eyes and pallid skin alerted me to the fact that his liver was deficient and needed medication. He was obviously suffering from a form of hepatitis.

I reached for my satchel of medications just purchased on this trip, and to my utter horror, it was missing. How could

I have forgotten the newly purchased medications 100 miles upstream in Leticia, Colombia? I was not prone to do that, but in my human weakness indeed I had. It was early enough in the day, so I had the yard man mix more gasoline and prepare the boat for a return trip.

That was a hard lesson to learn. From that point on I made sure that all items purchased were with me. Fortunately, I had left early in the morning, and even though the round trip took several hours, I could still get back there and return the same day. This was not the best way to do it, but Miguel was ill, and I needed to make the extra effort to help him. I found the satchel at the drugstore and quickly started my trip homeward. It was downstream and would not take quite as long as the upriver leg of the journey. There is no twilight on the equator, so at sunset it gets dark very quickly.

I was pleased, and I thanked God for His safety as I made two complete round trips that day. I was doubly thankful I could help Miguel and give him medication to bring him back to health again. He was very valuable to me in interpreting the Bible messages each Sunday to the Ticuna Indians. We take so much for granted. We need to ask the Lord to help us remember important things in our lives. This slip-up for me was costly and very time-consuming, and we almost lost a wonderful worker because of it. I learned my lesson. I wish someone had reminded me to bring the medicine as Paul had asked Timothy to bring his cloak. ***Bring the cloak that I left with Carpus at Troas when you come—and the books, especially the parchments.*** (II Timothy 4:13)

FIRE ISLAND AMAZON

―❦―

Near the mission station Port of Two Brothers there was an interesting island at the bend of the river. Locals told us several times that at various periods throughout the year one could see smoke coming from the surface of this small island or peninsula-like land along the shore of the river. I wish I had been an eyewitness of this.

I remember one time, for many days, we could hear the noise of a ship coming from down river. This was an unusual sound and persisted for days. Finally we saw this huge structure coming upstream. We noticed that smaller outboard motor boats were leaving and going along the banks of the river, apparently doing some kind of soil tests. We never learned the real significance of these, but by the ship's name, we knew it had something to do with petroleum exploration.

In the Amazon jungle, there are probably rich deposits of oil. We may never hear about it, but we believe it could be true. I wonder if the smoldering clusters of clay-like soft rock formations on that island are an indication that there is oil? At any rate, it was fascinating to listen to the folks that live there talk about this unusual activity upriver. It was just a short distance from where we used to live at the Port of Two Brothers. God's ways are so beautiful that even the unusual sights along the way are an indication of His great variety in the universe. *"For My thoughts are not your thoughts, Nor are your ways My ways," says the LORD. For as the heavens are higher than the earth, So are My ways higher than your ways, And My thoughts than your thoughts.* (Isaiah 55:8,9)

FLOATING ISLANDS

———⊗⊗⊗———

When I went on my first trip down the Amazon River by myself, I saw things that I will never forget. There were no places to buy gasoline along the way, so we had to take enough for our one-way trip up to Leticia, Colombia. Therefore, our boat was loaded with extra gasoline cans filled with the "magic stuff" that propelled the Evinrude outboard motor. At Leticia we purchased enough for our return trip to the Port of Two Brothers. The lesson I learned was that at times, the river was cluttered with all sorts of things. It was normal to see tree limbs floating leisurely along the river current. And there were entire trees that had fallen along the shore of the river, due probably to the soil erosion caused by the constant wear of the water against the bank. One has to be alert to these things. One may think with such a huge river, you could just go your merry way along with no concerns. That is not so. A hundred-foot tree is no plaything. Its branches could be submerged and extended way out from the trunk.

One floating object that always caught my attention was the "grass beds," or floating islands. These are made up of a variety of aquatic plants. Some have elaborate root systems;

others are more fragile. But with the combination of many varieties, there is a formidable mass of living things floating gently down the stream. Some of them can support the weight of a man, and in some parts of the Amazon river, deer have been known to be on these floating islands. This is the way some of these animals have changed their geographical locations, by hooking rides on the floating islands. I am sure they did not intend it this way, but we are inclined to think our Creator planned it all. Another sure thing is that snakes hook rides on these islands. I would never want to get into a situation where I was forced to take refuge on one of these islands.

So, piloting a small motor craft on the Amazon can be interesting. I actually enjoyed it, but I realized I had to be very alert to all the possible dangers. Besides the floating islands, I think of huge limbs or whole trees submerged below the river level. If you hit one of these at full speed, you would have a big problem. You learn to "read" the surface of the water. Sandbars are also a danger, and to run aground on one of these at full speed spells trouble. It was our custom to pray before we left on a river trip, and certainly when we arrived, we gave thanks to the Lord for His protection. I think of one of Paul's prayers in I Thessalonians 3:11, ***Now may our God and Father Himself and our Lord Jesus Christ, direct our way to you.*** We often prayed something like that as we ventured out to get supplies or whatever on that amazing Amazon River for a hundred-mile trip. Do YOU pray before you drive downtown or wherever you are going? It's a good thing to develop that habit.

A CLEVER DECEPTION

Late one evening a man appeared at our door at the Port of Two Brothers. Not many American–looking individuals did that, so it "snapped us to attention." The visitor had his arm in a sling and some scratches on his face. He nervously told us that while piloting a small aircraft headed to one of the towns along the Amazon, he had encountered inclement weather and had become disoriented. In this confused state he saw a clearing below and decided to land there because of an engine problem.

The problem was that this apparent dry lake was only a depression, a clearing filled with stumps and plenty of barriers. It was not good for landing with an airplane. The result was a very bumpy crash landing resulting in the destruction of the plane and injuries to the pilot. It was a miracle he even survived. Our visitor wanted to shower, and John Schlener gave him one of his shirts. As the man spoke, John had some "red flags" in his mind about his story. John let him sleep at his house but kept a vigilant watch over him all night in case he was up to something we did not know about. At this point the story gets a little fuzzy, but I believe John took our visitor to a town downriver from us where he could make arrangements for passage. While there John reported this questionable person to local authorities.

A footnote to this story is that the man was a fake. He was not a pilot and had no plane that he tried to land in a dry lake bed. Later it was determined he was wanted by authorities and was involved in some illegal activity. Perhaps you don't realize that when you pray for missionaries something like this could happen. But now you know. There are many deceivers in this world, and even the Apostle Paul spoke about this, especially in the realm of spiritual truths. He said, ***And for this reason God will send them strong delusion, that they should believe the lie.*** (II Thessalonians 2:11)

A BENT NEEDLE

John and Paul Schlener had a ministry with Ticuna Indians at the Port of Two Brothers. While they were on furlough, we had the privilege of working with this fine tribe. Medical work is usually part of missionary service.

One day a Ticuna man came seeking help with a pain "somewhere" in his body. I had no idea where the pain was or what caused it as he pointed to his stomach. Being an amateur at medicine, I had no clue what to do. I should have called Margie, who was a licensed practical nurse. Perhaps she had an answer. But I didn't call her. I told the Indian I would be glad to give him a shot that would take away his pain. Actually, that is what the medicine was – a painkiller. He agreed, and I prepared his injection. Remember, Ticunas are outdoorsmen. They are hunters and are used to roughing it in the jungles

I filled the syringe with medicine and cleaned the Ticuna's leathery arm with an alcohol swab. As I grabbed his arm and plunged the needle into the leather-tough skin, the needle bent to a 45° angle immediately. Boy, that guy has tough skin, I thought, and so I tried again with a different needle, and this time it worked. After just a few moments, I asked him about the pain he had. All he could do was slowly lift his arm that I had injected, and let out an agonizing "Ai. . . .Ai. . . ."(their method of indicating pain). In other words, he came for stomach pain, but after the shot all he was concerned about was the pain of the shot. He went away as happy as could be. We knew the pain was "transferred" from his stomach to his sore arm. We laughed about it and still do as we remember this incident. We are also happy to say how receptive these Indians were to the gospel. I had the privilege of teaching them each Sunday morning while the Schleners were on furlough.

A MEDICAL EMERGENCY
TRIP THAT SAVED A MAN

―⊷⊷⊷―

Often we were asked to take folks to the hospital in Benjamin Constant. Our good friend Henry, a German, lived in Brazil many years and was married to an Indian lady. He lived in a remote spot along one of the Amazon tributaries. Occasionally he would come to our station and request books. He was an avid reader and spoke English fluently. One day his family came with a plea for me to take him to the hospital in Benjamin Constant. He had a carbuncle on his posterior that was seriously in need of treatment. The trip to the hospital took several hours. He checked into the hospital and was there for a long time. On my regular trips to border towns to shop, get medicines and pick up mail, I dropped by to see him.

On subsequent trips I discovered that the problem was severe, and his life was hanging in the balance. We had visited many times, but this time I told him that I wanted to meet him in heaven some day. I asked him if he had ever personally invited Jesus to be his Savior, for the forgiveness of his sins and the assurance of life everlasting in Heaven. He said he had not. I asked him if he would like to, and he responded "Yes."

He prayed a simple prayer receiving Jesus into his life, and the transaction was done. He died in the hospital being saved spiritually; therefore the title of this article was fulfilled. I look forward to seeing him in heaven some day. What about YOU? God wants YOU to be saved like Henry. In the Bible look at the Gospel of John chapter 3 and verse 16, the most well-known verse in the Bible. It will tell you how to have eternal life and a home in heaven when you die.

IF THE CREEK DOESN'T RISE

A long the Amazon there was a never-ending quest to obtain food. Fish, a staple food for river dwellers, depended on the situation of the Amazon River or the many creeks that fed into it. And what I mean by that is that fishing depends a lot on whether the river is full or running normally. As a rule of thumb, fishing was not good when the river was swollen. For some reason I don't fully understand, the fish are less apt to bite under those conditions. Because of our workload and probably my own lack of interest in fishing, we would ask the Brazilians to fish for us and would pay them for their work. When we asked them to go fishing, if they had known this phrase which is the title of this story, they would have responded to me, "I will get some fish, God willing and if the creek don't rise." (Pardon the poor grammar, but that's the way the phrase is worded.)

During times when the creek rose and the fish were not biting, we prayed and trusted the Lord that somehow He would provide our needs through whatever means He saw fit. More than once we were thrilled to see a slow Peruvian river boat coming downriver. It pulled into our port, and I went aboard.

On one occasion I found a case of Kitut (Spam). You might say Ugh!! Not that!! Wait a minute. We prayed that God would send us something, so now we have it and should give thanks. I opened the case of Kitut, and now it's Margie's turn to create something edible and tasty from that canned meat product. Yes, she did. When that's all you have, it is amazing the cook's ingenuity in making all sorts of dishes from this stuff. We ate it baked, fried, cooked with other things, transformed, chopped up, sprinkled with jungle herbs, etc. Yes, we thanked the Lord for it as we asked His blessing at meal time. One day I went aboard one of these slow-going river stores and found a case of canned hamburgers from Argentina. What a gold mine! No, they didn't taste like burgers that come off a grill, but they were good.

Then the river started to go down. The rainy season diminished some, and once again fish appeared. There were many varieties of fish in the Amazon River at our front door at the Port of Two Brothers. Literally hundreds of varieties fill that river. The fishermen we hired always brought the prized one to us. What a treat! And on occasion, we got a turtle. Turtle meat is the best. We always gave God thanks for providing our needs. Yes, we even gave Him thanks for Spam. As Paul wrote: ***In everything give thanks; for this is the will of God in Christ Jesus for you.*** (I Thessalonians 5:18)

OUR FIRST NIGHT
IN BENJAMIN CONSTANT

When our time at The Port of Two Brothers ended, we moved to Benjamin Constant, approximately 2,000 miles upriver from the mouth of the mighty Amazon River. There was no doubt about it, we were in the jungles. Things are different there. The climate is certainly different, and we soon discovered things that we didn't expect. We hung our clothes in the closet at night and put our shoes on the closet floor. In the morning, on examining our clothes, we noticed white spots here and there all over the darker clothes, and looking inside our shoes, we saw that they were lined with a white layer of mold. We were surprised. The strange thing about this mold is that the longer we were there, the less we saw of it. So maybe we got moldy just like the stuff that was attaching itself to us.

OUR HOME IN BENJAMIN CONSTANT

REAL COWBOY IN BENJAMIN CONSTANT

Besides the mold, another interesting thing that plagued us was mosquitos. They were as regular as a clock in their appearance each evening. It amazed us how their built-in clocks worked. We thought those frail little guys would never be able to navigate in the strong winds that blew along the Amazon River. One night I focused the flashlight on my legs and saw that they were peppered with mosquitoes getting a good meal on me. The wind was fierce that night. How the mosquitoes fly in such a wind is beyond me! All these fierce attacks by mosquitoes remind us of a warning in Scripture about spiritual things. ***Be sober be vigilant, because your adversary the devil walks about like a roaring lion, seeking whom he may devour.*** (I Peter 5:8) With insects, you cannot be too careful, and you certainly cannot either with Satan, the enemy of our souls.

THE DAY THE WIND BLEW ITS TOP

───∞───

P robably any place can boast of high winds occasionally. Benjamin Constant certainly had its share of high winds. Generally speaking, we had it pretty good in the Amazon jungle. We had plenty of rain, which is why it is the world's largest rain forest. When it rains, it pours, and when it blows, it BLOWS. I don't remember many of the homes occupied by the local residents falling over or being badly damaged in wind storms. Maybe that is because of the way they are constructed. They had more "give and take" in heavy winds than typical North American homes.

Our simple school room/office in Benjamin Constant had a thatched roof. This kind of roof is very cool. I was working in my study one afternoon when a wind started up that was more than the usual tropical breeze. The roof structure was straining under the force of the wind. There was nothing I could do to stabilize the rafters, because I was alone. To climb into the attic of this small building was out of the question, and dangerous.

I was trying to figure out what to do, when the guard and caretaker of our fellow missionary's home and plane hangar arrived with awesome news. Breathing heavily, he advised me that the wind had blown the top off their house. It was a "butterfly roof." Each half of the roof was slanted downward toward the center of the house so it looked like butterfly wings. He said that as the wind tore the roof off, he could hear the nails coming out of the sheets of aluminum like popcorn. I hurried down with him to take a look, not expecting what I saw. The main roof was standing on edge against a palm tree. The house was now exposed to rain. Thankfully, no one was injured. It was an emotional moment when the missionary owners of this home returned to find their home so exposed by the high wind and rain. These words in Hebrews 13:5 bring comfort to us at all times, especially when tough times come: *Let your conduct be without covetousness; be content with such things as you have. For He Himself has said, I will never leave you nor forsake you.*

JUST FOR A GLASS OF WATER

W hen someone begins life in a foreign country, he usually has to make adjustments. We talked in another chapter about climate changes we must get used to. Because a foreigner comes with a background of his own customs, it is natural that many things will shock him.

We learned early on that water for the "outsider" must be treated or illness will likely result. Folks who live there have never had this problem, because their natural immunity is built into their system.

BOILING DRINKING WATER

Our senior missionaries gave us suggestions, and we chose what to do. We decided to boil our water, thus ridding it of some of the things that affect the missionary's health. In warm weather, large quantities of water are consumed, so we had to devise a system to keep us supplied with ample amounts of this precious liquid. In an appropriate vessel, we boiled water over a charcoal fire for about 20 minutes. This was done in a safe place where we could keep the process running smoothly. After the water cooled, it was stored in proper containers. We had to buy large amounts of charcoal for this process.

Water from our collection area (the roof of the house) was stored in a huge reservoir that would hold about 55 barrels of water. This water was already much better than the muddy Amazon River water. There were water filters that could transform Amazon muddy water into clean, pure water, but we discovered that they could get clogged with the impurities, so we discontinued using them. Boiled water placed in our Servel, the kerosene-powered refrigerator, was very refreshing. Water is a precious, God-given commodity. A lot of things we take for granted are not always available in other places. *As cold water to a weary soul, So is good news from a far country.* (Proverbs 25:25)

WATCH THOSE TERMITES

A lthough we are not builders, we were interested in the way missionaries constructed their homes. One couple in our town rented a home and later purchased it. Because the foundation was not termite proof, they had plenty of trouble. In their living room, the nice beams that supported the ceiling and walls were painted snow white. Later it was discovered that the beauty of the beams was only "paint thick." One day these huge beams gave way and collapsed, as the insides had been devoured by termites.

Can termites do that much damage? Yes. Scientists tell us that there are so many of these small creatures on earth, that the weight of all termites just about equals the weight of the human population. That in itself is a miracle. Because termites cannot digest what they eat, there are myriads of different organisms living inside them that do the digesting for them.

There are many varieties of termites. Over 20 varieties live in the Amazon rainforest. We were curious about the termite shield placed on top of the foundation stones around our house in Benjamin Constant This shield was a thin piece of sheet metal placed on top of each pillar and slightly turned down all around. Somehow the termite is not able to make the turn of getting up and over and around this piece of metal on the foundation stone. I guess you could say the termite could not turn the corner to make it up any higher. This is a classic example of man capitalizing on an insect's weakness or inability to perform a certain task.

Anyone interested in God's handiwork in nature can find a wealth of information about the complex termite family, including the way they build their nests, the tubes they make through which to walk, the amazing facts about one species whose nests are oriented to the compass, and on and on. We remember our son spotting a small pile of "sawdust" on the floor in our home in Benjamin Constant. I told him to look at the sawdust. It was made of thousands of very tiny perfectly round balls of wood. I then told him to carefully look up the wall above the pile of "sawdust," and there he found a very small hole a little larger than a pin-point. I urged him to just look at the hole for a while. He did, and soon he saw "Mr. Termite" place a micro pellet in the doorway (the very small hole) and kick it out onto the floor.

We wonder, don't we, why did God create the termite? He had something in mind, that's for sure. Look at this marvelous truth in the Bible. John 1:3 says: ***All things were made through Him, and without Him nothing was made that was made.*** All I know is that He made you and me so that we would become His children by trusting Him as our personal Saviour. Have you done that?

WASHING AND DRYING CLOTHES IN THE JUNGLES

———— ∞∞∞ ————

We washed clothes in a Maytag gasoline-powered machine. That was wonderful for us who had it. At the river's edge, national ladies used a simple flat board on which they pounded the clothes to help clean them. Another intriguing method was to make use of a certain plant. It, along with soap (if they have any) helps keep the white clothes whiter and the colored ones more vibrant. I cannot remember the name of this plant, but one of our former helpers in Benjamin Constant, Aldeney, told me it was from the bean family. All I know is that people's clothes always looked clean and bright. I often remarked how good they looked, because they were washed in muddy water. It is quite noteworthy to study all the things God puts in the world to help us in so many ways. I wish I were more knowledgeable and could write on the medical value of the Amazon jungle plants.

Now how do they dry their clothes? At our house we used a clothesline similar to the ones seen in the States. The Brazilians throw their clothes over bushes, a makeshift string, a rope, or a vine, or even place them in the windows of their houses.

Some soap the clothes and put them in the sunshine, and that draws out the dirt. When dry they are thoroughly rinsed and dried. They have their own methods of cleaning, and we admire their ability to keep their clothes looking so good.

WASHING CLOTHES

Jesus spoke of keeping things clean, but in John 15:3 He was referring to the spiritual part of mankind. He wants us to be clean because of His Word the Bible which cleanses us, and with sins forgiven and living for Him. *You are already clean because of the word which I have spoken to you.* (John 15:3)

WE ARE KNOWN BY OUR STEPS

It is true we are known by our steps. Across the street from our home in Benjamin Constant, a young man lay in his hammock. The only way he could swing himself in the hammock was by means of a string tied to one of the rafters and the other end to his hand. He was almost completely paralyzed.

As a younger boy, he had been hired by a company to clear the jungle to eventually make a landing field for airplanes. His work in swampy conditions made him sick. He was stricken with rheumatoid arthritis, which eventually left him confined to a hammock for the rest of his life. He never complained. He swung back and forth in his hammock by pulling gently on the string. A radio, his family, and his friends were the only things he had. The day President Kennedy was assassinated, I was visiting with him, and suddenly he said, "There is Mr. Arthur." I jumped up from where I was seated and looked out the window, and sure enough there was Arthur coming down the road. I asked Anthony how he knew it was Arthur. He told me he could tell by the sound of his footsteps on the path. I wondered how, because I hadn't heard a thing. Lying in his hammock all those years, he had developed an awareness of what was going on around him unlike anything I had ever witnessed. Several times while I was there, he mentioned by name others who were walking down the pathway.

God knows all about us. The Bible says in Psalm 37:23: *The steps of a good man are ordered by the LORD, And He delights in his way.* Also Job 34:21 says: *For His eyes are on the ways of man, And He sees all his steps.* He knows where we are and where we've been. He knows that all are sinners, and God wants to save you and take you to heaven some day. Would you ask Him to be YOUR Saviour now?

WORTHLESS MONEY
IN THE OFFERING BASKET

⟨⟩

Benjamin Constant is one of the last towns on the Amazon River in Brazil. On any Sunday we might have three or four nationalities represented in the services. The offering time revealed this weekly. Brazilian Cruzeiros, Peruvian Nuevo Sol ("New Sun") and Colombian Pesos filled the offering baskets.

In most countries there is a system of recycling old damaged money and getting it out of circulation so the government can issue new money. Unfortunately, in that part of the country this was unheard of. A Peruvian Nuevo Sol might be shredded into a form that was hardly recognizable. Adhesive tape, Scotch tape, glue, and just about anything was used to try to patch the pieces together. Sometimes we would receive just half or less of a paper bill. The only secure currency were coins, because they are more durable. When the church treasurer spread out the money to count, it was a sight to behold. The paper money looked more like something that had gone through a shredder. I doubt those who gave this money to the church would be allowed to use it at a bank.

WORN OUT MONEY

We used to sing a song, "Give of your best to the Master" and our people needed to learn that lesson in Christian giving. We were not hard on them, because they were learning, and in reality it was much easier to "get rid" of ugly and unpopular money at the church than any other place. We endeavored to teach them the truth of this verse: *So let each one give as he purposes in his heart, not grudgingly or of necessity; for God loves a cheerful giver*. (II Corinthians 9:7) I am quite sure that before long they all learned the right lesson as we taught biblical giving.

JUST IN TIME—SOMETIMES

—❦—

We can remember on several occasions receiving packages from the States with items we needed. When someone in Brazil was having a siege of sickness, it was amazing but certainly directed by the Lord that a package arrived with the right medication. One can only conclude the guiding hand of God was working to have the package include a certain item in the box. Even for the package to arrive in Brazil safely was a miracle. Many years ago, packages sometimes took months to get to their destination. When they did arrive, the contents of the package were just what was needed at that particular time. Many times tourists have appeared at a time when their talents were welcome for a special project being done by missionaries. The list goes on and on.

There are some humorous incidents also about packages. Well-intentioned donors added sticks of spearmint chewing gum to their packages, causing the cake mixes and other edibles to taste like chewing gum. No one ever dreamed this would happen when a box was sent. Humidity has an ominous effect on things. It will melt candy, promote mildew, and make many things unusable. But each time a package arrived, we thanked the Lord for the sender's thoughtfulness. In our modern day things travel by ship or air much faster, and these stories are not as prevalent.

We soon discovered a little-known fact about chocolate. It is a mystery how it happens, but there is, believe it or not, a tiny worm that lives on chocolate. We wondered why the chocolate bars had minute holes in them and there was a sprinkling of "dust'" (chocolate powder) inside the candy wrappers, and now we know.

One day a Brazilian ship docked at Benjamin Constant, and I went aboard to see what they had. My eye caught a beautiful wheel of snow-white cheese under a screen encasement used to keep the flies and other insects away. This was like compressed cottage cheese, and its flavor was heavenly (for a Norwegian). I took it home for us to enjoy for a few days. The next day I sliced a nice piece of cheese, and just before savoring it noticed that intermingled in the snow-white cheese were snow-white worms. In fact, it appeared there were more worms than cheese. Anyone with poor vision would not have noticed. Needless to say, that ended our cheese fest. And to think I had already eaten some the day before and it was sooo good. Oh, well, I guess I didn't suffer any bad effects. Even in our simplicity and ignorance God cares for us. We are so glad that He watches over us and helps us in all our infirmities, whether they are physical, mental or spiritual. ***My help comes from the LORD, Who made heaven and earth.*** (Psalm 121:2)

LITERACY CLASS FOR ADULT WOMEN

───⊶⊷───

O ur first years in western Amazon Brazil, 2,000 miles up the Amazon River in the town of Benjamin Constant, were spent learning the language better and getting acquainted with the people. Fairly soon we also started teaching the Brazilian boys and girls in school. While visiting with the ladies, my wife Margie learned that quite a few of them had not had the privilege of attending school as children. Quite a few of the Christian believers were disadvantaged, because they could not read the Bible in their own language.

MRS. LUZIA LEARNING TO READ

Margie started a class with these ladies to teach them how to read and write. This helped them in many ways, and especially to read and understand the Bible. She started with five ladies. Meeting regularly, Margie systematically taught them their own language. They all spoke Portuguese better than we did, and yet they did not know how to read it. You can only imagine the thrill it gave Margie as she saw them grasp their own mother tongue, recognize words, and slowly begin to read simple passages from the Bible and other textbooks Margie gave them.

One of her students, Luzia, was very eager to read the Bible. As she progressed in her learning, she told Margie one day, " I pray the Lord will keep me alive long enough to read the Bible through one time." What a practical goal she made for her life. This lady's son, John, came to the seminary of which I was director later and told us that his mother lived into her 90s. You can imagine how many times she had read the Bible. Do you read the Bible and profit from its teachings? I pray you do, for the Word of God is the greatest book ever written. *For the word of God is living and powerful, and sharper than any two-edged sword, piercing even to the division of soul and spirit, and of joints and marrow, and is a discerner of the thoughts and intents of the heart*. (Hebrews 4:12)

LOADED WITH CASH

—◦◦◦—

Living in a remote Amazon area has challenges that one would never think about when living in the States. Living in the part of Brazil so close to two other countries — Peru and Colombia — involved the use of three types of currency. Normally the merchants in any of these countries would accept cash, making the correct exchange rate.

Receiving American dollars was the trickiest. The black market operators have been always ready to get those dollars, but we as missionaries did not get involved in this aspect of money changing. The Brazilian government pretty well governed the process by which money could be exchanged. We discovered that the safest way to make these exchanges was to fly to the midway city of Manaus on the Amazon River. There at the Bank of Brazil, we could write checks and receive the official exchange rate and then return home. The return trip was not as easy as it may sound. We did a lot of praying for protection as we traveled on a PBY amphibian airplane with cash. The long flight from Manaus to Benjamin Constant was always a chore. With the money stuffed in about every place you could imagine, and on a "wing and a prayer" we made it home. Some money was used as "shoe insoles" inside our socks, and some was placed in luggage (close by). All in all we had to be innovative. You must remember that this happened years ago. We are sure that today with all the electronic advantages the world boasts, transfers are easy at banks and places of business. Every time we traveled great distances to exchange money, we were aware of God's protecting hand upon us. The last phrase of Hebrews 13:5 states: *I will never leave you nor forsake you.*

IT'S THE DECISIONS THAT GET YOU

—⚍—

When Margie was pregnant with our daughter Joy, we had an important decision to make. Would she go to our local hospital in Benjamin Constant or travel to Iquitos, Peru, for the birth? At that time, we were not comfortable about our local hospital, because of some administrative issues. In our field council meetings in Brazil, Fran Schlener coined a very astute catch phrase which we will never forget. She said "It's the decisions that get you." How right she was.

We decided on Iquitos, Peru, for the birth. Our mission had an established work there, with a Bible school and many local churches. We stayed with our good friend Jerry Russell during our time there. I had a severe case of boils at the precise time of Margie's delivery. To treat this properly took a great deal of time, given the fact I had over 50 boils on my body at all times. I boasted an overall count of 350 before it was over. We had our son Rawlie with us, and I cared for him while Margie was in the hospital. Joy's delivery was not without problems. The umbilical cord was pressing on Joy's neck. As we looked back on this event, we wonder if this was the start of her disabilities. I was present for her delivery just as I had been for Rawlie's birth in São Paulo, Brazil. The Iquitos hospital was simple, and fairly clean, and we were thankful to be in a place where there were fellow Americans, sympathetic to our problems. Margie recovered somewhat at Jerry's apartment, and then we returned to Benjamin Constant, a two-hour trip by amphibious plane.

The long episode began what would eventually alert us to the fact that we needed professional counsel regarding Joy's condition. Another story in this book entitled "An Unforgettable Trip Over the Andes" details more about this. God was good in giving us many resources in Iquitos, Peru, where Joy was born. The words of this song by Frances J. Crosby express our heart's emotions during these times:

> All the way my Savior leads me,
> What have I to ask beside?
> Can I doubt His tender mercy,
> Who through life has been my Guide?
> Heav'nly peace, divinest comfort,
> Here by faith in Him to dwell!
> For I know, whate'er befall me,
> Jesus doeth all things well;
> For I know, whate'er befall me,
> Jesus doeth all things well.

For You are my rock and my fortress; Therefore, for Your name's sake, Lead me and guide me. (Psalms 31:3) With Joy's birth in Iquitos, Peru we now had an international family: American, Brazilian, and Peruvian.

TWO AND HALF TONS OF BABY FOOD ON A JAPANESE SHIP

———— ∞∞∞ ————

J oy, our daughter, had terrible choking spells. Each bite of food caused her to choke. Anguish at our meals was hard to explain. We prayed our way through each spell. During our first furlough after Joy was born, I purchased Gerber baby food, which was much easier for her to ingest than what was available along the Amazon, and thus prevented extreme choking.

I decided to accompany our baggage to Belem, the port at the mouth of the Amazon River. The trip would be too hard for Margie, Rawlie, and Joy, so I went by myself. I traveled on the U.S. Argentina Maru (if my memory serves me correctly), a Japanese freighter with a limited number of first class passengers. This was an experience never to be forgotten, going through the Panama Canal Zone with those magnificent locks. I won't soon forget the time I disembarked at a small place, and to my dismay the garbage collectors were on strike. Garbage was piled up as high as the lower edge of the rain troughs on all stores. You should have seen the rats. What a mess it was!

After arriving in Belem, I went through customs. Time stands still, it seems, in some countries, and I had quite a wait to get our baggage cleared. I stayed with missionaries Stan and Pat Best. While waiting, I painted a sign for their church, upholstered furniture in their house, and did some minor electrical repairs. Finally we trans-shipped our baggage and that baby food 2,000 miles up the river to Benjamin Constant.

There's one more thing about the ship ride to Brazil. Other missionaries were traveling with me to this same city. On Sunday we asked the captain if we could have a gospel service and also a small portable pump organ for our music. He said we would have to wait, because the Buddhists were using it. We invited folks to the service, and to our delight, the president and his wife of the Panama Canal Company attended. That morning I spoke on Moses and part of his story from Exodus 2:3. When Moses' mother could no longer hide him, she made an ark of bulrushes for him, daubed it with asphalt and pitch, put the child in it, and laid it in the reeds by the river's bank.

God is good, because the Panama Canal Company president was very interested in oil in that part of the world. He was intrigued that Moses' parents used asphalt and pitch to protect their child's little ark. We were glad for another opportunity to preach the gospel while traveling to Brazil. Paul admonished Timothy, ***Preach the word! Be ready in season and*** out of season. Convince, rebuke, exhort, with all longsuffering and teaching. (II Timothy 4:2)

AN UNFORGETTABLE TRIP
OVER THE ANDES

—∞∞∞—

Our daughter Joy, eight months of age, was not well. As new parents, we did not know what was wrong. We lived in Benjamin Constant, Brazil. Our senior missionaries across the Amazon River in Leticia, Colombia, suggested we have her checked in Bogota, Colombia. They arranged the air flight for us, and we departed to see a specialist. The plane on which we rode was chartered to carry jungle animals to a zoo in Florida. We were surrounded by all kinds of creatures. Even tropical fish in special plastic bags took up space on the plane. Yes, boa constrictors were our traveling companions, too.

After a while, I looked out the plane's window and saw jagged snow-clad mountains. When I questioned one of the crew, he offhandedly explained that to economize fuel, this pilot does not go OVER the Andes but in between the high peaks as he heads toward Bogota. That was quite an experience. Because of our daughter's breathing problems, the Greek merchant who was chartering this plane graciously scheduled an ambulance to be at the airstrip when we landed. Thankfully Joy did pretty well on the trip, except for turning rather bluish. After the specialist examined Joy, he said to us. "You have a mongoloid idiot." Later tests proved this was not the case, but we were pretty devastated by his report. In fact, he said she needed a blood transfusion that very day. With this news, Margie and Joy left by plane the next day to our home in Ferndale, Washington, and our son Rawlie and I returned to close our mission station and join them later. This was another episode in the long story that would follow about our daughter's problems. God was leading in very definite ways, showing us at each step what to do and where to go. ***In all your ways acknowledge Him, And He shall direct your paths.*** (Proverbs 3:6)

ANEMIA: PHYSICAL AND SPIRITUAL

—⁂—

Rawlie and I returned to the jungles of Brazil from Bogota, Colombia, feeling rather lonely. It was in that city that the doctor had declared our daughter Joy to be developmentally disabled and dangerously anemic. Rather than risk a blood transfusion away from home, I sent Margie and Joy on the plane back to our home in Ferndale, Washington. God did a miracle on that trip. Our family doctor was waiting for Margie and Joy upon arrival, and after a blood test, it was concluded that she was in good shape and did not need a transfusion. See how wonderfully God answered prayer in such a short time? Communication was not simple in those days. I had to wait a while for Margie to transmit the news to me, and she had to wait to know we had arrived safely in Benjamin Constant.

The next Sunday, in Benjamin Constant, I preached in the evening service a message on spiritual anemia. I gave Joy's story and the reason for their trip home. I explained how God did a miracle in her blood while Joy and her mother were on the trip. The church was packed, with many visitors attending. I preached a simple gospel message and gave the invitation; the response was small. I was burdened and broken over our daughter's situation, and I used the moment to explain physical anemia to the ones present in the service. I explained that anyone who hadn't received Jesus Christ as his personal Savior was in a serious condition and needed help. There was a holy hush in the auditorium, and I emotionally told the story of our Joy. Once again I asked if there were some who would like to acknowledge they were sinners and in need of Jesus' cleansing power in their lives. Several raised their hands. I noticed the men were reticent in making up their minds. I pleaded with them to give their lives to the Lord, to be saved, and to live for Him. Then the Lord moved in our humble little church, and many people were saved that night. Someday in eternity we will know how many lives have been touched by our daughter's story. She could not talk nor even hear, but God has used her story to reach many. How we rejoice in this and give Him all the glory.

SHEPHERDS MINISTRIES

O ur world changed when our precious daughter, Joy was born in Iquitos, Peru, on October 31, 1959. Other stories in this book relate more of her story. Here we desire to write about the wonderful home where she lived for 45 years. Through the providence of God, this home opened for our daughter because of the kind help of Dr. Andrew Wood, the founder of Shepherds. This was her home until shortly before her homegoing on July 27, 2012.

The tender loving care Joy received there for so many years is beyond our ability to communicate correctly. We will never stop thanking Shepherds and all the good staff there who had a part in Joy's life. We know there were many throughout the years who helped her in numerous ways. She was not sup- posed to live past her fifteenth birthday, but she passed away at age 52. This was because of the magnificent care received at Shepherds. Joy was totally deaf and never spoke a word. However, in talking to the staff at Shepherds, most of them related how much Joy had taught them.

SHEPHERD HOME, UNION GROVE, WISCONSIN

Our deepest appreciation goes to Dr. Andrew Wood and the board at Shepherds for their years of working with us as they cared for Joy. In her later years Dr. William Amstutz was the president of Shepherds. Our sincere gratitude goes to him for the wonderful way he continued Joy's care at this special place.

A total surprise awaited me after retiring as pastor from First Baptist Church of Ferndale, Washington. I was asked to consider working with Shepherds as their West Coast representative. This position turned out to be one of the most rewarding things we had done in our years of ministry. We visited churches in eight western states, including Alaska, giving updates about the Home, requesting prayer and financial help for their needs. Our home was a fifth wheel trailer, and the Lord allowed us to do this for about 11 years. The last year was spent at home in Ferndale. President Amstutz and the board allowed me to remain there doing public relations work with the churches in these eight states. Their kindness in this was beyond our imagination. My wife, Margie, was very ill, and they wanted me to care for her but also maintain the relationship with churches we had visited in past years. It was a delightful year, and the graciousness of Shepherds in allowing us to do this is something we will never forget. Nor will we ever stop thanking the Lord for their extreme kindness in this offer.

When Shepherds was unable to care for Joy, because of more demands with her failing health, we were able to have Joy in a facility near our home, Christian Health Care Center in Lynden, Washington, until she passed away July 27th, 2012. Thank you, Shepherds, for the privilege you gave us to minister all those years because of your care of Joy. In Jeremiah 23:4 we read: *I will set up shepherds over them who will feed them; and they shall fear no more, nor be dismayed, nor shall they be lacking, says the LORD.* This is Shepherds' verse, and how true it is for the dear ones they care for. They have a Shepherd first in Jesus and also a wonderful place to live called Shepherds.

FROM JUNGLE TO SUPERMARKET

———✦———

In our area of Brazil, some 2,000 miles up the mighty Amazon River, food was always a concern to us. We enjoyed vegetables, but they were not plentiful. We did learn something, however, which was a great blessing at meal-time.

In America we had seen jars of palm hearts for sale. They were expensive, and we never bought them. So we really did not know what we were missing. I cannot remember the circumstances, but one day I decided to have a Brazilian who worked for us get some palm hearts. We learned that palm hearts are really the "unborn" (undeveloped) leaves of a palm tree. Inquiring of the local people which palm tree would provide this edible vegetable, we were told that açai palm was the one. I sent Pedro looking for some. It became a weekly ritual at our place. Pedro would cut down three Açai palms and extract the top part of the tree which contained the beautiful and delicious hearts we enjoyed so much. With some lemon juice squeezed on them, we had a very tantalizing addition to our meals.

In case you are feeling sorry for all those trees being cut down, I wish you could have flown with me about eight hours over the immense Amazon jungles to see millions of palms that grow in that huge forest. Did you happen to notice the name of the palm trees from which we took the hearts? The Açai berry is a very famous health food product used for many things here. It is sold in health food stores everywhere as an anti-aging medicinal product. It is used also for weight reduction and several other things. The locals used it to make a delicious drink. We have eaten ice cream with that flavor, also. We discovered long ago that the jungles where we lived contain enormous numbers of plants that are beneficial to health. *And out of the ground made the LORD God to grow every tree that is pleasant to the sight, and good for food; the tree of life also in the midst of the garden, and the tree of knowledge of good and evil.* (Genesis 2:9) So the very things we had around us go FROM JUNGLE TO SUPERMARKET –the title of this short story.

FLASHLIGHTS BEFORE L.E.D. BULBS

—✁✁—

W e have often thought how it would be living today in one of the towns along the Amazon River, where we worked for many years. Travel at night was not easy for our dear Brazilian friends. Some would come to church with little torch-like lamps fashioned from an evaporated milk can or something similar. The wick would be an old rag twisted into the small opening. The fuel would be either kerosene or diesel oil. These oil lamps were often the only illumination they had in their homes. But eventuially flashlights became more reasonably priced, and they took the place of the old fashioned lamps.

At church it was quite a sight to see people come into the building, get settled, and then methodically unscrew the battery cap and remove the batteries from their flashlights. Along the 2 X 4 boards in the church wall, one could see flashlights everywhere, all laid out with the batteries outside the unit. Folks conserved battery power this way, convinced it would drain the battery to leave them assembled. Who am I to judge? They had to be thrifty with batteries, which for many were a luxury, that's for sure. I would love to revisit these towns and experience the joy of folks in owning a flashlight whose bulbs would last almost forever compared to the old days of conventional light bulbs. The new L.E.D. bulbs have without a doubt revolutionized living in the jungles. When I think that at the economy dollar stores one can pick up all kinds of flashlights for a dollar, what a delight it would be to get them into the hands of our friends there. Who knows, maybe they do use them and have the luxury of better lighting to make their way in the dark to church and other places.

It gets so dark in the Amazon at night. A flashlight was a gift from God to our people to direct their way to church. Spiritually it was rewarding to preach Jesus, the Light of the world, to the Brazilians. ***Then Jesus spoke to them again saying: I am the light of the world. He who follows Me shall not walk in darkness, but have the light of life***. (John 8:12)

GASOLINE-POWERED WASHING MACHINE

———∞∞∞———

Wash day in Benjamin Constant was interesting. We were fortunate to have gas motors that powered our machines. This made a world of difference in the cleanliness of our clothes. The main ingredient on wash day was water. Even in a place where there was much water, the practical use of it was critical. Our home was constructed in a unique manner. The aluminum roof and gutter troughs on our house collected the water we used. The bathroom and shower room were especially constructed so that the top of it was a storage place for 56 barrels of water. That is a lot of liquid.

MAYTAG WASHING MACHINE

Water was heated in a 55-gallon barrel that had been cut in half, with a roaring charcoal fire underneath it. We cranked up the Maytag motor on our wringer washing machine, and Margie and her helpers did the rest. During the dry season when there was less rainfall, we sometimes had serious problems on wash day. I remember one time when things were really dry. We had to hire men to walk about a block and a half down from our house to the river's edge. Even there water was scarce. The water was not flowing, so it was getting stagnant and turning green. After filling several barrels, a lot of a Chlorox-type chemical was mixed with it to change the color and deodorize it before heating it for wash day. How thankful we were for rain and plenty of water when we had it. The large storage area above the bathroom provided water for flushing the toilet, taking showers, and for use in our kitchen. In the States we take so much for granted with all the luxuries we enjoy here. Even water is a luxury for some in Brazil. We valued greatly the water God sent us by means of rain so we could collect it in the huge storage tank built over the bathroom.

Jesus told a woman one day who came to draw water from a well, ***Whoever drinks of this water will thirst, but whoever drinks of the water that I shall give him will never thirst.*** (John 4:13,14) When a person receives Jesus as his personal Savior, he is drinking that spiritual water which brings eternal salvation. Have you received this blessing?

HANDLING RAIN IN THE TROPICS

I read that the total yearly rainfall in the Amazon rainforest can be up to nine feet. That's a lot of water! Most of the year in the jungles, it is warm or hot, but nights are often nice. Rains can come unannounced and so quickly that one is not prepared. I devised a method of storm shutters with a counterbalance system so we could easily lower and raise them. Our windows were screened (no glass) so we needed to protect our home when the heavy rains came. The shutters worked well, and Margie could manipulate them sufficiently to save the inside of our home from a flood when the wind and rain came. We were very thankful for them. When the former missionary, Lindsey, who built our house, lived in it, heavy rain and wind came one day and he was not prepared. The rain rushed in through screened windows and soon the house was flooded with water that had no place to go. Lindsey ran for the brace and bit, and drilled a large hole in the living room floor to let the water escape. That's not the best way to control water, and that's why I made the shutters.

Water is a blessing. The aluminum roof of our home conducted rain to troughs and from there to huge holding tanks.

Every time it rained intensely, we knew the 55-barrel capacity tank would be full. That would be useful for flushing the toilet, taking showers, and washing clothes, and it would also provide drinking water for us.

Benjamin Constant was known for its muddy streets. After a rain it was very hard to walk to church less than a half block away. We carried clean shoes and changed into them when we got inside the church.

The Amazon River is very wide, even 2,000 miles up where our town was. In these heavy storms, the river sometimes rose over a yard deep in one night.

At a Brazilian funeral one day, the men tried to lower the casket into the hole when I finished preaching, but the hole was so full of water that they had to dip the water out with gourds. It took a long time, but finally the casket was covered with mud and the service was ended.

During a tropical rainstorm at church, the noise made it impossible to preach and be heard. We had nice roofs on our church and home, but most people had only thatching. When woven properly on long poles, thatching provided a dry interior for the homes. One thing we know for sure as we read the Bible, God **sends the rain on the just and the unjust.** (Matthew 5:45) Rain is a blessing from God, and we have seen how people respond to this great blessing.

MIRACLE OF THE FREEZER

⸺⸺

L iving in the tropics brings exciting challenges. We learned before we went to the Amazon jungles that Servel refrigerators are wonderful. Then we purchased a stove that also ran on kerosene, and it looked just as nice as one in any kitchen. Both of these ran on kerosene, one to make things cold, the other to heat and cook food. Amazing, isn't it? Storing a Servel refrigerator while we were home for a year had its drawbacks, until we learned to "burp" the machine when we returned before using it again. That's right, turn it upside down and allow those chemicals that produce the cold, when heated, to "burp," and normally it would do fine for the next four years.

One day as I was purchasing a cold bottle of pop in the corner store near our place, I noticed that the glass pop bottles were floating in cold water in the dispenser. My mind raced. I imagined how one of these machines could be used without water. I ordered one from the pharmacy in Leticia, Colombia. These freezers came from Sweden. I put kerosene in, lit the wick, and waited for it to get cold. But I did not put water in it. Guess what! The thing got really cold. I put in a thermometer to check, and it was about 5 degrees. Now I had a place to store fish and beef. Before, we had to purchase just enough to use daily. When our fellow missionaries heard what I had done, they all bought freezers, and what a blessing it was to have a place to preserve food. One more thing I did. I ordered Kellogg's breakfast cereal and distributed it to our mission stations. They really liked that and from then on had me order it many times. I had a desire to help fellow missionaries who lived downriver from us. For them to have some of the "goodies" we had was an enjoyable thing for us. I hope you feel the same way about things in life. In Galatians 5:13 the Apostle Paul concludes the verse with an interesting phrase*:* ***by love serve one another.***

INGENUITY AT WORK ON THE RIVER

———⚏———

W e never cease to be amazed at how human ingenuity plays a part in everyday life in the Amazon jungles, both on land and on the river. A friend from an Amazon tributary was visiting me and told me this story: One afternoon a midsized canoe stopped at the front of his house. A man came up and clapped his hands. That's the Brazilian "doorbell." He asked permission to spend the night there, because his little Swedish outboard motor had just lost its propeller.

Hospitality is one of the strong points of Brazilians. There is always a welcome to anyone who drops by. The guest asked my friend if he had a certain piece of hardwood lying around that he could use. He did, and the guest borrowed a machete and began whacking away at this very tough piece of wood. He began to whittle, and he transformed this rugged piece into a crude propeller. Hours went by, and this piece of wood took on a pretty good shape.

HAND-CARVED PROPELLER

After shaping the propeller, he borrowed a screw driver and placed the point of it in a brazier containing hot coals of charcoal. This brazier is the household "stove." Each time the screwdriver got very hot, he pressed it against the center of the propeller and twisted it slowly to burn a hole in the wood. This process went on for a long time. Finally he had burned a hole completely through the propeller. Next morning, he went to his canoe, slipped the prop on the motor shaft, secured it with a pin, and off he went. My friend gave me the prop, which is pictured here. What ingenuity this man displayed! There are countless illustrations of this. We should never take God-given abilities for granted. In reading through the Bible, I was impressed how God gifted artisans in the Old Testament to make things for the Tabernacle. Even if a person seems naturally talented in a given thing, I hope he and we together will just thank the Lord for this gift given them. ***And in the hearts of all who are skillful I have put skill, that they may make all that I have commanded you.*** (Exodus 31:6)

UNACCUSTOMED CUSTOMS ALONG THE RIVER

―――❦――――

I soon learned as a missionary conducting funerals in the upper Amazon, that things are done differently there than in the United States. When a person dies, a wake is held usually in his or her own house. The body is placed on a flat surface with candles and small dishes of salt along with some flowers. People come and go all night paying their respects. Bodies are not embalmed, so everything has to be done within 24 hours. While the wake is going on, friends or hired persons are in the back of the house building a crude casket. In non-Christian situations the men drink heavily while building, and therefore the product usually shows the results. At the funeral of a child, I soon learned that mothers never go to the service. They remain at home while the procession to the cemetery takes place. If any who encounter the procession would like to view the deceased, the procession stops, the lid is removed, the body is straightened to look better, and flowers are put in order. Then the viewing takes place. This is very common.

Cultural practices vary. At a funeral held at a cemetery downriver, the body arrived and with much difficulty was unloaded from the boat. After the service, a long line formed at the casket, and each person took the hand of the deceased and shook it. This was a formal way of saying "goodbye." As in America in former days, at the conclusion of the service each person takes a handful of dirt and throws it on the casket in the grave. Now everything is so neat and orderly at the cemetery, there is no dirt to pick up. We learned in our ministry both at times of death and other situations to ***Rejoice with those who rejoice, and weep with those who weep.*** (Romans 12:15)

WAR ON MALARIA

———————

In the Amazon area of Brazil where we lived, there were many mosquitoes. I remember telling folks about screens on the bedrooms in our home in Benjamin Constant. At about 5:45 in the evening you could place your hand on the screen while standing inside the house. In a few seconds when you removed your hand there was the shape of your hand outlined on the screen. Multitudes of mosquitoes immediately landed on the screen to suck your blood. We were very thankful for window screens. Brazilians used mosquito nets for their safety.

The Brazilian government sent crews into all parts of the Amazon to help cut down on the mosquito population. They sprayed insecticides, and it really helped. It killed not only mosquitoes but also other insects. Chickens would eat the dead or dying insects, and then they got sick. So there were negative repercussions from this drive to cut down on malaria. But overall it was a good program and helped the people greatly.

I volunteered to send blood samples to a government agency in Manaus, testing for malaria. I had a dispensary at our house where folks came for help. I collected blood, sent each slide properly marked and packaged to the agency downriver from us. I kept records of each person, and we then waited a few days or weeks for the report. If a person needed medication, it was included with the report. Then I contacted the individuals and dispensed their medication. After treatment, another specimen was sent to the agency to check the person's progress. This was a rewarding service we could do, and we were pleased to be able to cooperate with the officials in combating this devastating fever that plagues so many in the Amazon.

We learned early on that one cannot be too careful when it comes to caring for your health. Insect repellent, although harmful to the body, does work. Care at night with mosquito nets or just living in a screened house is so important. At any rate, we figured we should do all we could to protect ourselves and leave the rest to the Lord. We served in Brazil with I Corinthians 9:22 as an encouragment to continue on: ***To the weak I became as weak, that I might win the weak. I have become all things to all men, that I might by all means save some.*** This was our prayer.

PESKY INSECTS

I n this small story I will only mention a few of the insects that thrive in Brazil's obliging climate. The roach is probably one of the most prolific insects on planet earth. We have seen many different kinds in our experience in Brazil. When we had gospel services back in the jungles while living in Benjamin Constant, Amazonas, huge flying roaches often crashed into the light of the Coleman lantern or onto me while I was preaching. They are ugly, and no one enjoys getting hit by one. In our bedroom we often had them roaming around at night. They loved to live in the drain pipes of our shower room. While showering, one might experience the terrible sensation of feeling a roach crawl up your leg.

Mosquitoes are a constant concern; because of the malaria threat, we had to be very careful. There are probably as many suggestions on how to keep these critters away from you as there are people on planet earth. Everyone has his or her own idea of what to do. I thought that heavy winds on the Amazon River bank one night would be a sure thing to keep them away. When I focused the flashlight on my leg, there were a myriad of them, testing the flavor of my blood. How could a tiny frail insect even fly in strong winds? I don't know the answer, but I know they do.

Both Margie and Rawlie experienced two varieties of insects that bore into their flesh and laid eggs. The one attacked Margie while she was washing clothes in the Maytag washing machine outside. Healing was a long, arduous process, because this hideous insect kept enlarging the hole into which it had dug itself. Rawlie experienced the agony caused by an insect that seems to bother mostly feet. After the eggs had been deposited under the skin, they hatched, and these worm or maggot creatures created much pain. To this day the only cure is to "dig" them out with a sterilized needle. This not-so-pleasant task was performed many times on our son. The constant vigil that kept us alert to these destructive insects reminded us of our spiritual warfare and how our ***adversary the devil walks around like a roaring lion seeking whom he may devour.*** (I Peter 5:8)

POWER OF THE GOSPEL

⸺❦⸺

The Apostle Paul in the New Testament makes this statement: For I am not ashamed of the gospel of Christ, for it is the power of God to salvation for everyone who believes, for the Jew first and also for the Greek. (Romans 1:16) Fellow missionaries Dale and Martha Payne invited us to their station some 200 miles downstream from Benjamin Constant, Brazil. Dale wanted me to wire his house and at night conduct evangelistic meetings at his church. I was delighted to do both, so Margie and I traveled there to begin our work. I am not an electrician, but Orville Floden in Leticia, Colombia, was, and he drew out the entire wiring diagram for Paynes's house. All I had to do was follow instructions. My dad had taught me to do this long ago.

The wiring went well, with only one mishap. The ladder on which I was standing slipped one afternoon and sent me tumbling about 6 feet to the ground. The ladder scraped my leg badly, but thankfully I was able to preach each night in the Baptist church of Santo Antonio do Iça. God blessed His Word, and quite a few trusted Christ as their Savior. One young boy who received the Lord was Mark, the Paynes's son. We thank God for that salvation.

Another salvation took place that week that I had not remembered. Many years later, Antonio wrote and told me I had led him to Christ during that week of meetings. I frankly forgot that incident, but Antonio did not. That young man went on to study at the seminary in Manaus. Paraphrasing his letter, he said something like this: "Mr. Ralph, I studied, graduated, and God sent me out to start new churches. By His grace I was able to start four or five churches along the Amazon River." I was deeply humbled by this letter, and I give all honor to the Lord for allowing us to serve in Brazil and be used in furthering the cause of Jesus Christ. ***For I am not ashamed of the gospel of Christ, for it is the power of God to salvation for everyone who believes, for the Jew first and also for the Greek.*** (Romans 1:16)

QUICK TRIPS

—⚬⚬⚬—

Before missionary pilots came to the Upper Amazon, travel was slow and tedious. With outboard motor boats and sufficient fuel for the trip, we would set out for the long journey. Margie would pack a lunch with plenty of drinking water. Then off we would go to get medical supplies, groceries, and mail. Those trips were almost always eventful.

The pontoon-equipped planes were a blessing. One could make a round trip in hours compared to days in a river craft. Hank Scheltema and Terry Bowers were the pilots who transported us to our desired locations. Reliable fuel was always a challenge to the pilots, and even docking the planes was a continual concern. I remember when one of the hangars was being planned. Huge trees were felled and floated to the port in front of the pilot's home. Cleverly the workers joined these huge logs together to make a ramp and a platform on which to "park" the aircraft. Then the appropriate roof and siding to protect it was constructed.

On one trip I noticed that we were at a great altitude over the massive Amazon jungles. The huge Amazon River down there looked like a boa constrictor slithering along. The pilot asked me if I had noticed how high we were above the jungle. I affirmed with a "yes," and he then explained why. With only one engine, your success of reaching a destination is pretty slim in case of motor problems. He went on to say that at that great altitude it would be more likely possible to reach the mighty Amazon River, which we could see winding its way through that impressive jungle forest. The plane could glide, hopefully, to an appropriate section of the river and touch down there. It all made good sense to me. I also prayed we would not have to do what he just described as an escape route.

For medical emergencies and many other purposes, the planes were a blessing, and we were thankful for them. This, too, is another matter for prayer as you remember your missionaries. My father-in-law, George Monroe, did not like to fly. He always used a Scripture verse out of context to describe his feelings about the subject of flying. He would quote only part of Jesus' words, *Lo, I am with you always.* (Matthew 28:20) He would always emphasize the word "LO". However, each trip we made was always given to God in prayer.

REVIVAL AT YOUTH CAMP

———— ∞ ————

O ur purpose in Brazil was to teach people the Bible so that they would understand God's love for them and receive Him into their lives for eternal salvation. This happened all during the twenty five years we were there. At services on Sunday and in Sunday school classes, Vacation Bible School for children, and in a host of other ways, we taught the Word of God to Brazilians. During the summer, we had summer camps at different places away from our town. This involved transporting the young people by river launch and smaller private boats 100 miles downstream to the spot chosen for this camp.

We were in the middle of the jungle at a little village. The kids were sleeping in hammocks in thatch-roof buildings. During the day we planned all sorts of activities for the campers, including Bible classes. The study was on the Holy Spirit. At night the preacher brought a message on some aspect of the subject taught during the morning classes. At the conclusion of camp I was honored to bring the last message before leaving the next day for home. As I developed the theme of the Holy Spirit, it was obvious that the attention of the campers was unusual. When I gave the invitation for those who desired to know more about or personally receive Jesus Christ as personal Savior, I did not expect what would happen. All of the campers were ready to make a decision. Campers were in lines to talk to the counselors about the decision they were making. That was a memorable evening. It was obvious the Lord had sent revival to our youth, and it was all in answer to fervent prayer. Many were praying, and God answered.

The effective fervent prayer of a righteous man avails much. (James 5:16)

SEE YOU TONIGHT!

———⁕———

A long with a fellow missionary we would travel to an Amazon River tributary doing evangelistic-medical work. We were able to help the Brazilian Department of Health by giving vaccines and medications while visiting on these rivers. Each house visit was accompanied by a delicious cup of coffee both when we arrived and when we left.

Besides visiting and helping with health issues, we invited people to a gospel service. We would conduct this in a home upstream from where we were visiting. After visiting all day, we headed to our meeting place. We traveled quite a while to reach this house. It was already dark, because there is no twilight on the equator. We pumped up our kerosene lamps and went up into the house. I, because of my size, had to be careful going up those steps, for fear I might break them.

As soon as we got into the house and got the lamps adjusted and sat down, I looked around and saw people we had visited earlier in the day. How did you get here before us? You didn't paddle your canoe around our diesel launch. You can't go that fast! Then out came the truth. The river we were traveling on is snake-like, with multitudes of turns. Picture this: at each turn in the river, local folks would drag their canoe across a short distance and be back on the river way ahead of where they crossed. They just kept doing this and were able to reach their destination much earlier than we.

That night we learned something interesting. As we sat waiting for folks to come to our meeting, we could hear, in the distance, canoe paddles slicing into the water, propelling the crafts along. I mentioned this to our host, who quickly told me who it was we heard paddling. "How did you know?" I asked. Then he said that each person who slams his paddle into the water has his or her own sound. So they can readily know who is paddling the canoe. Isn't that amazing? What a great spiritual lesson. The Bible says, ***Till the LORD from heaven Looks down and sees***. (Lam 3:50) Many other verses tell us He sees and hears. Aren't you glad God sees us? We cannot hide from Him.

HIGH-TECH MACHINES OF LONG AGO

---⊗⊗⊗⊗---

When we arrived in the Amazon Rain forest to serve the Lord, we were amazed at all the advances made in technology. Compared to the advances of today, they may seem fairly crude, but we never cease being amazed at the ingenuity of the human heart. When Margie needed a permanent, we were told that down on the boardwalk in Benjamin Constant, our town, there were those who could help her. Sure enough, we looked for someone and she got a permanent. There was a fantastically arranged machine with wires coming out. Strange-looking endings on the wires were the curlers. There was no regular electricity in Benjamin Constant in those days, so this contraption must have been powered by charcoal, alcohol, or something else. At any rate, the heated elements, affixed to the hair, accomplished what the ladies desired—curls. It was quite a sight to see all those wires attached to the curlers leading to a central nerve center that provided heat to curl her hair.

When I had a serious tooth problem, I found relief across the Amazon River in the city of Leticia, Colombia. There the dentist took his patient right on the sandy ground, just up from the edge of the Amazon River. I wondered what the dentist's method would be, and soon found out. A pole mounted on a round base platform and a conspicuous pedal were my clues. The dentist would pump this pedal, and with the series of gears it would rotate the bit at the end of the flexible cable. Believe it or not, this thing worked. What an amazing piece of equipment to do his dentistry, without even electricity. Now I admit that I prayed he would have a steady foot and keep that bit twirling at the highest speed possible. Any change in the movement or foot pumping on the pedal would drastically change the velocity of the bit that was grinding away on my decayed tooth. I was praying he would have no distractions and suddenly stop the drill deep in my tooth. It was so long ago I really cannot remember if he used a pain killer to deaden the tooth, but I am sure he must have.

By contrast, I want to say that when we moved to the larger city of Natal, Brazil, we had as our personal dentist one of the finest orthodontists in Brazil. He had been awarded prestigious acknowledgments worldwide for his expertise in dentistry. We always gave the Lord thanks for providing the right people at the right time to care for our physical needs. *In every thing give thanks: for this is the will of God in Christ Jesus concerning you.* (I Thessalonians 5:18)

7TH SEPTEMBER HOLIDAY

———∞∞∞———

This date marks Brazilian Independence Day. It is an important day, and our Baptist school in Benjamin Constant celebrated it with great enthusiasm. On that day, the big event was a parade. All schools participated in this, and the townspeople came out in mass for this patriotic occasion.

Our school put time and much preparation into our program. It was a sacrifice for many families to provide their students with uniforms for the marching parade that day. My wife Margie researched each year for this gala celebration. Special skits and programs were held in our church before or after the parade on this special day.

BRAZIL INDEPENDENCE DAY

Practicing for the parade required much time and discipline. When the day arrived, enthusiasm ran high as city and government officials turned out for this special day dedicated to Brazil's Independence.

We were proud of the students who represented our school each year. They were sharply dressed in white uniforms and proudly displayed the Brazilian flag as they marched through the streets. At the conclusion of the parade, a special program was presented. Important military figures gave messages appropriate to the occasion, and city officials chimed in with well-worded speeches about the duty of citizens to represent their country well. Sometimes there would be city-wide picnic-like parties for the celebrants. At other times, participants would assemble at the place they represented and have parties. Street vendors were out in full force selling every imaginable treat known in this part of Brazil. Our students went to the school or church and continued on with festivities of that day.

It is hard to imagine what it must have been like throughout all Brazil those days. We were about 2,000 miles up the Amazon River. The excitement there was no less than in huge cities where millions gathered for parades, programs, and picnics. As citizens of another country, we were so happy to be a part of Brazil's independence celebration. It meant a lot to us to be able to respect and participate in the freedom they enjoyed. And because of this we were there to help train young people in the school to be good citizens of this great nation. We wanted our students to be well trained and educated. Our church was there to give them spiritual guidance and prepare them for life in Jesus Christ and the salvation He offers to all who trust Him. We are reminded of this as we read, *All Scripture is given by inspiration of God, and is profitable for doctrine, for reproof, for correction, for instruction in righteousness, that the man of God may be complete, thoroughly equipped for every good work.* (II Timothy 3:16-17)

SHOWERS OF BLESSING

―――∽∾∽―――

Living in the tropics, believe it or not, the water some-time seemed to be too cool for comfort. I know the kids in the Amazon surely didn't feel that way, because it is a little warmer in the river. But the rain water we collected in a 56-barrel cement tank above our shower and bathroom, was cool, making showering quite uncomfortable.

Long ago, experts in Brazil figured out a way to make water more enjoyable for bathing. They have an electric shower head which screws onto the shower pipe to deliver heated water. At first I thought to myself, "Wow! I'll get electrocuted doing this." But when we realized that probably millions of Brazilians had these gadgets in their homes, we were more encouraged to try one at our home. I was able to find the necessary appa-ratus and installed it in our shower. The day for the big test came. Remember, we generated our own electricity and had to be careful that not too many lights, motors, or other things were turned on when we took a shower. That shower head took plenty of electricity. What a treat it was to inaugurate this new "toy" at our home some 2,000 miles up the Amazon. A late afternoon shower was a blessing. We made sure we timed our showers so the electric shower would have the priority. We would start up the light plant and enjoy our shower. It was so refreshing in the tropical heat. Yes, it was a shower of blessing. And in Ezekiel 34:26 we find this phrase: "there shall be showers of blessing." We also often thought this when the refreshing rains fell on us in Brazil. Are you thankful for the things God gives you? *And I will make them and the places round about my hill a blessing; and I will cause the shower to come down in his season; there shall be showers of blessing.* (Ezekiel 34:26)

THAT'S USING YOUR HEAD

———◦∞◦———

We love Brazilians. They are such fun-loving, genuine friends. We have learned so much from them. God was good in calling us to work in Brazil for twenty-five years. Soon after arrival in the Amazon area, we were intrigued to see how folks carried things on their heads. I think if I did that, I would have a headache. And I have never had a headache. From small loads to large, we were amazed how they used their heads.

A family who lived downriver from our church in Benjamin Constant always came early for the services. One of the younger of the siblings carried the Bibles for his family – yes, on his head. There were five or six Bibles balanced on his head, and he was walking along like an acrobat on a high wire. How did he do it? Why didn't they fall? They are expert at doing this.

CARRYING WATER

I wish I had a picture of this. Margie and I were in a single engine airplane making a trip to a nearby town where I was to conduct evangelistic meetings at night for our fellow missionary and to wire his house for electricity during the day. We sat in this pontoon-equipped aircraft trying to get off the water. The pilot tried everything, and nothing worked. The pilot decided something must be unloaded to make it lighter. Friends living along the river who knew the pilot sent their sons to unpack the weightier items so we could fly. The plane finally made it into the air. We looked down and saw our good friend Antonio carrying a toilet upside down on his head (like a hat) back to the plane hangar, about one-half mile upriver. We will not soon forget that. The Scriptures admonish us to have patience. We agree that our Brazilian friends seem to have more than I do. They demonstrate it every day. ***You have need of endurance.*** (Hebrews 10:36)

THE ARM OF THE LORD
AND "ONE ARM"

<hr>

We should never be amazed how God works in lives, but we are normal, and this is a natural reaction. One day when John Schlener, fellow missionary, was at the hospital bringing a sick person for treatment, we saw the hand of the Lord in perfect timing. A man from Benjamin Constant was also at the hospital emergency because he lost his arm in a saw mill. He needed blood immediately. Hearing this, John offered his blood, and this heroic deed saved Ávito's life. A chain of events followed but ended delightfully when this man received Jesus as his Savior. He later became a deacon in the Benjamin Constant Regular Baptist Church.

Ávito was a committed Christian who lived his testimony on the job. A carpenter by trade, he amazed us by the way he climbed around houses he was working on. With only one arm, how did he do it? To make his occupation even more intriguing, he drove nails into boards with his bare hand to start them, using the hammer to finish the job.

Ávito had a special place in our lives because of what he did one day. The young people and adults from our church were having a picnic on a nearby sandbar. I was shuttling people back and forth from the mainland out to the sandbar. On a return trip to the sandbar, I could tell the mood was somber. I soon learned that our very young son Rawlie had jumped into the water, supposing it was shallow. It was over his head and he began to drown. Mr. Ávito came to his rescue and with his one arm pulled Rawlie to safety. How we thank the Lord for this man who was alert and able to save our son's life. I appreciated Ávito's love for the Lord. He was a deacon in our church. We thank the Lord for men of his caliber as leaders in the church. And I think of John Schlener, who was in the hospital at exactly the right time to give his blood to save this man's life.Then to think that later on he would receive the Lord. I am reminded of Paul's words, *I have become all things to all men, that I might by all means save some.* (I Corinthians 9:22)

SIDEWALKS IN THE JUNGLE

———∞———

When we use the word "jungle," we are referring to the general area of the mighty Amazon basin. In our town of Benjamin Constant, some of the buildings had a cement porch and entry way into the building. But as I recall, there were no sidewalks made of cement. We had the famous boardwalk of Benjamin Constant which went right down to the edge of the river. It was well made, but as its name suggests, it was a board walk. Around our house in the rainy season, which it seemed was most of the time, was a muddy mess. One day I decided we would change that and make sidewalks so we could have access to all our buildings around, including our house. We seem to like things to be comfortable, don't we?

SIDEWALKS IN THE JUNGLE

To begin we had to make our own bricks or hire someone to make them. There are no rocks or crushed gravel in the Amazon. Sand was plentiful along the river. Bricks took the place of gravel. Because there were no lumber yards, we had to have 2X4's or other size pieces cut by hand from trees in the jungle. After laying out the position of our sidewalks, the forms had to be made, and then work began. In areas where water needed to pass from one side to the other, we had to have clay pipes made and placed properly to conduct water. So with bricks at the side and on the bottom as foundation material, the real work began. Prior to this, cement and sand were brought to the site. With the cement placed in these forms, our worker, Pedro, smoothed the surfaces, and the job was pretty well finished. The next morning we noticed that an intruder like a worm had dug its way across the sidewalk. But sidewalks are better than mud any day. It was fun having those walkways around the house, to our workshop and school-office building. And we can assure you it kept a lot of dirt and mud out of our front and back porches. Before the sidewalk, we had to be so careful how and where we walked. The same applies to us spiritually. We must be careful of our walk so that we please the Lord always. I trust we will all do this today. His word reminds us, ***that you may walk worthy of the Lord, fully pleasing Him, being fruitful in every good work and increasing in the knowledge of God.*** (Colossians 1:10)

SNAKES ALIVE!

Two thousand miles up the Amazon River in the town of Benjamin Constant is where we lived. Because we taught school, ministered in the church, did medical work and many other things, our schedules were tight. We hired workers to help us around the house when needed. On this particular day I had the men clean under the house. In the Amazon, houses are built on pillars about a foot and a half high. This helps the house "breath" underneath and provides limited storage space. I had hand-cut (sawed) cedar boards stored there.

One day as the men were working, I could hear them give a low-key laugh. Ordinarily one would think that is okay. But I sensed something was wrong. After a short time I stepped outside and asked Paulino what was going on. My intuition paid off. He told me nervously that our son Rawlie, about two years old at the time, was under the house and was intrigued by a beautiful snake. The fiery red skin of the reptile was captivating, to say the least. The trouble is, this snake is one of the most venomous in the jungles. The bite of this snake would kill a man in 15 minutes.

PAULINO KILLED THE SNAKE

I needed God's wisdom how to handle this. I spoke to Rawlie calmly, asking him not to touch the pretty snake. I dared not scare him or the snake. Paulino with great care grabbed the board and pulled it out slowly with the snake perched on it, all coiled up and ready for action. A deft blow of the machete killed the snake, and Paulino had broken out in a profuse sweat. How thankful I was to hear nervous laughter and see Paulino's courageous action. This was another vivid reminder of how important it is to pray for missionaries. One never knows what they may be experiencing at any given moment. The Apostle Paul always requested prayer of his readers, ***Finally, brethren, pray for us***. (II Thessalonians 3:1)

OPPORTUNITY FOR EVANGELISM
ON A SURVEY TRIP

⸺◈⸺

A survey trip in the upper Amazon area was an under-taking that had to be planned carefully. I wanted to look at a town downriver over 500 miles from us. I decided to go on a small Brazilian boat. For a foreigner it is always a challenge to do this, given our height, weight, and sleeping accommo-dations aboard a small boat. Also, the food is a challenge because we are not accustomed to eating all the things they do. The captain of this boat was traveling with his wife and very small son. The boat was spacious enough for me to enjoy some time on the deck viewing the scenery. I also spent hours visiting with the crew and owner of the outfit. One day he took me into his bedroom, where his family lived. Even though the boat was small, he had a Japanese generator going 24 hours a day and his bedroom was delightfully cooled by refrigeration. It looked as if his bed was king size. It was enormous!

The food was pretty good. They served a variety of good fish. I had to be careful not to drink the water. Brazilians could handle it, but not Americans. I drank bottled pop and water that I knew was safe. Their coffee was delicious, and I had plenty of it.

When it came time to sleep, many were out on the deck with their hammocks, but I was given a very small place where I could stretch out a little and try to sleep. The room was hot, and I was not too keen on opening what little ventilation was available for fear of huge mosquitos. So I suffered it out for the few nights I was onboard.

When we reached the city I wanted to survey with the hopes of taking the gospel to it someday, I was cordially received by a man who had a large meeting place. I stayed there and noticed he was setting up for a special service. I later learned that it was a religious group. They had a Bible on the main center piece, and he openly told me their organization was seeking the truth of life. He opened the door in a marvelous way for me to present the gospel to him. I asked permission to step to the altar they had set up and read from that book (the Bible). He gave permission with delight. I carefully opened the book to John 14:6 and read to him Jesus' words: ***I am the Way, the Truth, and the Life, no man comes to the Father but by ME.*** What an awesome opportunity it was to present Jesus Christ to this man! I honestly felt my mission of the survey trip was rewarded, if I did nothing more than witness to him and his organization. We are so thankful for the way God opens doors to present the gospel.

RUBBER TREES

───⊗⊗⊗───

Brazil at one time furnished a lot of raw rubber for the world. We met old timers in Manaus who worked in this trade for years, developing a great rubber producing industry.

Man's innovations are always intriguing. The process through which rubber goes is very interesting. The tree trunk is cut with a slit in a downward direction. A container is placed at the lower end of each cut to catch the gleaming white fluid. When the containers are filled with the magic ingredient, men gather them, and another process takes place. A fire is built and then smothered, to produce thick smoke. The rubber liquid is poured at the midway point of a pole layer by layer. As each layer of liquid is placed, it is passed through dense smoke, causing it to partially set it so it adheres to the first layer. After a tedious ordeal, this latex takes on the shape of an oblong ball which adheres securely to the pole. It is marketed in this way. The buyer cuts open each ball of rubber to make sure the farmer has not added any illegal weight to this product.

RUBBER TREE

Where we lived, Brazilians made all sorts of things from this raw rubber: shoes, gloves, balls, strips of rubber for sling shots, containers to hold liquids, and many other things. With their ingenuity, they took liquid rubber and made many useful objects. Years ago, Ford Company started rubber plantations, but they were plagued with tree disease and many other hardships. The plantations did a lot of good for Brazil until eventually Ford sold out. After this, Brazil started anew on the plantations, and we understand the industry is presently doing well. Synthetic rubber is also very widely used now.

I never cease to be amazed at God's handiwork in nature. Imagine these magnificent rubber trees. And to think He gave man the ability to eventually learn how to use this tree to bless millions of people all around the world with products made from it. That makes me very grateful for a God who cares that much for us to think of all these added things we so often take for granted. God's Word states that, ***By Him (Jesus) all things were created that are in heaven and that and that are on earth.*** (Colossians 1:16)

ATTENDING CHURCH IN THE TROPICS

⎯⎯⎯∞⎯⎯⎯

The Regular Baptist Church of Benjamin Constant, was the name of the church where we preached and taught in Brazil in our early years as missionaries. The building was basic, with classrooms and an auditorium. The men of the church had a work-day each week to keep the place looking nice. Benches in the auditorium were very simple, with no backrests. Most of the benches were occupied in the services, because attendance was good. There was nothing special about the floor, except one could see the ground below through the cracks. The church was elevated off the ground so air would keep things as dry as possible underneath. That's why you could see the ground through the spaces on the floor.

BAPTIST CHURCH IN BENJAMIN CONSTANT

Children would often come barefooted; older children and adults wore flip flops or sandals. On a rainy day, worshipers cleaned their feet and shoes the best they could before entering. The custom in churches in those early years was NOT to provide hymnals or Bibles. Each person bought and brought a song book and a Bible. It was fascinating to witness the "pecking order" in families when it came to carrying Bibles. Often we saw an individual with any number of Bibles carefully balanced on his or her head, bringing them to church. This always amazed us. Apparently having one's hands free was a status symbol people enjoyed.

At night when people came to the service, those with flashlights removed the batteries and put them on a 2X4 cross member of the church wall. Brazilians always did this in order to not wear out the batteries. In the larger cities we were astounded to see cars driving without their lights on, apparently to save battery power.

Brazilians love to sing. We were often told by women who washed their clothes in the river that they could hear the believers singing gospel hymns. One gets used to the cries of babies in the service. (It was also not an unusual sight to see a mother hold her baby out the window, allowing it to "do its business" in order to keep things dry in the church.) There were no screens on the windows, and we were glad for this. Because of the tropical heat, ventilation was important. With open windows and doors, however, comes another undesirable: mosquitoes. Our believers occasionally felt the need to spit, and they stepped to a window to do so. The people react automatically to foul odors by spitting. I am inclined to believe that through the years some of these customs have diminished.

The church was equipped with storm shutters to help protect the building in heavy tropical winds and rain. They were a great blessing, that's for sure. During a heavy rainstorm it was impossible to speak or be heard in church. The roof was made of aluminum sheets, and the noise of rainfall on it was unbelievable. Brazilian believers love to go to church. They are great at singing, and they do it with great enthusiasm. In Hebrews 10:25 we read: ***Not forsaking the assembling of ourselves together, as the manner of some is; but exhorting one another: and so much the more, as you see the day approaching.*** We hope you enjoy the fellowship in a church. If you don't attend, why not start next Sunday?

OPERATING ROOM DOOR LEFT OPEN

∞∞∞

In Benjamin Constant, where we lived for several years at the beginning of our missionary service in Brazil, there was a hospital. According to the standards of other places it was probably not the best equipped or run hospital in the country, but when one considers it was located some 2,000 miles up the Amazon River, I think it was pretty good. We made many trips to this place from The Port of Two Brothers and Benjamin Constant.

Prior to an upcoming hernia repair on a patient, the hospital doctor asked our fellow missionary if he would take a movie of the surgery. Arrangements were made, and I helped get things ready for this project. Even though it was isolated, this hospital had most of the basic equipment for such surgeries. It was obvious that in order to properly film the surgery, some adjustments would have to made in the operating room. These being made, the day arrived, and the surgery began. We didn't know the man, but that makes no difference. Lighting was correct, the camera tripod was in place, film was on hand, and the operator was prepared for his task. In the nice air-conditioned room, which was a treat for us, the environment was pleasant.

However, as the filming progressed, different angles were needed to properly chronicle the procedure. Yes, we had to open the door to be able to get the right shot of the surgery. Oh, no, we forgot that when you open the door, the temperature rises in the operating room. This made no difference to the surgeon, so it was okay with us. With the door open, flies found their way to the scent of blood. After a while, the odor was not pleasant in the room. I believe my colleague who was filming was a wee bit squeamish and maybe faint-hearted at this juncture. Admittedly I did not enjoy it. This filming of the surgery took three hours. The hospital room was a mess, and flies were everywhere, but at least the doctor's wishes were respected; he got his movie. As missionaries we are driven by the words of Scripture, ***Therefore we make it our aim, whether present or absent, to be well pleasing to Him***. (II Corinthians 5:9)

If we can please the Lord through all these efforts to reach people for Christ, that's what is expected of us.

I'LL BE BACK WITH ONE MORE

———— ∞∞∞ ————

Sometimes God sends blessings in big doses. In our work in Benjamin Constant, a couple of Ticuna Indian fellows started attending our church services. At the first invitation given for people to respond to the message of the gospel, these boys raised their hands. At the end of the service, I had a serious talk with them about their decisions. They definitely knew they were sinners and wanted to invite Jesus into their lives. They needed His forgiveness of their sins and eternal life which He promises in the Bible. We were happy with their commitment. The next week the two brothers brought another brother along. After the service this young man received the Lord joyfully. We were delighted that now there were three in that family who were Christians. They lived downriver from our town, so each week they had to leave quite early and paddle their canoe for a long trip to get to church. The interesting thing about this was that they were always on time and eager to learn more about their newfound faith in Christ.

The next week these three brothers brought another brother, and he also received Christ as his personal Savior. We were amazed how these conversions happened so rapidly in one family. The next week their sister came, their only sister. She listened attentively to the gospel message, and at the invitation she was wonderfully saved. You can imagine the encouragement this brought us, seeing a family united in Christ, coming to church, and growing in their knowledge of spiritual things. After about two weeks, these five young people brought their mother, and yes, she was saved also. What a blessing! Before we end this story, let us say that their dad also was saved. So here we had a fine Ticuna Indian family united in Christ. We learned that after the first two boys got saved, they went and witnessed to their next brother, who was convinced he too should be a Christian. The same thing happened to the next brother and later the sister and mother. These folks had learned very early in their Christian experience the joy of telling others what Christ did for them. It was a powerful example to witness and was a help to many in our church. This family was very faithful in their attendance and growth in spiritual things. I had the privilege of starting an evening Bible study with the boys. They were a tremendous encouragement to us in our ministry. We will never forget the lesson they taught us in having a passion to see all their family become Christians. I pray this will encourage you, dear reader, to turn your life over to the Lord and then get busy telling others what you have done. ***The LORD has done great things for us, and we are glad***. (Psalm 126:3)

CORNER GROCERY STORE

The corner grocery store in the Amazon jungles is not necessarily on the corner. It could be almost any place. And it certainly does not look like a grocery store you are used to. I believe the corner store in the jungles is an "institution" in itself. It is almost the life-line for poor people who live around it. I was amazed how much stuff could be placed in such a small space. But the magic of the store came alive when a person could go there to get a pop bottle filled with kerosene or diesel fuel for the lamps at home. This was the intrigue of the corner store. You did not have to buy in quantity. In fact, few people could, because they did not have much money. So when a housewife needed two eggs, she could go there and pick them up.

One great advantage of the corner store was that many of the locals had charge accounts at these places. It was very convenient to drop in, pick up three cups of flour or the local farinha (meal) made from the cassava root. Fishing gear, rope, and about anything else you could imagine would be available. I don't know where they put all this stuff or how the owner could have kept track of it, but he did. A man walking to work drops in and picks up a cigarette to smoke on his way to work. On and on it goes.

The name of these stores in Portuguese, at least way up the river where we lived, was "botequim." A dictionary would indicate this to be a bar, but in the language of the people of the upper Amazon, it could be that or just a store. It is true, liquor was sold there, and some of the stores had their own personalities, and drinking would take place in them. Some had very low-key cafes also where you could drink coffee and have a piece of bread or local fruit which was sold there. Indeed, the corner store was an institution, and a highly intriguing place to visit and just watch the flow of traffic in and out. The corner store was also the focal point of most of the town gossip and local news.

You will read in another story that it was in one of these corner stores I saw a machine filled with water with pop bottles floating in it. That's how they cooled their drinks. I took the idea from that and got one of these coolers. They ran on Kerosene, believe it or not, and would keep our meat frozen to below zero. What a wonderful discovery it was when I decided to use it without water. What a miracle machine for storing our fish and beef! You can read more about this in "Miracle of the Deep Freeze" in this book.

I know that volumes could be written about the corner store, but suffice it to say that it is a lifeline to these dear people in towns along the Great River. We were glad there was one right across the street from us in Benjamin Constant, and believe it or not, it was ON THE CORNER. Many poor people took advantage of the corner store because at least they had credit with the owner. Jesus warned that the poor would always be with us. I am so glad these corner store owners were kind to them. And we should be too. *For the poor you have with you always, but Me you do not have always.* (John 12:8)

DOWN THE ROAD AND INTO THE JUNGLE FOR A RODENT

—⚬∾⚬—

My custom was to have early morning Bible studies with the men of our church before they went to work. The long trek along the trail and into the jungles was always intriguing. One cannot imagine the beauty and interesting sites along the way. And the sounds are most captivating coming from the myriad of animals, birds, and other creatures that entertain the trekker.

Arriving at the thatched roof house, I carefully climbed the ladder, which was made with limbs nailed to two upright poles. With my size and weight, it is a wonder I made it to the top without breaking some of the rungs. This was a breakfast meeting, and we gathered around the dining table and began our meal. The hostess, wife of one of our believers, prepared a very nice breakfast. Our cold drink was a delicious "aba-catada." This is an avocado mixed with milk and sugar and is very delicious. No meal would be complete without coffee, and it is always good. But what about the main dish? On this particular day we had fried eggs and a slice of meat that was white and about the size of the palm of your hand. No knives were provided, just a medium-sized tablespoon. So I used it to cut the meat, and it was so tender no knife was necessary. I asked the hostess the name of the meat, and she said it was paca. If we had been new to the Amazon, I probably would never have figured out what this was I was eating. Paca is part of the rodent family. So for breakfast that day I had rat meat. I must confess it really was delicious. Would you like to try some? When God created the heavens and the earth, including all these amazing animals, He said it was good. ***Then God saw everything that He had made, and indeed it was very good. So the evening and the morning were the sixth day.*** (Genesis 1:31) When you pray for God's blessing on your food, remember that in the jungles that might mean bless the rodent (rat) food, dear Lord.

THE COOLEST PLACE
ON THE HOTTEST DAY

———∽∾∽———

The Amazon humidity mixed with high temperatures can give a heat that is unequal in intensity. We all know that air in motion is more cooling than dead air. That's the reason we use fans. When we traveled on the river in our speed boat, we always felt refreshed by the humid air surrounding us, because we were in motion. In Brazilian homes we noticed coolness unlike what we had in our house with our aluminum sheets for roofing. Thatched roofs definitely are cooler than other types of roofs. In northeast Brazil, in downtown buildings, sometimes we felt almost cold as we entered them. What made the difference? At night brick and stone buildings absorbed the night coolness, and during the heat of the day they were as "cool as a cucumber."

On a very hot day in the Amazon, I was looking for a certain kind of wood in the jungle. In my boat I traveled to a spot on a tributary of the Amazon, tied the boat to a tree, and walked into the jungle. It was low-water season, which made it easy to work my way into the jungles, because all the underbrush was cleaned out, leaving a semi-moist, mud-like surface to walk on. The jungle "umbrella" made it delightfully cool. On the hottest day one CAN find a cool spot. I guess you could call it God's air-conditioned jungle blessing for me that day.

I dreamed of ideas to give us air in motion during siesta times. What about a fan blade powered by counter balanced weights that at least give a few moments of air movement even without electricity? Someday someone will invent it. But cool refreshing space is a great blessing on a blistering hot Brazilian day in the tropical rain forest. Have you thanked God for the refreshing times He has given you? It makes me think of a famous Psalm, *He makes me to lie down in green pastures; He leads me beside the still waters.* (Psalm 23:2)

DON'T PLAY GAMES WITH SNAKES

My friend Orville left his town, Leticia, Colombia, for a business trip to a nearby place in Brazil. His boat, with an Evinrude outboard motor, was his transportation. The Amazon River is wide, sometimes two miles or more. As he traveled along, he encountered all sorts of stuff floating in the river.

River travel can get monotonous. Sometimes things change and life gets more interesting. Orville looked ahead and saw a large snake making its way across the river. He decided to have some fun. Taking aim with his boat going full speed, he visually measured the half-way point of the boa constrictor. Then with determined hands on the steering wheel, he said to himself, "I'm going to cut that fellow in half with the propeller right now." With a dull thud sound, he hit the monster full speed, saying to himself, "That is one less snake in the Amazon." and he continued his journey downriver.

Quite a while elapsed before Orville in some strange way "felt" a presence in the boat with him. Of course he was all alone. He reluctantly looked over his right shoulder and to his horror, the large head of a mighty boa constrictor was inches now from his head. What had happened? When he tried to cut the snake in half, the snake hit against the lower part of the engine, escaping the propeller, and crawled up it as a "tree" to gain access into the boat. It was slowly making its way to the driver for an encounter. Thinking quickly, Orville reached to his left side and retrieved an oar and with his left hand deftly applied a hard blow to the snake's head, stunning it into unconsciousness. Never again did he repeat this trick.

When you pray for missionaries, ask the Lord to give them common sense in all they do. It is no wonder we are advised about the tricks of our enemy as written in the Bible: *Be sober, be vigilant; because your adversary the devil, as a roaring lion, walketh about, seeking whom he may devour.* (I Peter 5:8)

AN UP-IN-THE-AIR GARDEN

———❧———

In the upper Amazon town of Benjamin Constant, vegetables were not easy to find or grow. Vegetables in the diet are important, and missionaries sometimes found a way to provide these necessary items for their families. The Lord knows we wanted to stay healthy. He gave us common sense to have an innovative idea to solve the problem.

As I pondered one day, I realized that growing vegetables on the ground would not work because of all the things that could interrupt their growing cycle. We did not have the luxury of hydroponics, either. One of these problems was stray cattle and other jungle animals that might want to experiment with whatever is growing. All the living things in the dirt would also be a deterrent to growing a product. I had a brainstorm which I am sure was not original. I elevated the garden, putting it at eye level or higher, so cattle could not eat the plants. Sturdy posts were placed at the four corners, and a substantial box was placed on top. The earth was treated by separating it and letting it dry out and thereby ridding it of some of the living organisms which would doubtless feed on the root system of the growing plants.

ELEVATED GARDEN

You may ask what we grew in this elevated box. We planted *couve*, the Brazilian word for collard greens. It was a prolific survivor when grown this way, and we certainly enjoyed the wonderful fresh vegetable. Gardening obviously demanded attention there in the Amazon jungles. We had to water our garden by hand, because there was no running water. We had to check it often to be sure no animal or pesky insect was invading our treasure. Yes, missionaries must do other things besides preach and teach. They have to provide for their family. The following Scripture phrase comes to mind when I think of our vegetable garden: *If anyone will not work, neither shall he eat.* (II Thessalonians 3:10)

AMAZON LUMBERJACK

I cannot do justice to this subject, so I will give a small segment of it as told to me by a Brazilian logger. Everything in the jungle takes a long time. Men who select and cut timber are a special class. Logging is done in the dry season, and men who do this work are astute by any measure. These men know the jungle like the back of their hands. An area is chosen where felled trees can be maneuvered tediously to a larger tributary that flows into the Amazon River. The loggers' work is extremely dangerous. They have practically no machines, so almost everything is done manually.

After arriving at their chosen spot, the loggers set up camp, and bright and early the next morning, the work begins. Trees are chosen and men begin the job of cutting them down. It still remains a mystery to me how they do this. When the first tree is down, then the next one is chosen and felled. It goes on like this for a long time. After cutting, the jungle floor has to be prepared for the next step. The cutters have to have a sixth sense, to know what to do. When the main clearing is done to their satisfaction, the next part is hardest – waiting. What are they waiting for? They wait for tropical rains. In the rain forest, rains are hard and often. The main channel of the Amazon River rises considerably during the rainy season. This means all tributaries do likewise. Water comes down in torrents, tributaries fill, and banks overflow. This is what the loggers are waiting for. They are happy when the jungle floor begins to flood. As it does, the magic happens for which they have been waiting. The huge trees begin to shift a bit as the water lifts them. Eventually these huge mammoth trees are floating. Now begins the unbelievable job of maneuvering the trees to the Amazon River.

I wish I could have personally watched this process. With hours of tedious and strenuous labor, they float these huge hulks of lumber through all the thick jungle litter and finally out to a smaller tributary. They then tie the logs together and have a tug boat tow them to the Amazon, where again they are securely tied and start their journey of hundreds of miles to the sawmill. These brave men face all sorts of obstacles in order to make a living for their families. Their hard work reminds us of God's word to the first inhabitants of the earth. *In the sweat of your face you shall eat bread Till you return to the ground, For out of it you were taken; for dust you are, And to dust you shall return.* (Genesis 3:19)

CHARCOAL CHARLIE

———— ◦∞◦ ————

We are always impressed by how God programs people into our lives. As a missionary pastor of the Benjamin Constant Baptist Church, I witnessed God's grace displayed in the members. Aniceto was one of these choice persons. Because we boiled water for drinking, we used lots of charcoal. Aniceto made charcoal for a living, so we bought it from him. Aniceto, or Charcoal Charlie, as we called him, would come to our home to sell us more charcoal as we needed it. He had a special place where he made charcoal near his home. It is quite interesting how they gather the proper wood, place it in depressions in the ground, and ignite it. Then they cover it with dirt, and a ventilation system is used to keep the subdued fire going. Aniceto was an expert and knew the precise timing in this process of making charcoal. The smell is unique and everyone knows what is being done by the odor that fills the air.

Charcoal is used in many ways. We used it mostly for boiling drinking water. The ladies in our area used charcoal irons for ironing clothes. It was quite a sight to see large, heavy irons "powered" by charcoal. They were very effective. At our house we were more modern and used gasoline-powered irons. They did a good job.

Charcoal Charlie came to our house often, and when I asked how he was, his answer was always the same: "I am not very well, thank the Lord." What a profound testimony this was! Aniceto was not well physically, but he kept busy and considered it a blessing from the Lord that although not well, he could keep going. We all can learn a lesson from him in this. The Apostle Paul said it well: ***Not that I speak in regard to need, for I have learned in whatever state I am, to be content.*** (Philippians 4:11)

BAMBOO RAKES AND CHAIR SEATS

Even though we did not know how to do many things, it was fun learning along with our Brazilians, helping them produce something practical. I am not a carpenter, but I decided to teach our handyman how to make chairs. We drew up plans, and he shaped the legs and assembled them. I had decided we could make the seats with a woven material from the jungles. The Brazilians would know what kind would be practical, so I sent one to find the right material. He chose the right kind of vines and eventually wove them into very attractive seats for the chairs. Now it was possible for him to make these for others if he chose to do so.

MAKING BAMBOO RAKES

In Benjamin Constant there was much bamboo. One day I had an idea that our yard man could actually make and sell bamboo rakes. This adventure was a lot of fun. Peter cut the bamboo, and then chose the length of the tines. With a blow torch and a pipe securely fastened to the workbench, we heated the ends of the strips of bamboo. When the bamboo was very hot, and using layers of cloth (so as not to get burned), we shaped the hot strips over a hot pipe. In a short time they took on the proper shape. Then all he had to do was fan the shaped strips and secure them to a smaller bamboo as the main handle of the rake. When the product was finished, it actually looked similar to a rake one could buy at a garden supply shop.

Through the years we discovered several things that a person could make on his own and thereby help with his finances. We wanted to teach our dear Brazilian friends the value of work and what it would mean to them if diligently pursued. In the Bible we read: *He that tills his land shall be satisfied with bread.* (Proverbs 12:11)

BAPTISM SERVICE IN THE RIVER

—⊶—

I learned as a young person that not all churches have baptistries, the tanks that are built into some churches. I was baptized in Phoenix, Arizona, in an irrigation ditch. Our churches sometimes used the larger canal for this purpose. In Brazil, especially in the upper Amazon, we surely did not have such accommodations as baptistries in the church, so we used the Amazon River. At these church services, many of the towns-folk attended and witnessed what was going on. We are sure many were just curious. People who have personally received Jesus Christ as Savior are baptized as a public demonstration of their faith in the Lord. It is a very meaningful service for those who participate and for the witnesses. Candidates for baptism would carefully make their way down the steps that were previously embedded in the mud floor. The side rails give stability, and the one baptizing had a back rest as a security so he can perform the baptism. In other words, in case piranhas are interested, it was wise to have a quick escape planned. Piranhas don't normally attack, but occasionally they do, and it was good to be prepared.

BAPTISM IN THE RIVER

Long ago when we had these services at the river's edge, not too far from the Baptist church, a lot of people attended. It was noteworthy also that this was not a casual occasion. The ladies wore dresses and the men were nicely groomed.

Before the baptism, the pastor would give a message or short meditation. There would be singing by all and prayer. As each one was baptized, many times the group would clap and give vocal expressions of joy.

The Bible teaches baptism, and believers in Brazil were carefully instructed in the biblical teaching on the subject. For them it was a public testimony of their personal faith in Jesus Christ, and their pledge to live their lives for the Lord and be a witness for Him. Have YOU made that decision as a believer to be baptized? *Go therefore and make disciples of all the nations, baptizing them in the name of the Father and of the Son and of the Holy Spirit.* (Matthew 28:19)

CHICKEN HATCHERY – JUNGLE STYLE

M y wife Margie home-schooled our son Rawlie. To help with some of the home projects, I decided to build a homemade chicken incubator so Rawlie could trace the formation of a baby chick in the egg. I started with a frame box with one shelf in it. On the rear of the box I put an Aladdin lamp, which was normally used for illumination at night. Placed in the incubator, it provided heat, which is needed to similate the mother hen's temperature. We kept the wick very low and with a thermometer gauged the warmth perfectly. A mother hen's body exudes moisture as she sits on the eggs, so we used a spray bottle to apply the moisture artificially twice daily. A mother hen also turns her eggs to keep the heat distributed during incubation. I used a piece of heavy wire the shape of a large letter U. Once daily I pulled that gently under the eggs, and they were turned by the movement.

Now the fun starts. As the chick was being formed in the egg, we would take a flashlight and shine it through the egg. Soon we could see the heart pumping. Then the baby chicks hatched, and we cared for them. Often the grown birds provided meat for our Sunday meals in the Amazon. We also had chickens that did their own incubating, and it was fun watching them care for their babies. One of the hens was better than the rest at raising families. We named her Veronica. Jesus compared the relationship of the mother hen with her chicks to the relationship He desires to have with us: ***Jerusalem, Jerusalem, the city that kills the prophets and stones those who are sent to it! How often have I desired to gather your children together as a hen gathers her brood under her wings, and you were not willing!*** (Matthew 23:37)

CONVULSIONS AND THE MIRACLE
AT THE HOSPITAL

---∞∞∞---

O n a very rainy day in Benjamin Constant, Brazil, I was concluding a burial at the cemetery. We could not get the casket into the grave hole, because the hole was full of water. With gourds, the men frantically bailed out the water and shoved in wet slimy mud over the crude casket. The service was ended, and I headed home.

Soon I was met by a small boy on the very slippery jungle trail, telling me to come home quickly because our son was sick. Arriving home, I found our house filled with Brazilian believers, all praying for Rawlie. In the kitchen, my wife was holding him, only the whites of his eyes showing.

HOSPITAL IN BENJAMIN CONSTANT

It was a desperate situation. I asked our helper boy to get our motor boat ready with gas, and we went down to the boat house to try to get him to the hospital. Carrying our son on the slippery pathway to the boathouse was a task.

As we traveled the mile or so to the hospital by river in our boat, Margie at one point said "He's dying." I said to her, "Someone is praying for us." As we approached the entrance to the hospital, the door closed. The doctor decided that it was all he would do that day. We were devastated. But by the providence of God, an army official, a doctor, who was being treated for malaria of the brain, heard what was going on and unlocked the door from the inside and treated our son on his own. Talk about miracles! God prepared a dying doctor to save our son. We thank God for miracles. A phrase from Mark 7:37 comes to mind when I think of this incident: *He (Jesus) has done all things well.*

CONVULSIONS AND
THE MIRACLE IN AMERICA

—∞∞∞—

When we were home in the States for our regular furlough, we spoke in churches, giving reports of our ministry in Brazil. At a church in Phoenix, I was asking people to pray regularly for missionaries, because you never know when they might need your help in prayer. We have always emphasized this. I told them about the time Margie was sure that our son was dying on the way to the hospital and my assurance that someone was praying for us.

At the conclusion of this meeting, a lady came up to us and asked more questions about that trip to the hospital. I remembered pretty well when it was, and we talked for a short time about the incident. The lady was visibly touched by our story because of the time element. She told us, "For some reason on such and such a day I was awakened with a profound burden to pray for Ralph and Margie in Benjamin Constant." As we compared notes and time differences, we realized she was praying for us almost to the minute when Margie voiced her emotional concern about our son's life. How wonderful it is to have people in fellowship with the Lord so that they can be reminded at the precise time when an urgent need is present in someone's life, even though they are thousands of miles away. As we traveled to churches to share our ministries in Brazil, we always urged Christians to continuously pray for the missionaries with this verse: ***Brethren, pray for us.*** (I Thessalonians 5:25)

COFFEE AT ITS BEST

—⁂—

Two of us were on an evangelistic-medical trip up one of the many tributaries of the great Amazon River. We had left the port of Benjamin Constant the night before and had spent the night a few miles up a smaller river. Our custom was to visit as many places we could each day, inviting people to the gospel service we held at night. Along with this, my colleague would do any necessary medical and dental work the people needed, including delivering babies. We travelled in his medical launch.

When we arrived at the first house for a visit, the people there quickly told us they knew we were coming. I asked them how they knew. They told me they could tell by the sound of our launch diesel engine that it was us. Each boat has its peculiar sound. Sound carries extremely well over water. We were amazed.

Customarily the housewife in each home offered us a cup of coffee as we entered and again as we left. They are very hospitable. At one home, the wife put raw coffee beans into a 5 gallon kerosene can cut in half lengthwise, and roasted the beans over a charcoal fire, adding sugar as they heated until they were pitch black and the smell was "killing." Then she transferred the beans into a grinder that uses a disc system to pulverize the beans almost to the consistency of powdered sugar. She then brewed the coffee and offered us a cup. You cannot imagine how delicious this was! It is impossible to have coffee any fresher than that. It was in Brazil that I learned to drink this wonderful brew. This hospitality was shown us in each house we visited. In another story we tell of the evangelistic meeting we had at night along this tributary river of the Amazon. These people exemplified Paul's admonition: ***Share with God's people who are in need. Practice hospitality.*** (Romans 12:13)

A FUNNY BRIDGE

———⊶⊷———

House maintenance is perhaps a little more difficult along the Amazon than in the States. We discovered that paint must be of a very high grade or soon mildew would be eating away at it. We purchased expensive paint to keep our house in good condition. Mold in the jungles has a way of devastating things very quickly.

We repainted the kitchen, including the floor. We found a good grade floor enamel that was super for the cedar boards. It is so hard to function properly when the kitchen is out of use. I finally got half of the floor painted its nice gray color, and this half was dry now and usable. To get over to the dry part of the floor, I made a bridge, carefully constructing it so it would be sturdy, wide, and easy to navigate over to the newly painted surface. As a precaution I made a simple sign that instructed anyone in the kitchen to stand steadily on the bridge and walk carefully to the dry side. For some reason, one of the girls who helped Margie in the kitchen with meals, approached the bridge, read the sign and did the following: She removed her sandals, looked intently at the bridge, and then straddled it and walked on the wet paint to "dry ground".

I don't think she put her sandals back on, because at this point her feet were wet and a gray color. And so went life in the Amazon. We never knew what a day would bring. But we did know, and still do, that, ***This is the day the Lord has made, we will rejoice and be glad in it.*** (Psalm 118:24)

A HARD NUT TO CRACK

Other than the cashew nut, I wonder if the Brazil nut is the next favorite of many people. Where we lived, in Benjamin Constant, majestic Brazil nut trees were everywhere. They are immense, some reaching the height of 160 feet. Early on in our life in the jungles we learned to respect this tree, especially when the fruit was ripe. If a falling nut pod hits a passerby, it would kill him instantly. It is dead weight, and as it falls the velocity increases. Men working during harvest-time use very long poles. I still don't understand how they manage them because of their extraordinary length. They must use extreme caution, always looking upward. We hope they have good eyesight, for this is no work for one with poor vision. Not only are they cutting loose the clusters of nuts, but when they fall, they must take extreme care to follow them to the ground.

An interesting aspect of this Brazil nut tree is the way God planned for the flowers to be pollinated. An orchid flower that does not grow on the Brazil nut tree is necessary for attracting large colonies of the only bees that are able to pollinate the Brazil nut flower. The female of this species of long-tongued bees is the only bee on earth that has enough strength to lift the coiled hood on the flower and a tongue long enough to negotiate the complex coiled flower.

God has designed this unique nut to be well protected. It grows in a large, fibrous pod that protects the treasured nut inside and cushions it from the impact of its great fall to the ground. Removing this thick, fibrous casing, reveals a hard shell, inside which are the Brazil nuts. This shell is very hard but not too thick. It is almost like hardwood. When polished and shellacked, it makes a beautiful showpiece. Our Creator God has put inside each shell between eight and twenty-four nuts depending on the diameter of the pod. We understand that each size always yields the same amount of nuts. To get to the nuts, you must break yet another very hard shell which encases the meat itself. We used hammers to break through this very hard shell. A Brazilian friend of ours showed us how they do it. With his fingers on the flat edge of the nut, he struck the nut against a hard surface, and it broke open. I would not suggest trying this. Indeed, this nut is protected so thoroughly that we have never seen anything like it. In a similar manner the believer in Jesus is protected. ***Our lives are hid with Christ in God***. (Colossians 3:3)

A JUMBO OF A TREE

———⁂———

Our first days in the Amazon town of Benjamin Constant were filled with exciting new discoveries. There is so much to learn about life in a new place. We moved into the house our fellow missionaries built, but who had since moved to work with an Indian tribe downriver. There were tall, beautiful symmetrical trees at the front of our house. We had no clue what they were.

JUMBO TREE

As months passed we noticed these trees were flowering, and soon the ground was covered with a beautiful layer of very small red petals. It was a sight to behold. God's beauty was displayed on the ground in the form of a beautiful carpet of flowers. As the trees developed, in a few weeks a nice red apple-size fruit was present in abundance. The missionary ladies soon discovered that this delicious white-meat fruit was quite similar to an apple, and when seasoned appropriately, could be baked as a wonderful "apple" pie.

At night "visitors" liked to enter our yard and help themselves to this prize catch. Returning from church, we would often see people in the trees, gathering, to their delight, as many fruit as they could cram into their pockets or throw to their friends on the ground. We decided to put an end to the stealing. On a given day we would announce the great "jambu" distribution. This is the name of the fruit in Portuguese. In English it is red wax jambu. It is hard to believe that so few trees could give so much fruit. In a place where money was not abundant and these God-given trees yielded so prolifically, we wanted to share them with the townspeople and not allow them to take them at night. One day we picked the trees, completely filling many washtubs. These we distributed to all who wanted them. Everyone was content, and we were too. How gracious of the Lord to provide these prolific fruit-bearing trees in the middle of the jungle. *Let the earth bring forth grass, the herb that yields seed, and the fruit tree that yields fruit according to its kind, whose seed is in itself, on the earth; and it was so.* (Genesis 1:11)

A PAGE FROM THE DIARY

⸻∞⸻

Living in the upper Amazon area of Brazil near the frontier of Peru and Colombia presented many challenges. Being much younger also contributed to a much busier schedule. I looked back in our journal and read page after page only to discover that we did a lot of visiting, both in the hospital and in private homes. Because our main mail supply was in Leticia, Colombia, we made numerous trips to get and send mail. Being a border town, Benjamin Constant also had access to more imported goods than other places along the river. In Leticia, the choice was even greater. I bought a lot of "goodies" in that town. Once I stepped into a store and saw an entire shelf of Peter Pan peanut butter. I told the clerk I wanted it all. Our senior missionary living in this town knew about my purchase before I reached his home later that day. My only response was that he lived there and could buy it at will. When I saw it, I wanted it all. It was also easy to distribute to other missionary families downriver who would really appreciate it.

OUR MAIN TRANSPORTATION ON THE RIVER

The trip from our town in Brazil to Colombia was usually eventful. So many things can happen while traveling in a small motorized boat. Sudden wind storms can create waves that are overwhelming. Rain can soak every inch of us. Motor failures or challenges can also keep us on the alert.

One day as we were traveling with several passengers, a dogfish jumped into the boat and proceeded to slap me several times on my leg. I am glad he did not choose to bite, because he had very sharp teeth.

We never wanted to get caught in the dark, either. There is no twilight in the Amazon, and when the sun goes down it's like pulling the shade. It is dark. We always gave thanks to God for His protection for us as we traveled. I am glad we learned to do this, and we are thankful for many who prayed for us. Peter tells us, *Casting all your care upon Him, for He cares for you*. (Peter 5:7)

SEVEN CLASSES IN ONE

Two of our ministry goals in Brazil were to evangelize and to give the Brazilians an opportunity to get an education and be productive citizens of their country. To help us accomplish these goals, we conducted services in the Baptist churches and also taught school. It was fun teaching children the basics of education: reading, writing, and arithmetic. Each of these studies would help them for the rest of their lives. Margie used our front porch as her classroom at first. It worked well and was ventilated, so it was cool in that hot climate. She basically taught preschool equivalent courses.

MARGIE'S CLASS IN SCHOOL

My study (classroom) was a thatch-roofed building with windows on all four sides. The desks were arranged in five rows from front to back. This allowed me to teach using the old-time one-building, one-classroom education system. The five grades were challenging to these American missionaries, but God graciously helped us educate the children.

After one of our students graduated from the elementary course, I noted he was back on the jungle paths playing soccer. I called him in and said I would teach him the "ginasio" course, which is similar to our high school. He agreed, and he sat directly in front of my desk. So I taught grades one through five in front of me, and the high school series right in front of my desk. To my left I taught our son's kindergarten class.

Believe me when I say Margie had her hands full with those rambunctious preschoolers and I with my six classes in the Portuguese language plus our son's class in English. But it is amazing how well it went. Sebastião, the high school student, has thanked us for the training we offered him. He went on to seminary, graduated with high grades, and then he went to university and graduated there the same way. He is now a pastor in Manaus, Brazil. We are proud of him and so thankful for the privilege of investing our lives in his early education. He surpassed us in his academic achievements, and we are happy to have been part of the process which got him to the position he now holds. At this writing he is a pastor and teacher in the Amazon Federal University in Manaus. He also directed a seminary. He was not the only one who went on to further his education. Joao (who also directed a Bible school in Manaus), Clovis, Narcisio, and others are just a few of those who graduated from our Escola Batista in Benjamin Constant. We are grateful to God for giving us the opportunity of being part of this process. Again we are reminded of Paul's teaching, *And the things that you have heard from me among many witnesses, commit these to faithful men who will be able to teach others also.* (II Timothy 2:2)

A CLOUD OF BUZZARDS

—∞∞∞—

S ometimes you can witness a sight that is incredible if you are in the right place at the right time. We never cease to marvel at God's workings in nature. In Benjamin Constant, where we lived along the Amazon River, we had such an experience. One day in the back yard of our home I happened to glance up at the sky and saw something I will never forget. Had I waited long enough I would have noticed thousands of buzzards, because the sky would turn dark with them.

This mass of flying buzzards was not going forward in a straight line, but in a huge swirling motion as they moved in the direction of "up river." I was curious how so many could gather and what their motive was for being high in the air and moving with such determination in one direction. I asked the locals the meaning of this and was told an amazing story. Each year hunters go far upstream to the headwaters of some tributaries of the Amazon River in search of alligators for food and hides. As they catch and butcher the animals, much of the beast is left to rot in the hot Brazilian sun.

A BIG ALLIGATOR

Because of God-given instincts, the vultures seem to have a communication system second to none. Their *GPS* systems are right on. They know when to start their trek to the cache of food. In huge circles, thousands of buzzards move slowly but deliberately in the right direction seeking their reward up river. It must be a sight to see thousands of birds land on these sandbars for a meal. They are doubtless a real nuisance to hunters. One wonders how far the birds can see across the jungles and if they can smell their meal. At any rate, isn't it amazing how God cares for His creation? Job was aware of the awesome wonders of God's handiwork in nature when he wrote this: ***Who teaches us more than the beasts of the earth, And makes us wiser than the birds of heaven?*** (Job 35:11)

Let us thank Him, for we know He is in control.

A DIFFERENT WAY TO LOSE WEIGHT

———❦———

Living 2,000 miles up the mighty Amazon River had its challenges. Our home was comfortable, and we tried to improve it by adding things to make it better. We decided that walking in the slimy mud around our house should end, so I made cement sidewalks. I am sure that was an innovation for our neighbors and friends in town. We also had a diesel-powered generator for our electricity. That meant we could actually have showers heated by electricity. Does that sound dangerous? It really wasn't. Our generator was located away from the house in order to cut down on the noise. The trek back there to shut it off each night got tiresome, so I made a remote shut-off that worked fine.

But before I installed the remote shut-off, one night I stepped off our porch onto that nice sidewalk which led only partway to the generator. As I glanced down in the subdued moonlight, I saw the dark form of a snake making its way across the sidewalk. Focusing the light, I discovered it was poisonous. Just seconds before the snake encounter, an acute pain streaked across my chest from my left shoulder at an angle over my chest. Immediately I thought I was having a heart attack. It is funny (I guess) what one can think of in moments like these. From that moment, I decided to lose weight. Did I need to? I think so. I weighed over 275 pounds. So my diet began. That year I lost 86 pounds, but I did this without giving up desserts. That is a terrific way to lose weight! I never will forget that episode and the Lord's gracious reminder for me to lose weight. Subsequent medical exams revealed no problem with my heart. But just think, a snake started that process. As a missionary pastor I should have thought of this prior to the incident with the snake. We are definitely instructed in God's Word that our body is the temple of the Holy Spirit (I Corinthians 6:19). We should take care of it.

MIRACLE SPARKPLUG

———⊗⊗⊗———

Every time we set out on a trip up or down the Amazon River, we expected something to happen. Navigating the river takes some learning. I certainly tried to observe the senior missionaries as they worked their way in and out of islands and around the sandbars and all the stuff that floats on the river.

One day I had a serious problem with our Evinrude outboard motor. I tilted it up and saw nothing out of order. Then I removed the motor case and noticed the spark plug had popped out of the engine. Because of poor gasoline, we always carried extra plugs. But the spark wire was still connected to the plug, and the plug was out of the motor. On close examination, I noticed that the threads were ruined where the spark plug should be screwed in. Away from help, alone on the river, what am I going to do? It's always good to PRAY, asking God for wisdom. I did. I cannot blame the Lord for giving me this idea, but I thanked Him that it did work and got me home. I took part of the spark plug box and carefully placed it in the spark plug opening on the motor. Next, I took the plug, and with great care, started screwing it in place, making its own threads in the heavy carton paper I had placed in the hole. When it was screwed in completely, I placed the spark wire on and cranked the engine, and it started! And the miracle is it kept going and got me home. What a miracle! God is good and helps us; even when things are not supposed to work, they do. So please remember to pray for God's wisdom to be given to His servants, the missionaries. *For the LORD gives wisdom; From His mouth come knowledge and understanding.* (Proverbs 2:6)

COTTON IN MY EARS

———⟨∞⟩———

Before we had mission airplanes to transport families, we were dependent on commercial airlines. We were grateful for the plane that was the lifeline for folks along the great river. It was called a PBY Catalina.

Our town of Benjamin Constant was about 1,000 miles upriver from Manaus. Aviation fuel was brought by barge up river to various stations to refuel planes. Barrels, each holding 55 gallons of fuel, were stored in a spot near the river. When a plane arrived, the barrels of fuel were taken to the floating airplane dock. A special pump took fuel from the barrels to the tanks on the airplane wings. A chamois filter was used to keep water and other impurities out. You can see how necessary a floating dock was. When the river was low, the dock was lower than the level of our plane terminal.

Traveling in a PBY was an experience. As we entered the plane, we were given cotton to place in our ears to protect them from loud noises. When the plane started and the pilot throttled its engine, the noise began. Whisking over the water in itself created quite a noise. Because the plane actually floated on water, sometimes we could not even see outside because our window was under water. The noise was deafening. Thank you, cotton. If the weather was hot and no wind was blowing, it was harder to get the plane off the water. Sometimes the pilot would have to make many attempts before lifting off. Once airborne, all was okay. But when we landed again, we were glad for cotton. It helped to buffer the ear-splitting noise of our aircraft and its friction against the water. I am so glad the Lord is the engineer of our bodies. He expects us to care for them the best we can. In 1 Corinthians 6:19-20 Christians are told, ***Or do you not know that your body is the temple of the Holy Spirit who is in you, whom you have from God, and you are not your own? For you were bought at a price; therefore glorify God in your body and in your spirit, which are God's.***

SEAMSTRESSES WITHOUT PATTERNS

When we arrived in Brazil, my wife, Margie, soon learned some interesting things. We had been instructed by our Mission to take adequate supplies with us, which we did. We used steel barrels to transport our items to Brazil. Soon after getting accustomed to life in the jungles, Margie needed an article of clothing and inquired where she could buy it. The answer was fast, "You can't buy any clothing here." The stores only sold material by the meter. After picking the material, she then went to a recommended seamstress and explained what she wanted. The seamstress just wanted a picture of the dress. Margie returned home and was so thankful we had brought several Sears catalogs with us. She thumbed through the books until she found the desired picture. Returning to the seamstress, Margie showed her the picture, and the dress was soon made. We were always amazed by the innate talent God gave these ladies.

Another subject Margie learned many things about was cooking. If the recipe called for shredded coconut, the cook would have to obtain a whole coconut, crack it open, and shred the meat manually. What about lemon juice? Go to the tree and pick a lemon and juice it. All flour had to be sifted in a very fine screen to clean out the live material. Worms, eggs, and other creepy critters lived in the flour. Recipes calling for milk were made from powdered milk. Most of the milk we used was from Denmark. We bought huge cans of it, and when the cans were empty used them to store flour and other perishables that needed to be kept dry.

Missionary ladies became experts in discovering substitutes in their cooking. We love stuffed bell peppers. A vine-vegetable is plentiful in the Amazon called xuxu. With some ingenuity, Margie made stuffed green peppers with it. They are actually pale green and smaller than our green peppers, but delicious. Oh, I forgot to say that you can't go to the store and buy hamburger. You needed to plan ahead for that. We had to purchase the meat and grind it. Then we kept it frozen in our special Electrolux deep freeze that was powered by kerosene. What a blessing! Every day in Brazil was an adventure. The Bible says in Psalm 118:24, *This is the day the Lord has made, we will rejoice and be glad in it.* We considered each day a gift from the Lord. There was so much to learn and it was exciting. I trust you can enjoy your days because the Lord has given you this joy.

THE THRASHING GECKO

———— ◦◦◦ ————

Geckos are interesting reptiles. At night one is awakened by the sound of something hitting against the picture hanging on the wall. You shine your light on the picture but see nothing unusual. When you turn the picture around, showing what's behind it, that tells the story. There was a light colored, bug-eyed gecko with a half-swallowed cockroach in its mouth. The noise you had heard was the gecko thrashing back and forth trying to swallow the roach. We never complained about this particular noise in our house, because we knew it would mean one less cockroach.

The geckos were our helpers, and even though seldom seen, they were especially busy at night. I rarely saw one in the daytime. It is interesting to watch them move around. With suction-cup toes, they climb walls with the greatest of ease. When they capture their prey, those suction-cups secure them to the wall while they are attacking. The gecko itself was not messy, and when it attacked a roach, the roach was swallowed.

The only thing we had to get used to was the sound of the gecko enjoying his meal. With time we no longer heard them. They were welcomed guests in our home.

We are sure that many who have suffered sleepless nights have claimed Psalm 127:2: ***It is vain for you to rise up early, To sit up late, To eat the bread of sorrows; for so He gives His beloved sleep.***

THAT'S A BETTER SHOT

———⊷∞⊷———

Every four years, before departing for our home in Ferndale, Washington, we attempted to take more pictures. We used these for slide presentations of our work in Brazil. Sometimes things did not work out as planned, but at least they were part of our missionary career days in Brazil.

At the Naval Base in Natal, I was innocently taking pictures of the attractive landmarks, statues, and beautifully kept landscapes around the base. I thought to myself: "The folks at home will be happy to see such nicely kept facilities as these." My picture-taking adventure was going well, when all of a sudden a military person walked across the street and asked what I was doing. I quickly explained my desire to take pictures to show at churches when we were in the United States. Well, it was obvious I was in trouble for filming a government facility. And it was even more serious because I am an American. The officer immediately demanded I turn over the camera, which I did. I was then escorted to the security office, where an explanation was in order. I apologized for doing anything not permitted and suggested they remove the film from my camera. After some lengthy conversations, it was finally decided that this photographer was not trying to sabotage the Naval Base by revealing things but just wanted to share pleasant scenes with his friends in America. It was a great relief the way they treated me.

On another occasion, I was filming in a town in the upper Amazon River area of Brazil. At a certain place I stopped to chat with the man in charge, who had a revolver in its holster on his hip. I suggested we step outside, where I would take his picture using his office building as a backdrop. On the way outside, I discovered something which normally would not have overly alarmed me. He had been drinking, and the aroma of liquor was very obvious. He wanted to stand and pose with his revolver in hand. Because he was inebriated, I knew this could be a problem. In fact, as he pulled his revolver out of the holster and prepared his pistol for shooting, he pointed it directly at me. By that time I was sweating, and not because we were in the tropics. I asked the Lord for wisdom to know what to do. I knew I had the promise of God's Word: *If any of you lacks wisdom, let him ask of God, who gives to all liberally and without reproach, and it will be given to him.* (James 1:5)

I told the gentleman that if he pointed toward his right, that would make a much better picture and I would be happy to send him a copy. He was delighted. He moved the gun from pointing straight at me, to his right, and I took the picture. All I could do was thank the Lord for preserving my life from what could have been a disaster.

NO MONKEY BUSINESS

—⊶∽⊶—

Margie's mother visited us in Benjamin Constant when our children were young. It was delightful having her with us as she was such a good sport even though past retirement age. On a trip downriver, we had motor trouble, so I pulled up to the bank of the river among some bulrushes. We prayed, drank some water, and enjoyed sandwiches Marge had prepared for our trip. I changed the spark plugs on the motor, hoping that would make the motor run better and get us to our desired destination. Thankfully, it did,

THATCH ROOF HOME

In the Ticuna Indian area of Santa Antonio do Iça, we stopped at the missionary station of Betania. We visited our missionary colleagues and then visited a Ticuna family who lived in a thatched-roof home. As we were talking, I looked up and saw a long rope-like cord hanging from the high rafters of the house. At the lower end a blob of something was tied to it. Upon closer examination, I determined it was a monkey. Yes, a sun-dried monkey. It was stored in this manner to keep jungle rats, mice, and other creatures from eating it. It was a very clever idea. I asked the owner if he would sell me this choice piece of meat. He kindly consented and took it down for me. Later we took it to our home and slipped it in our Perfection kerosene oven. This made the monkey meat hygienically palatable, and we enjoyed this delicious meat for lunch.

In our home we always pray before partaking of a meal. We were grateful to the Lord for creating things we could eat. The Apostle Paul on a ship that eventually ran aground and broke up, did this. ***And he. . . .took bread and gave thanks to God in the presence of them all; and when he had broken it he began to eat. (Acts 27:35)*** I don't suppose that bread was very fresh, and the word may just refer to whatever they were eating, but Paul prayed before eating. That's what is important - giving thanks to God for the provision of our needs.

UP AND UP IN THE AIR

—∞∞∞—

I have never been the best flyer in the world. Motion sickness has always plagued me. When the single-engine aircraft came to our ministry in the Amazon, I realized I had to get accustomed to occasional air trips. Usually my weakness was controlled by closing my eyes and trying to relax. Actually it worked all the time, as I never really had any mishaps.

Flying over the jungles in Brazil was an unforgettable experience. It is beautiful and breathtaking. Because our pilots flew quite high over the jungle, the snakelike Amazon River looked small winding its way along the endless miles of green jungle. The vastness of the Amazon is almost overwhelming as one looks at the horizon, and the greenness never ends.

On an important flight we encountered some breathtaking views of clouds and even some lightning activity in the distant formations. Visibility was a must as we travelled over the vast jungle areas. Occasionally we would see a clearing, indicating there was a house and alongside a plot of ground for the family garden. If our elevation was not too high, we could even make out the form of humans who were curiously gazing upward to see our plane passing over.

As we continued our journey toward our destination, there was a huge column of clouds that was impressive. It appeared to be several hundred feet wide, and its height without end. Our pilot asked me to look at the altimeter on the plane dashboard. He was getting closer to this column of clouds, and I wondered what he had in mind. All he said was, "watch that altimeter." Soon it was obvious we were not going to skirt that chimney-like cloud but go right into it. I prayed silently as the pilot did exactly what I thought he was going to do. He headed directly into the cloud, and soon we were enveloped by these ominous puffs of clouds. Not being able to see a thing but whiteness, I had no idea what the pilot was thinking. He reminded me again to look at the altimeter. The needle went crazy as we were caught in an elevator-like trip upward, something I had never experienced before in a plane. The altimeter had jumped to a very high reading in a matter of seconds while the plane was caught in this unbelievable updraft. To my amazement, the plane eventually came out of the clouds. Now we were at a much higher elevation, which the pilot had desired. He had done this on purpose to gain altitude without using much aviation fuel. He accomplished his purpose, and I learned a lesson on the mighty power of clouds and thermodynamics.

In retrospect however, I often wondered if that was a wise thing to do. I can visualize a mishap in our elevator ride, and perhaps losing control of the plane. I am not a pilot and know nothing about this subject. If we had crashed, I am quite sure it would have been difficult or impossible to find the wrecked airplane somewhere in the vast impenetrable Amazon jungle. It may be out of context, but this verse in Deuteronomy 33:27 means much to me when I think of that incident: ***The eternal God is your refuge, and underneath are the everlasting arms.***

THOSE PESKY ROACHES

We soon learned that roaches have a survival rate that is phenomenal. These disease-carrying insects are nasty and live everywhere. Taking a shower in the jungles could be an experience. How often we glanced down only to discover one of those ugly things emerging from the drain pipe. If you were not careful, they would make a beeline for your leg and ascend it gracefully to escape the rushing water.

We were always careful with our food, making sure everything was covered properly so roaches could not invade it. Screen boxes with short legs placed in small cans of water helped keep roaches and ants out of food. The water would keep the ants out and the screen shut out the roaches. It was a never-ending pursuit to discover ways to discourage roaches from entering places they should not be. Another precaution we learned quickly is that all dinnerware and utensils needed to be carefully stored. Nothing is more disgusting than to find a roach at the bottom of a glass, cup, or pan you are using.

Finally, we learned that some insects we detested were actually "helpful" in other ways. Ants, which are a pest, would clean up the roaches we killed during the night in our bedroom and bath. We spotted little areas of sawdust-like debris, and knew the ants had been busy during the night. When you dressed in the morning, it was a very good idea to inspect your clothing before putting it on. And please check your shoes before putting them on. Roaches like darkness and may be down inside your shoe.

Keeping roaches under control is as hard as fighting the forces of evil in this world. It is a never-ending task, but God provides help for those who seek it. Joshua was an encouragement to his people and we can be comforted by his word as well: ***And Joshua said unto them, Fear not, nor be dismayed, be strong and of good courage: for thus shall the LORD do to all your enemies against whom you fight.*** (Joshua 10:25)

SLEEPLESSNESS

An annoyance at bedtime is tiny green frogs. They are normally out of sight, but at night they start to play. They are small and you can hardly feel them land. If they land on you, it gives you a clammy wet-like sensation. At times we focused the flashlight and found them on our pillows.

Roaches are an aggravation at bedtime. They like the dark, and when you least suspect them, they appear. Many times during the night, we would have the sensation of an intruder in our bedroom. I remember on a moonlit night as I turned over in bed, I noticed something dark on my pillow close to my face. Turning on a flashlight, I saw a huge roach that had been there already trying to work on my mouth or somewhere on my face.

Mosquitoes, if left alone, will hound you all night long. We soon learned the habits of these miniature creatures and how annoying they can be. Before going to sleep, we found them and killed them. As soon as you swat at a mosquito, you can be sure it will land very soon. This enabled us to find most of them before bedtime. To cut down on the mosquito population, we shut the bedroom doors early in the evening.

We used insecticides very sparingly, because the fumes they create are injurious to health, and we heard reports of their causing hepatitis.

There are things we never got used to, but in part we had to or we'd never sleep at night. We are sure that many who have suffered sleepless nights have claimed Psalm 127:2: ***It is vain for you to rise up early, To sit up late, To eat the bread of sorrows; for so He gives His beloved sleep.***

A SACRIFICE NOT MANY WOULD MAKE

—∞∞—

In our years serving in Benjamin Constant, we witnessed many tangible demonstrations of sacrifice. The church had many members, and they attended regularly. Torrential rains are very common in that part of the world. Many times we trudged through thick slimy mud just a short distance from our home to get to church. We had to carry extra shoes to change into when we got there. We thought of those dear people who didn't have the luxury of two pairs of shoes or those who were barefoot.

One Sunday morning, the rain was coming down in torrents. We wondered if anyone would come. Finally, they started to show up. On a wet day in the jungles it can be surprisingly cold for those who are not accustomed to cooler temperatures. Quite a few members lived back in the jungle beyond what we would call the "city limits." We supposed they would not come, because the small rivers and streams swell in heavy rains. We were surprised to see some who live way back arriving for Sunday school. When questioned how they made it, this was their story: "We arrived at the creek, and it was filled with water. We could not wade across. We made a decision to come anyway. We removed our clothes, made them into a bundle, held them above our head the best we could, and got across the creek. Then we put our dry clothes back on our wet bodies and finished our trip to church." Do you know anyone who would do that? Those Brazilian Christians were heroes. We admire them for their faithfulness and their desire to attend services. These people taught us a real lesson. I think of the words of Christ: ***Whoever can be trusted with very little can also be trusted with much, and whoever is dishonest with very little will also be dishonest with much.*** (Luke 16:10)

AS BIG AS A BARREL

Even though I used to be as big as a barrel, that is not the subject matter of this story. The big question is how to get your belongings to another country and keep them safe. We learned from other missionaries to use heavy metal barrels. First we had to find them, which was not always easy. To store things in them it is best to have heavy plastic liners. Later we were able to buy ready-made liners, but at first I made them. I made bags out of heavy plastic and used heat to form them. When we packed, we also placed silica gel inside to absorb any moisture. We packed our barrels carefully and were certain to number them, label them, and securely lock the clasp shut with a padlock. Sometimes we welded the clasp shut so it could not be opened. We never knew how these barrels would survive through customs in Brazil.

BARRELS TO SHIP OUR GOODS

In Benjamin Constant we kept our barrels in the attic of our house to provide as much heat as possible in that humid rainforest area. The heat helped keep them dryer. I remember I had one barrel filled with shoes alone. My shoe size was not available in Brazil, so we had to take 4 years' supply with us. I had to have a mix of heavy boots, dress shoes, and ordinary shoes. All we needed to run our household was crammed in these barrels.

Through the years, we used the empty barrels to store water in and for other purposes. A half barrel was used for heating water for washing, etc.

An interesting side story of these barrels is that one year we had reports that one of Margie's helpers was at youth camp very well dressed. I should say that youth camps in Brazil are that way. Young people wear their best clothes to camp. We had never seen anything like it in the States. This particular individual apparently was using clothing that others thought belonged to Margie. It was true, and she was living high on the hog at camp at Margie's expense. This person had gone into our attic and taken numerous items of Margie's clothing from a barrel and wore them at camp. We were very sorry she did this. She asked forgiveness, and we granted it. We remained friends with her and her family. The biblical precept is so true that says, **Be sure your sin will find you out.** (Numbers 32:23)

OFF TO SEMINARY

───❀❀❀───

Because we taught Brazilians in our school in Benjamin Constant, we followed their development. Through ministries in our church it soon became evident that some young people were gifted to be servants of the Lord. When their schooling was completed as far as we could take them, some were chosen to have further education at Berean Baptist Institute and Seminary in Natal, Rio Grande do Norte. It was our pleasure to send some away to this distant city and school. Not long afterward, we ourselves were transferred to Natal and worked in the seminary.

What a joy to see the young people develop as they studied secular subjects and then went on to seminary for theological training. Margie and I were privileged to be a part of their training process. It has been encouraging to see them go on for further education and into ministry. Some took secular employment and did Christian ministry also. Sebastião and Narcizio were two who went from Amazonia to Natal. They were bright young men and did well in their educational pursuits. We followed Sebastião, who returned to the Amazon River town of Manaus where, besides his secular accomplishments, he became the pastor of a large Baptist church. He also directed a seminary in that city.

While we were in Natal at the seminary, one day we heard a knock at the door, and here was another of our students from Benjamin Constant. What a thrill to see him! He had traveled thousands of miles with the intent of studying with us. He graduated from our seminary and went to the city of Manaus and was involved in a seminary or Bible school in that city. We had a real interest in this young man because Margie taught his mother how to read and write Portuguese when she was in her 70s. His dad was a deacon in our church in Benjamin Constant. What a small world, and we rejoice to see how these fine people continue serving the Lord. We were privileged while in seminary ministry to help train men for the ministry. This reminds us of Paul's instruction when he said, ***And the things that you have heard from me among many witnesses, commit these to faithful men who will be able to teach others also.*** (II Timothy 2:2)

BIG MOVE TO THE CITY

———✦———

We enjoyed our life and ministry in the Amazon jungles. The people were fun-loving, many were receptive to the message of the gospel, and we enjoyed being involved in school ministry teaching Brazilian boys and girls.

Many miles (or kilometers) away from Benjamin Constant, on the Atlantic coast, is the city of Natal, Rio Grande Do Norte, Brazil. The director of the Berean Baptist Institute and Seminary, Carl Matthews, had a heart attack on a routine trip to the post office, and not many hours afterward he was graduated to glory to be with the Lord. His death was a big blow to the city of Natal, where he had been given honorary citizenship and special recognition for his noble work during the building of the air base near Natal during the war days. Bill Branda was the acting director after his death and held this position for some time. ABWE (Association of Baptists for World Evangelism) contacted me about serving as director, but we really had no interest in leaving the Amazon area of service. During our furlough, I was approached again about it, and finally, after prayer and much thought, Margie and I made the decision to accept the invitation.

Moving from Benjamin Constant, Amazonas, Brazil, to Natal in Northeast Brazil, was a big chore. Everything we had was for life in the tropics. Even the logistics of moving so far across the country was overwhelming. But we dug into our new project with enthusiasm, knowing the Lord had something great for us in the city, just as He had in the jungles. The barrels were filled and boxes made for other items. We sold things no longer needed in the big city, said our good-byes, and headed for Natal. Leaving our friends, the churches, and our home was not easy. These had been the first ten years of our missionary career. In our ministry we referred to and used more illustrations of life in the Amazon than any other place in Brazil.

What a contrast it was living in the city compared to the jungles. We purchased a used Kombi (Volkswagen Micro-Bus). We were amazed at the store owner's trust in the foreigner. I told him that as soon as I received the money I would pick up the car. He emphatically told me to take the micro bus and when the money arrived, bring it to him. He requested no signature, phone number, or home address. I thanked God that our American friends in this city had such a good reputation. It reminds me of a Bible verse that shows the trust we have in the Lord. ***The LORD is good, A stronghold in the day of trouble; And He knows those who trust in Him.*** (Nahum 1:7)

LIFE IN THE BIG CITY

————∞∞∞————

Moving from the jungles to the city was an experience we will never forget. When our baggage from the Amazon arrived, we had the colossal job of getting it into storage and then finding a place to live. Our missionary colleagues cordially invited us to stay with them, and that was very nice.

Living in the big city was new to us after jungle life. To find our way around town was a learning process. We had to find out where particular stores were that had things we needed. The location of government buildings, the post office and grocery stores, and where to buy other incidentals, were parts of our introduction to the city of Natal.

Eventually we rented a home on the seminary campus and were soon doing our teaching ministry at the seminary. Working with young people was a challenge and a great blessing. Each had come to improve his education and prepare to serve the Lord. Each missionary had classes assigned to him or her, and we studied very hard preparing for our classes. It was rewarding to see the growth in the students' lives. There were many school activities which kept everybody very busy.

Brazilians take their national holidays seriously, and we kept very busy arranging special programs and making signs and placards for every event.

At the seminary, life was never monotonous. We spent hours in personal preparation for our classes. At one time Margie did all the book work for the school. As director of the seminary, I had to deal with many legal matters, and Margie helped by working out the payrolls for the teachers. Having employees there involved many crucial legal ramifications, and we consulted appropriate sources to keep all that in order.

As the school nurse, Margie had her hands full at times with certain illnesses that spread among students living together in rooms. She had to be knowledgeable about what medications were available at local pharmacies and to have a supply at the seminary.

Our students went out each weekend to minister in churches all over the state of Rio Grande Do Norte. We were always in awe, thinking how dedicated these young people were to be so willing to travel to distant cities and towns to minister in many churches. Most would travel on Friday and return Monday. Each Tuesday morning during chapel times they reported on their ministries. How thankful we were to hear of conversions in the churches. Many of these students were young men, too young to be doing what they did, but we admired them greatly for ministering in a mature way.

We recently found one of our former students on Facebook, and it was a delight to correspond with him and learn of his years of service in one of the churches he worked in when he was a student at the Berean Seminary.

Margie played piano for the seminary choir, whose director was Dick Matthews. They traveled to many churches giving concerts and were a blessing everywhere they performed.

It is no exaggeration to say there was never a dull moment in seminary life. Margie and I counted it a privilege to have spent fourteen years in this ministry. Illness demanded we return to the States, but what a thrill it has been to hear reports of how God is using the Berean Baptist Seminary to touch lives in northeast Brazil. We will never forget our years spent there. Margie and I took seriously the words of Paul: ***Let a man so consider us, as servants of Christ and stewards of the mysteries of God. Moreover it is required in stewards that one be found faithful.*** (I Corintians 4:1)

CAMP AT LAKE BONFIM

———∞———

The seminary was blessed to own property at beautiful Lake Bonfim. This lake, about 35 miles away from the capital city of Natal, where we lived, was an important part of our ministry. This property was used for church camps, seminary retreats, men's and women's retreats, and for many other occasions. Seminary students were used as counselors at the camp. Transportation became a major factor during camp season, so Margie and I and others spent a good deal of time transporting campers from the churches and counselors from the seminary to the camp.

CAMP AT LAKE BONFIM

God worked in wonderful ways during camps. Many adults, children, and young people were saved there. When the seminary had its retreats, there was always a challenge and a colossal job of getting the cooks, supplies, etc., to camp. Swimming was the main attraction, but many other recreational opportunities were available. We also made emergency trips to town taking people to the doctor, hospital, or other urgent appointments. In those days there were hardly any telephones, and no cell phones. As I recall, there was one phone in the caretaker's home, and it did not always work. Bill Branda, a missionary, invited his parents from the States to come to Natal. Mr. Branda, senior, built a windmill that pumped water from the lake to fill tanks on higher ground. Having gravity-fed water lines was a great help to camp life.

Then there was the drama of watching the lake water level rise and eventually take over cabins built on the shore. I remember one time visiting with one of the cabin owners and watching the lake water lapping up and splashing against the windows. Eventually that lovely cabin fell, destroyed by waves beating constantly against the cabin.

Lake Bonfim provided a wonderful retreat and vacation spot for missionaries. We went there several times for our vacation. The cool breeze from the lake and the calmness of the surroundings made it an ideal place. Even on vacation, we kept busy. Our son took along work for Trans World Radio and helped greatly in handling the correspondence we received for this radio ministry. Margie read, and I also helped with the radio work.

We were told when we first came to northeast Brazil, that Lake Bonfim had medicinal qualities. The clear water and perfect temperature made it ideal for swimming. It was always cooler at this camp property than in the city of Natal. No wonder it was such a favorite place. In the beginning there were few homes along the shore. Now it is filled. In nearby Parnamirim there is an air force base, and when it was dedicated, we understand the president of the United States visited Camp Bonfim.

I am reminded of the words of Jesus to His disciples on one occasion when He knew they were tired and needed some rest. ***And He said to them, "Come aside by yourselves to a deserted place and rest a while." For there were many coming and going, and they did not even have time to eat.*** (Mark 6:31)

PROJECTS WITH OUR SON

—⁘—

R awlie chose to attend high school in Fortaleza, Brazil, some 6-8 hours by bus from Natal, our home. When he went away to study, we told him to feel free to come home as often as he wished. Bus travel was easy and inexpensive, so he took us up on that and was home from time to time.

I thought it would be a good idea for us to have projects to do on some of his trips home. We converted a pump organ into an electric instrument to make it easier for Margie to play at church and other functions.

RALPH & RAWLIE MAKING AN EVAPORATION COOLER

Another project we tackled was making an evaporative cooler for our house. We thought that other missionaries, particularly in the interior of the state, where it gets very hot, would like to use them in their homes. If we lived there, we would have used this type of cooling system, as it's so simple. We started with a frame box, made 2-3 inch walls on three sides, and filled them with shredded wood, called excelsior. We found some in Natal used for packing and protecting shipped items. At the top of these three sides of the box, we ran pipes with minute holes drilled in the bottom side. They were connected to a water source. The box was closed so air could enter only through these excelsior walls dampened by a trickle of water that kept them wet. It is remarkable how much hot air is cooled as it is sucked through these wet pads by a fan mounted inside the box. We installed this unit outside the house right next to one of our bedroom windows, and what a difference it made for sleeping on warm nights. These were two projects Rawlie and I enjoyed doing together. Rawlie was very handy, and I could give him projects of wiring different machines and fixing things. He was good at all of them. We did several others while he was in high school. Even though as parents we often felt we did not do justice in rearing our children to the biblical principle found in Ephesians 6:4, we pray that our efforts were honored by Him. The verse reads: ***And you fathers do not provoke your children to wrath, but bring them up in the training and admonition of the Lord.***

MIND-READING FURNITURE MAKER

———⦿———

When we arrived in Natal for our new ministry at the seminary, we had no furniture. We left it all at Benjamin Constant, knowing that shipping it would be too expensive. There was another reason also. The tables and chairs were well worn and undoubtedly mildewed from being in the tropics. We chose to start over and buy new things. In a larger city there were many options. We asked a lot of questions and even went on walking trips in the section of town known for the production of furniture. We spotted a place, asked the owner some important questions, and went home to make our decision.

We looked through catalogs, drew crude pictures, and jotted down our thoughts and questions. We decided on a certain type of dining room table whose extension leaves would be self-contained, folding up into the table rather than being separate. We didn't purchase a manufactured table by some big company but ordered it handmade by a craftsman whom we nicknamed Eight-and-one-half-fingers. I guess you figured it out – that's all the fingers he had after losing the others in his trade. With everything in hand, we headed for his shop.

When we saw him, we explained we wanted a special table, to which he replied, "I know," and proceeded to show us what we wanted. To this day we really do not know how he knew this, but in subsequent visits to his shop, we ordered more things which he made to perfection. We were very pleased with his workmanship.

I wish we could have brought this table home to the states, because it was indeed a work of art. This furniture maker was truly an interesting man—a great craftsman. We think of him and all the others with whom we came in contact while in this city. The Lord has commissioned all His children (Christians) to be witnesses for Him no matter where we are. We pray that the words spoken and the Gospel tracts distributed, brought people to a knowledge of Jesus Christ. I trust we will see many of them in heaven some day. Will we see YOU? This verse comes to mind when I think of the workmanship of this cabinet maker in Natal: ***Whatever your hand finds to do, do it with your might; for there is no work or device or knowledge or wisdom in the grave where you are going.*** (Ecclesiastes 9:10)

BEREAN BAPTIST SEMINARY

———◦∞◦———

Berean Baptist Seminary and Bible institute, located in the beautiful city of Natal, Rio Grande do Norte, Brazil, was training ground for many Brazilians pastors, missionaries, and laypersons. It was our privilege to work a number of years there, a few of which I was asked to serve as the director. The buildings were in a very high profile section of town. In fact, we were told that the intersection at which it was built was one of the busiest in the city. When the number of cars increased in this town, we knew it was so. It was necessary to clean the window screens often, and the first swipe of our cleaning cloth revealed a dirty black smudge. We wondered how good it was to be breathing this stuff.

BEREAN BAPTIST SEMINARY

This Seminary, started by missionary Carl Matthews, was a lighthouse for training. Only eternity will tell the impact of this place in the lives of those who studied there. Many churches were founded in Brazil by students who received their theological training there.

It was thrilling to hear the Tuesday morning reports at the chapel as seminarians returned from their assignments in different parts of the state. By the world's standards these men were too young to pastor churches, but they were the ones who were in training and willing to do the work. It was a blessing to hear reports of souls being saved. I, too, was able to go many times to churches about four hours away from the capital of Natal, to minister. I usually made the trip by bus and returned early Monday morning. Sometimes we drove our car and took students with us. Some of our articles tell of these eventful trips which we hope you will enjoy hearing about.

We are thankful that the seminary, even though it has moved from the location where we served, is still going well and training men and women for the ministry. Our purpose was to train men and women and equip them for evangelism and service for the Lord. The words of II Timothy 2:2 motivated us to continue in this vital ministry. *And the things that you have heard from me among many witnesses, commit these to faithful men who will be able to teach others also.* **(II Timothy 2:2)**

SENDING STUDENTS
TO THE SEMINARY

———∞∞∞———

G od gifts missionaries with special ministries, and we saw this early in our work in Natal, Brazil. In the interior town of Carnaubais, a couple, Fred & Virginia McClanahan, from our mission, worked fervently and made an impact on that town and the cause of Christ in many places. This town had many possibilities, because years ago American companies encouraged people to cultivate and care for a special tree that was grown in that area. Carnaubais, the name of the town, tells you what it is: carnauba wax. This product grows in only a few places. Hard, yellow-brown flakes are obtained from the carnauba palm leaves by collecting the leaves and beating them to loosen the wax. Then they are refined, and the wax is bleached. This wax is used in making many things we enjoy daily. Look it up on the Internet and you will be amazed. One of the most well-known products we associate with this is carnauba wax used to brighten and preserve paint finishes on automobiles.

This town named for the palm tree where it was produced, was where Fred and Virginia McClanahan served. They had a passion for young people to get an education. In the course of their years, they sent quite a number of students to the Berean Baptist Seminary in Natal. These young people's dedication was a direct reflection on their excellent training in the Baptist church under Fred and Virginia Clanahan's leadership. In many places around Brazil today there are pastors and Christian workers who were sent by this couple to Natal to study and be prepared for Christian service. We thank God for them.

Fred's wife Virginia died, and later he married Janet. They both continued the fine work of training young people to serve. Fred is gone now, and Janet continues giving herself to students in the state of Ceará. Jesus exhorted His own in Matthew 6:19-20, ***Do not lay up for yourselves treasures on earth, where moth and rust destroy and where thieves break in and steal; but lay up for yourselves treasures in heaven where neither moth nor rust destroys and where thieves do not break in and steal***. Certainly these dear missionaries gave of themselves for the cause of Christ, thus laying up treasures in heaven. May we all follow their example.

A STUDENT LEARNS
AN IMPORTANT LESSON

———— ✆ ————

When I was directing the school, I used students to do jobs for me personally. This provided help to me and a little spending money for them.

One of our young men was sharp, good-looking, and fairly arrogant. This is not to say that we all are not arrogant, to some degree. I asked "J" to disassemble a drawer lock, lubricate it, and replace it. I suggested he mark the pieces so reassembling would be easier. Later on that day he produced the drawer, complete with the lock he had serviced. And then in a very casual manner he handed me some brass pieces, including screws and other unidentifiable parts, with the comment, "These were left over."

This was my teaching moment. I explained to him that there are no "leftovers" in lock assemblies. They are one unit, working exactly as the designer intended. Anything left over would contribute to the malfunction of this item. I also asked if he had diagrammed, labeled, and numbered the parts as it was disassembled. He readily admitted he had not.

"J" learned a lesson that day. Our lives are like that lock. There are many facets to each life, and God designed us for a reason. When we think we can put everything in its proper place without His help, we lose. He also learned that instead of self-reliance, he should have labeled the parts so he would not have leftovers. In life we wonder how many leftovers we have because the Lord's help was not sought in putting our lives back together after some circumstance. Remember God's word in Proverbs 3:5-6: *Trust in the LORD WITH ALL YOUR HEART, AND LEAN NOT ON YOUR OWN UNDERSTANDING; In all your ways acknowledge Him, And He shall direct your paths*.

CEDARVILLE COLLEGE STUDENTS' SURPRISE

———⟨∞⟩———

We were delighted to have students from Christian colleges in America visit the seminary in Natal and minister with their music. When the groups arrived from Cedarville College, we had orientation classes to acquaint them with life in a foreign country. We counseled them about water and the wisdom of drinking water that was safe. Brazil had very good bottled water, and we learned early to use this when traveling. Untreated water is one of the main causes of severe discomfort experienced by many visitors to other countries.

We were blessed by the music of these dedicated students who paid their own way to Brazil and who were willingly serving the Lord. We took them on tours to interesting places, which included the School of Music, where they performed for students studying in this very well-known place.

One of the highlights of their tour, we are sure, was the beach. Natal has at least 20 beautiful, white, sandy beaches. The swimming was delightful, and the students thoroughly enjoyed it.

We divided the visitors so each missionary could interact with members of the choral group. Margie, my wife, was impressed by how much these young people could eat. She made cream puffs along with many other exciting and delicious treats to accompany their meals. They all loved them!

When they arrived, the students were a bit taken aback to find themselves in a city. They had thought of the mission field as a place of jungles, snakes, and a more rough type of living. We reminded them that they would have the opportunity to visit these kinds of places on their trip. The fact remains that although this was a city, they were in a foreign country. The students boasted they saw no difference between our city and other cities around the world. They were happily enjoying life, food, fellowship, and the wonderful weather.

But in less than three days, the majority of these robust students were flat on their backs in bed suffering acute stomach disorders or diarrhea. We are sure they must have remembered that they had said, "It didn't even feel like they were on the mission field." Thankfully Margie nursed them back to health, and we know they all learned some important lessons about sun exposure, eating habits, and general hygiene. Needless to say, they were surprised with this sudden health problem after only a few days.

Soon they were brought back in service, and the churches where they ministered were blessed. The Christians in Acts 8:4 were busy. It says: ***Therefore those who were scattered*** *went everywhere preaching the word*. What a blessing to see these young people eager to tell others of their faith in Jesus Christ. We hope that you, also, are such a witness.

EVANGELISTIC CRUSADE

＊

After much prayer, our Rio Grande do Norte, Brazil, council decided to attempt an evangelistic thrust for the entire state where we ministered. Fred Orr was contacted to be the speaker. He was Irish and ministered in a different area of Brazil. His first wife had died, and later he married a Brazilian from the Amazon town of Benjamin Constant.

The Lord led in positive ways for us to accomplish our dream of covering the state with the gospel message. Doing this required much planning. A large auditorium was rented in downtown Natal in a central location that was accessible to all. Many committees were appointed to work out the details of each step of the program. Volunteers received training in personal evangelism, and teams were organized to travel to all churches in our fellowship in the state. The teams met with the evangelist, and itineraries were set up for the entire length of the program. Our master plan called for the team to visit all our churches and have evangelistic meetings. Local churches were prepared for their meetings by advertising in their towns.

Marvelous stories were related by teams as they held campaigns in churches. The number of conversions and life-changing decisions by folks in these places was encouraging. When all churches in our fellowship had completed their meetings, the city-wide meeting began in the capital city of Natal. Ample advertising preceded the opening day. Music was an important part of the program. The seminary provided support, and vocal numbers were performed by local pastors and laypersons. Fred Orr preached powerful messages, and the results were rewarding. Prayer played an important part in this campaign. It was obvious that if the Lord was to work in our city, we needed to bathe everything in prayer.

DEAF MAN'S "HEARING AID"

Only the Lord knows the real outcome of this effort. One thrilling story came from a church in the interior. The granddad of one of our seminary students was an unbeliever. He had been witnessed to many times, but each time he rejected the gospel. After hearing the gospel presented in the local church, he still did not respond to the salvation message. The team left his city saddened that he and others for whom they prayed had not made decisions for Christ. Outside the city they felt led of the Lord to return and talk to João de Deus (the man's name means – "John of God"). The Holy Spirit wonderfully worked in his heart, and he was ready to make this decision. These words of Scripture are so true as we heard of his salvation: ***Likewise, I say to you, there is joy in the presence of the angels of God over one sinner who repents.*** (Luke 15:10)

João de Deus was very hard of hearing, and his grandson worked out a system in the church for him to use one of the loudspeakers (a smaller version). This was connected to the main system with a long wire reaching the place where he was seated. What a sight it was to see this handsome white-haired man with the speaker against his ear listening intently to the Word of God! His conversion was worth all the effort of the campaign.

ASLEEP ON THE JOB

—∞∞—

S eminary life is challenging and fun. What a joy to work with young people dedicated to serving the Lord! Students in training go through many experiences in the process. Besides classes, which require much homework, sometimes there is employment, practical work assignments in churches, and much more. Some of the students taught released-time classes in schools, and others traveled to distant churches on weekends to preach, teach, and visit.

Dick Matthews, son of Carl Matthews, who founded the seminary, was the choir director besides all the other things he did at the school. When we arrived, Margie helped by playing the piano. Although she claimed not to be the best musician, she was the only one at that time who played. I personally think she did very well, and without her the choir would have had to sing without accompaniment. Choir rehearsal also demanded a time commitment by our students. When you put all these things together, our hats go off to our students. Some students were not trained in music and had to learn a lot of fundamental facts. To sing parts in the choir, each group had to learn to harmonize, and all this took practice. We were thankful for Dick and Margie, who spent hours in these rehearsals to produce the fine music they presented.

After what was a very busy day, we went one evening to Dry Lake Baptist Church in Natal. The crowd was large, the pastor introduced the guests, and Dick had the seminary choir sing.

During one of the excellent choir numbers, I happened to notice one tall girl's slight motion. She lightly swayed as they sang. This would not have been unusual in some songs, but it was not the practice of this choir to do much moving while singing. I noticed that Helen's eyes were closed. I glanced again and to my utter surprise, she had fallen asleep while singing. Galatians 6:9 urges, ***And let us not grow weary while doing good, for in due season we shall reap if we do not lose heart.*** Poor Helen got very WEARY that night during the concert. In retrospect, it was humorous, although I am not aware of anyone ever detecting this besides me. I hope not, because the choir was great and their music honoring to the Lord.

FLAT ON THE GROUND

———⊗⊗⊗———

As a representative from Berean Baptist Seminary in Natal, I was asked to attend an important meeting in Juazeiro do Norte in Ceara, Brazil. Our sister Bible school was founded in this city by Baptist Mid Missions. We were dealing with the TEE program used to teach theology by extension courses. This school's campus was large and spacious. The missionaries laid a great foundation in this part of Brazil, and the training program was excellent.

During these special meetings we were tied up most of the day. On a break, I took a walk across the extensive campus. I was not prepared for what followed. In a strange way I was distracted by a sound I could not identify. What was it, I asked myself, quite bewildered by this fast-moving event. I looked up and saw a black "cloud" that turned out to be African bees. The only thing I instinctively knew to do was fall FLAT ON THE GROUND. I did this, and a heavy cloud of flying bees made a sound I will never forget as they passed over me. I am eternally grateful they did not decide to "land" at that moment. We know that the instinct of these vicious insects is to attack anything that is close and alive. When the dreadful buzzing of these hundreds of thousands of bees subsided, I got up from the ground and made my way back to the meeting, grateful nothing serious had happened.

When a missionary friend and his family were away on a weekend vacation, they hired a friend to watch their home. One afternoon he witnessed something unforgettable. While looking outside from a screened porch, a bunch of killer bees attacked their German Shepherd watchdog. There was nothing he could do, and the dog was dead in 15 minutes. We learned quickly to respect these critters. It reminds us of our enemy the devil, about whom the Bible states, ***Be sober, be vigilant; because your adversary the devil walks about like a roaring lion, seeking whom he may devour.*** (2 Peter 5:8)

FLAT TIRES

———⊗⊗⊗———

In our ministry in northeast Brazil, the missionaries were scheduled to visit different interior churches throughout the state. The purpose of these trips was encouragement and evangelism and to give support to these churches. It was our turn to go to Caicó, located 135 miles from the capital city of Natal, where we lived. This was a family trip, so Margie, our son, and I went alone. Many times we took seminarians who ministered to churches on each visit. But this time it was our family.

On the trip there, we had a flat tire. When we arrived at the church, we were shown our accommodations, and they were very adequate for us. There were plenty of hooks for hammocks, a must in every place in Brazil. It makes it much easier to travel, as each person carries his own hammock. There was a simple bathroom and a place to shower. This was a luxury that many places did not have. The usual method of bathing was using a half-gourd to dip water stored in a huge clay container, and even this was a blessing after a long, hard, dusty trip on the road.

Our time at this church was a blessing. We were invited to people's homes for meals. We had to be careful not to drink the water, which for the "outsider" could cause stomach upsets, because it had not been boiled. Brazil sells bottled water, so we used that. The folks were very hospitable and cordial. We enjoyed our time in their homes. Two of our seminary boys were from this town. One had received the Lord through listening to our "Voice of the Bible" radio program sponsored by our seminary.

In our living quarters, the outside city noises were prevalent. The homes were built close together, almost touching one another. We heard the voice of a girl who was obviously in distress. Later we learned she was developmentally disabled. In those days she was kept in a cage to control her. Because we also had a developmentally disabled daughter, our hearts went out to this girl and her family that did not have the resources we did. Our weekend trip to this church went fast, and we returned with joy in our hearts for the privilege of preaching and seeing people come to the Lord in this nice church that kept going for over a year, even without a preacher.

The trip home began Monday morning early. Remember, it is only 135 miles to our home, but the road is not a freeway, and the bumps, boulders, holes, and litter surprised many. We had three more flat tires on that trip home. It took us 11 hours to go 135 miles. Travel in Brazil in those days was interesting, and one needed a sense of humor to be prepared for the unpredictable. Also we needed to commit our way to the Lord. We always looked forward to these trips, as they motivated us to keep on ministering. And we were thankful to the Lord for a safe journey. Before each trip we prayed, asking God's direction on our travels. ***Commit your way to the LORD, trust also in Him, and He shall bring it to pass*** (Psalm 37:5) We still do that for every trip, even if it's only a mile downtown. Do you?

FORGIVE ME

—⊷∞⊶—

When we arrived in the big city, Natal, after living in the Amazon for 10 years, we had much to learn. Many people came to our door asking for financial help. We struggled with what to do, because we sincerely wanted to help, but it was impossible to help everyone, even if we gave only a small amount to each one. A friend in Natal from whom we purchased our paper in large quantities for seminary use told me that at least 300 people a day came to his place of business asking for help. This is not a problem peculiar to Brazil. In the States, we had requests similar to those in Brazil, but not in such great numbers.

Women would "borrow" newborn babies and carry them from door to door as "bait" to motivate people to give financial assistance. The human heart is amazing in all the innovative ways it figures out how to make appeals for money.

How do you deal with this never-ending challenge? We asked questions and observed how the Brazilians handled these situations. To our amazement, we heard over and over again the word "Perdoe" from those being asked for money. This word means "Forgive." We noticed that after an impassioned plea for money the person being asked would simply say "perdoe." With this, a beggar moved on without the slightest bit of hesitancy. So we learned that in most cases that's all it took to get a beggar to move on. If we actually knew the person asking for money, we would feel free to give him assistance, but for the most part we just said, "Perdoe," and they moved on.

We reminded ourselves over and over again that we were in Brazil to bring people the gospel of Jesus Christ. When we asked them to forgive us for not being able to give them money, it was wonderful to be able to present to them the gospel of salvation, and that they could receive forgiveness of sins by receiving Jesus as their personal Savior. The Bible refers to Jesus, *in whom we have redemption through His blood, the forgiveness of sins* (Colossians 1:14)

PUMP ORGAN GOES ELECTRIC

———⊷∞⊶———

In Natal we had a pump organ that folded up, looking like an "oversized suitcase." It was a little awkward to tote around but a delight to use in the church services. Our son Rawlie was attending high school in Fortaleza, to the north of us about seven hours. I decided that father and son could do a project together when he was home for a visit. I had a "brainstorm" of electrifying the organ instead of having my wife pump feverishly on two pedals. We started with an Electrolux vacuum cleaner. It required a power transformer so the 110V machine could operate with our 240V power source in northeast Brazil. I connected the vacuum hose to the bellows of the organ with a valve so it could be used either as a pump or electrically, as the organist desired. But remember we are not trying to vacuum the organ, so I connected the hose to the outlet end of the Electrolux so it would blow air into the bellows.

PUMP ORGAN MADE ELECTRIC

Now we faced the problem of regulating the volume. When Margie wanted to play softly, how could we achieve that? After some thought, we came up with a speed control foot switch from a White sewing machine. Some electrical manipulations to connect this apparatus into the electric supply line, after the transformer, accomplished the task. Now all she had to do was to let up a little on the "accelerator" and the music was softer. We had lots of fun with that machine in church. People really enjoyed seeing and hearing it. Music is a wonderful way to worship the Lord, and we are glad we could use this machine, as Margie played it so well, to the glory of the Lord. I Chronicles 13:8 records how King David used instruments to praise the Lord: ***Then David and all Israel played music before God with all their might, with singing, on harps, on stringed instruments, on tambourines, on cymbals, and with trumpets.***

WE DIDN'T LOCK THE DOOR

———⚬⚬⚬———

No matter where you are, the unexpected can happen. Our missionary co-worker and I went to a nearby city five hours south of Natal. There we needed to transact some business and do necessary shopping for the seminary. The trip was uneventful. We arrived in Recife and then stopped for lunch before doing the necessary errands. The city of Recife was big and busy, but we found a good place to park our Volkswagen bus. After lunch, we headed for the car. To our consternation, we found the door unlocked and the contents missing. Yes, all our luggage, including our Bibles, was gone. We prayed that the thieves would at least read our Bibles. As I remember, quite a few class study notes were in my suitcase. I had hoped to get in a little studying while gone. Both of us were tall and not necessarily dainty in size. How would we ever find clothes to fit in a store to get us through this short stay? We tried but had to resign ourselves to the fact that we could not find adequate clothing. We would have to make do with what we had on. It was disheartening to lose our baggage. We cannot remember if we locked the doors. Perhaps seeing the baggage was too tempting for the thieves, so they just broke in. In that particular vehicle it was impossible to hide items. They were fully visible to the passersby.

On another occasion, we were host in Natal to one of the Trans World Radio workers, a Christian ministry that broadcasts programs produced by our seminary in Natal. At the seminary our radio staff answered the Portuguese mail in exchange for airing seminary programs. We had a very good relationship with Trans World Radio. The gentleman who was head of the São Paulo division of this station left our city and flew to another on the coast of Brazil. When he got into the airport, he realized he had left his tape recorder on the taxi seat. In a city with hundreds of taxis, where would he start trying to get it back? This recorder was not a dime-store variety, but one that was equal in price to a brand new Volkswagen "bug" vehicle. Imagine losing something that valuable. God definitely intervened, as the taxi driver contacted the airline, and it was returned to our friend. This in itself was a miracle. I wonder how often God works for us in ways we don't even know about. In Romans 8:28 we are instructed: ***And we know that all things work together for good to those who love God, to those who are the called according to His purpose.*** Many may have difficulty trying to understand how God does this, but believe me, we take great comfort in this wonderful verse.

THOUSANDS ALIVE IN THE CEMETERY

———— ∞ ————

November 1 and 2 are very important days in the religious culture of Brazil. All Saints Day and the Day of the Dead are commemorated by the entire nation. Christians use this opportunity for a time to witness to many hurting people as they remember their departed loved ones.

At the seminary, our choir practiced long hours to fine-tune appropriate songs to sing at the service. Believers invited us to conduct a gospel service at the gravesite of their loved one or friend. Our choir would sing, and a pastor would give a gospel message. This would be repeated many times throughout our time at the cemetery.

To prepare for this event, much work was involved. First, a schedule was made and students would volunteer to take positions at the cemetery's main entrances. They were responsible for their position for one hour or more, and then the next person would take over. Countless thousands of people came through those entrance gates. There was much talking and plenty of dust, and it was very hot. This duty started before daybreak and finished late at night. Many volunteers were necessary to carry out our program.

One of our main ministries on this day, besides the gospel services, was distribution of gospel tracts. At our seminary, my offset press was used to print the seminary address on over 100,000 gospel tracts. I discovered how to do this in order to eliminate the time-consuming and very tiring process of hand stamping each tract.

Before this day, thousands of people came to the cemetery to clean, whitewash, and make ready the tombstones and places where their loved ones were buried. The cemetery looked very nice those two days. You must remember that religion without hope is the reason we engaged in this ministry. We were able to minister to many lonely hearts who were uncertain about the spiritual condition of their loved ones. They came that day to give their respect and honor to their loved ones. We are thankful for the multitudes who heard about Jesus Christ and the salvation He gives to all who will receive Him personally into their lives, and for the forgiveness of sins and eternal salvation with Him in Heaven. What a privilege it was to witness to thousands who were alive in the cemetery. *And you He made alive, who were dead in trespasses and sins.* (Ephesians 2:1) This is what Jesus does for those who receive Him as their personal Savior.

TRANS WORLD RADIO

———⁂———

At the seminary we produced a radio program called The Voice of the Bible. This program was transmitted by Trans World Radio to Portuguese-speaking people all around the world. The transmitting station was located on the island of Bonaire in the Netherlands Antilles.

We had an agreement with this station that they would transmit our program and we would pay for the service by handling the Portuguese mail. The address of our seminary was given out, and we in turn received thousands of letters with questions, requests for Bibles, and many other things. As director, I had a staff of 15 students to handle the influx of correspondence. I read all the letters and categorized them for the staff to answer.

It was an exercise in patience and seeking God's wisdom to know how to decipher different handwritings from all over the world. With the Lord's help, we accomplished this. Bible teacher Pastor Ribamar was a gifted man of God with the ability to teach the profound truths of Scripture. Another important resource person was Pastor Xavier, who answered all the complex and varied Bible questions listeners sent in.

We greatly valued these men. The staff of 15 students and our son Rawlie handled the mail pretty well. We had to have that many typewriters and a repairman who kept them in running shape all the time.

Only in eternity will we know the result of these years of messages that went around the world to Portuguese-speaking populations. We do know that many came to faith in Jesus Christ and countless others were strengthened in their walk with the Lord. Trans World Radio, one of several Christian broadcasting services, has been greatly used of God for proclaiming the gospel around the world. We are so thankful for the time God allowed us to be a part of this ministry. The phrase of a song we used to sing is, *Give the winds a mighty voice, Jesus saves, Jesus saves*. Through the means of radio, thousands heard the gospel message of salvation through Jesus Christ.

WHO IS THE DRIVER?

———◦∞∞◦———

Working in a seminary requires cooperation by all staff persons. When a trip was planned, certain students were chosen for the trip and given responsibilities both for the trip and for when we arrived at the church where we would be ministering. And we must not forget the driver. Several staff members took turns as drivers, and therein is the reason for this story. When each trip was planned, whether an outing to a church for ministry or a recreational trip to the beach or some other attraction, something interesting happened. The curious Brazilian students had one question: Who will be our driver? You might ask, what difference does that make?

Well, to the students it made all the difference in the world. You see, each of us has his own personality and way of doing things. The Brazilians took note of this very quickly. So each time an event was planned, the question arose about the driver. As time went on, we finally learned why they asked such a question. There were three main drivers: Agnes Haik, Bill Branda, and myself. They represented three different types of personalities and ways of doing things. One of these things we call "punctuality." If Agnes Haik was the designated driver that day, the students knew pretty well what time they should get to the departure point. The same applied for the other two.

Would you know it, I had the reputation for being the punctual one. The students knew that when the time was set, they had better be there. In a land that does not always get up tight about being on time, you can be sure I was a challenge to the students. I imagine many of them would rather have had the other two drivers. They never did tell me this. In the idiomatic expressions of the Portuguese language, the students would say: "terrivel" when referring to my punctuality. It really means "terrible," but it is not all that negative in the context of their culture. So Agnes, Bill, and I were known by how important each of us considered and obeyed departure times. We look back and smile on those wonderful days and the delightful students. I wonder if the Apostle Paul's words, can be applied here somehow? ***Redeeming the time, because the days are evil"*** (Ephesians 5:16)

UNFORGETTABLE TRIPS
IN NORTHEAST BRAZIL

———— ❦ ————

Traveling with the seminarians to assignments was an experience never to be forgotten. Returning to Natal late one night from a Sunday meeting, we were driving the monotonous miles. But seminary students are young, energetic, and full of joy. Many times they sang all the way home. That night in the distance, we saw something in the middle of the road. As we got closer, we saw that it was a big branch of a bush thrown across the highway. We went around it. Sure enough, there in the distance was another. We knew we had better be cautious, because this was a warning. The next pile of branches almost covered the entire width of the highway. We had to stop and survey the situation. There just beyond this last pile of branches was a huge hole. A section of the road was completely gone. How thoughtful of someone to warn us. This is the way it was done in Brazil. Without those warnings we would have careened into a cavernous hole in the pavement. That night we were thankful that we could get around the damaged spot. Sometimes, one has to return or try to find a detour around these spots. If you are not acquainted with the surroundings, it is very difficult to continue on.

After a full day of ministry in the city of Caicó at the Baptist church, a student and I were on our way home to Natal. There were several small mountain twists and turns in the long road home. Out of nowhere an animal darted across the road in our pathway and hit the front right of our Volkswagen "bug." Instantly we saw that the headlight had been damaged. It was working, but its light was not focused on the road. Without proper equipment, we were in trouble. I had a "brainstorm." We pulled over to the side of the road but were not out of danger, because the road was narrow. We had to pick some vegetation along the road and cram it in and under the damaged light, raising it up to a level that would focus it on the highway. We had to adjust it a couple of times, and finally we got back to the seminary.

On another trip, our Volkswagen Kombi's engine gave out near an interior town. We pulled into the agency, and in 45 minutes another engine was installed and we went on home. These engines are amazing; they are so easy to remove and replace. We were thankful for such an easy fix (except financial) to our dilemma. Every time we traveled, we committed our trip to the Lord, and I firmly believe that prayer should be a vital part of every waking hour. Paul expressed it best, ***Pray without ceasing.*** (1Thessalonians 5:17) One never knows what's ahead.

EMBARRASSED? GET USED TO IT!

———◦∞∞◦———

Brazilian customs are rich, and we were the recipients of many interesting and kind gestures that are part of the Brazilian culture. Soon after getting settled in Natal, we opened a bank account at one of the branches in our city. Because of our involvement at the Seminary, we were obliged to make repeated trips to transact business dealings with finances. As is true with most banks, there are lines. I can remember standing in a long line of folks desiring desperately to be waited on. To my astonishment, a lovely employee of the bank approached me carrying a tray with an attractive demitasse cup on it plus a steaming pot of great Brazilian espresso coffee. At first a little embarrassed, I wondered what I was to do. All those people in front of me had been waiting longer than I. There were many behind me. Why was I chosen for this blessing? I learned that day, whether we like it or not, that Brazilian courtesy demanded they show this very kind attention to a foreigner who was one of the bank's clients. I accepted the delicious cup of coffee, sweetened exactly to my liking, and in front of all those people, tried to act like I was truly enjoying it. As a matter of fact I was. With time I learned that this was a Brazilian custom and I had better get used to it.

One day as I entered a new branch of a savings and loans bank, the manager, a lady, stood on a chair and motioned to me, even calling me by name the instant I walked in the door. There were many people there, but she was beckoning me to come to the front. I was impressed that she knew my name, first of all, and then that I would be singled out to come to the head of the line. Embarrassed? Yes. On and on these stories go. When our son, Rawlie, accompanied me back to Brazil to help with closing our apartment, selling and packing goods for a permanent return to the States, he needed a driver's license. We went to the licensing department and, as usual, were standing in line, waiting our turn to be waited on. Then unexpectedly, a young lady who attended our church, an employee of the licensing department, approached us inquiring why we were there. After we told her the reason, she left but soon returned and had us follow her. We found ourselves seated in the main office. Wow, how did this happen? Brazilian custom and courtesy. After explaining our need for Rawlie to have a driver's license to help me with my work, we watched this man reach under his desk and push a call button. Soon another employer of the company appeared. He was told to prepare paperwork for the license. Rawlie was photographed, filled in the papers, signed his name, and soon had a plasticized driver's license. The most amazing thing about this was that it had an expiration date of more than 10 or 15 years in advance. We could hardly believe this. Oh, I forgot, we were served coffee there also. We learned the biblical exhortation, ***In every thing give thanks, for this is the will of God in Christ Jesus concerning you.*** (I Thessalonians 5:18) God was again bringing us into contact with people to whom we could also show kindness. We witnessed to them the love of God and thanked them for their kindness to us.

THE PRESIDENT IS COMING

⸺◦⊱⊰◦⸺

One day President Ernesto Geisel (the 29th president of Brazil) visited Natal. You can imagine the preparation made for his trip. The town was spiffed up as we had never seen it before. Things were painted, streets were marked appropriately, and signs galore were displayed. Huge banners waved over the streets and individual houses. Places of business had their own greetings for the president.

For the seminarians it was an exciting time. Our students made special signs. When the day arrived, all were at their best in front of the seminary, which is right on the avenue where he would pass. The students looked sharp as they waited almost at attention for our prestigious president's arrival.

As in all important arrivals, the preparation was enormous. From the airport several miles away, the entire route had to be made secure with proper police inspectors and plenty of service-men stationed at strategic positions along the way. The president's entourage was impressive. In those years there were not a large number of cars in Natal and certainly not many that were such luxury vehicles as his.

At approximately the announced time, give or take several hours, the beautiful black cars appeared on Avenida Hermes da Fonseca, where our Seminary was located. Wearing uniforms and lined up along the sidewalk next to the seminary, the students gazed intently at the limousine in which their president was riding. They hoped to catch a glimpse of this important man. Cars were moving slowly, and we are sure the president ordered this so he could greet the thousands who were awaiting his arrival. Thankfully, our students were not disappointed. As President Ernesto Geisel was within viewing distance, we could see him waving at us. What a personal touch he gave us that day! We were waving at him, and he returned the favor. It was very special, and we will never forget this. This was about as close as anyone could get to an important person like this.

This reminds me that someday our King, the Lord Jesus, is coming, and we need to be ready. We're looking forward to this important event. We're ready, and we hope you are too, having trusted Jesus as your Saviour. ***Therefore you also be ready, for the Son of Man is coming at an hour you do not expect.*** (Matthew 24:44)

THE MAGIC OF PRINTING

———⚭———

Any missionary will attest to the usefulness of machines to help them preach and teach the Word of God. Especially in Natal at the Berean Baptist Seminary we were thankful for machines. In the Trans World Radio ministry of answering the Portuguese mail, we used 15 old typewriters to get the job done. A serviceman who ran a typewriter repair shop kept our machines going, and we appreciated his good work.

Printing study books for the seminary was a constant challenge. Using manual typewriters kept us busy long hours. We received a special gift one year that enabled us to purchase a new IBM Selectric typewriter. In its day this was considered an amazing machine. After a while, another gift made it possible for us to get one for Margie, also.

Before copy machines were made, we used mimeograph machines to print our material. We passed through several evolutions of these machines, also. At first it was the old hand crank mimeo. We were thankful for them, and year by year the stencils cut on the typewriter improved, which made the mimeograph process easier. Then we purchased a machine that cut stencils electronically. So all we had to do was type a nice copy with the IBM machine, and this stencil cutter would burn a stencil and make perfect copies. Then mimeo machines became more sophisticated and electric, so we didn't have to crank them. The next improvement was the offset press, which surpassed them all. What a blessing!

But did you notice that we predated the digital and computer age on the field? We did not have the capabilities now enjoyed in almost every office. But it was great having what we had, which enabled us to do all the necessary printing jobs.

Let me add a footnote to this short story by telling you what we did before typewriters and mimeo machines were used in northeast Brazil. In the earlier days, Christian workers could scarcely afford machines. I taught the seminary students how to use the hectograph process. This used a gelatin-like substance in a pan onto which a paper was placed which had been prepared with a special ink. The ink is absorbed onto the surface of the gelatin, and the desired paper is placed on this surface and then carefully removed. The paper printed by the ink on the surface of the gelatin is the finished product. About 30-80 copies could be made at a time. In the era before all the fancy machines, this was a mighty helper to those who wanted multiple copies. We taught the seminarians how to make the gelatin and where to buy the special carbon paper-like stencils and how to make it work. We encouraged the seminarians to get the gospel out in any way they could, even using these methods of duplicating the message in printed form.

We also had to use in those early days plain carbon paper. This was a tedious process, and many copies could not be make. But we did the best we could with what we had. In the Apostle Paul's day, everything had to be hand-written. What a blessing to use such modern methods. Paul wrote in II Timothy 4:2: ***Preach the word! Be ready in season and out of season. Convince, rebuke, exhort, with all longsuffering and teaching.***

THE MIRACLE OF THE OFFSET PRESS

———∞∞∞———

At the Berean Seminary in Natal, Brazil, we did a lot of printing. We produced lessons, tests, syllabi, gospel tracts, programs, schedules, letters, and a host of other things. While home on furlough, we met a dear man, Sam Parvin, who was interested in our situation and gave the seminary an offset printing press. I went to his place in Idaho, and he spent hours showing me how to run this machine. I recorded his instructions with a tape recorder to help me when we returned to Natal. Sam was kind enough to dismantle the machine and ship it to us. We were so thankful.

We tried to wait patiently for this treasured package to arrive, and it finally did. We wondered how much difficulty we would have getting it through customs. We took the necessary papers to our local authorities in Natal and presented them to the customs officer. In fact this man was top man in the chain of command. We prayed and waited to see what he would do. He noticed we were from Berean Baptist Seminary, and he made this remarkable statement: "I graduated from this school." Could it get any better than this? Yes, it could.

Not only was there no custom charge, but our next surprise was around the corner. Several weeks passed, and I wanted to get the press unpacked, assembled and working. About this time we had a visitor come to the seminary who had been a camp director for years in the States. His name was Eldon. The day he came to our seminary, he casually asked if there was anything he could do to help us. When I mentioned the newly arrived offset press, his reaction was remarkable. He had worked on the same model of machine and knew it frontwards and backward. He spent the next several days assembling this machine and putting it in working order for us. Isn't the Lord's timing perfect?

The press was a vital contribution to our ministry at the seminary. We are so grateful for God's servants, like Sam, who are sensitive to needs such as this. We think of the Apostle Paul, who apparently left his Bible and writing material at the last place he visited. He wrote to Timothy, ***Bring the cloak that I left with Carpus at Troas when you come—and the books, especially the parchments.*** (II Timothy 4:13) I am so glad we had such good equipment to help us as we prepared young men and women for the ministry with printed material.

HOW YOUNG IS YOUR PASTOR?

———✲———

When we joined the faculty of the Berean Baptist Institute and Seminary in Natal, Rio Grande do Norte, Brazil, our eyes were opened to how the Lord's work was done in that part of Brazil. It was our privilege to teach Personal Evangelism to the freshman class. Little did we know the full impact our young people were having throughout the state. If you look at a map of Brazil, specifically the state of Rio Grande do Norte, you will see that its general shape is that of an elephant. I can only say that we had a gigantic opportunity before us as a seminary, and certainly the task was huge. Our students, very young in those early days, were actually coming to complete their high school studies and move on into the institute training and seminary education. Throughout the state there were churches in many of the distant and nearby towns, but the crying need of the moment was leadership. Most of these churches had no pastors. In a way they depended on the seminary to send young people to help them in their ministries. To the credit of our students, they were more than willing to help. We are sure the things they learned during the week were put into practice in the churches each weekend. It was in reality on-the-job-training for these dedicated students. The churches were so thankful to have them. These students were being stretched to the limit in performing ministries way beyond their actual training. The key was their willingness to go and serve. All week they were in classes, and then on Friday or Saturday they traveled to various churches throughout the state. The trip alone was taxing. Many times they had to stand up the entire four or more hours because of crowded conditions on the bus. Not all churches were that far away, but many were. The girls went to churches nearer the seminary to teach classes and help with visitation, etc.

SEMINARY CLASS

The Tuesday morning chapel at the seminary was a blessing. These young people would give testimonies of the weekend activities in the churches where they ministered. Every week was a different story of God using them in special ways. The souls saved each week were encouraging. These young people were in their teens, and I still am in awe as we recall how dedicated they were and how marvelously God used them. I wonder how many of our teenagers would do what they did? Recently we heard from one of our students who now is in his 50s. Little did we realize he would return to the church he served in as a student to become pastor for many years. This is very rewarding. The ministry of training young people for the Lord's service is so important. We endeavored to follow the Apostle Paul's instruction when he said, *And the things that thou hast heard of me among many witnesses, the same commit thou to faithful men, who shall be able to teach others also.* (II Timothy 2:2)

MAYBE MORE IS BETTER

—∞∞∞—

M argie's School of Missionary Training and licensed practical nurse credentials helped her minister to our seminary students and aid them with their health problems. The students came from all sorts of backgrounds and from many different places. Their everyday health concerns were a challenge and required depending on the Lord for wisdom.

Years ago, my dad was given the formula for a simple medication which heals and soothes "owies" quickly. Fortunately, we had ample supplies of this medicine, simply called in our family "Pop's medicine." Both in the Amazon jungles and in Northeast Brazil we used it generously.

The students had very little money to spend on much of anything. Margie tried to teach them that a small amount of ointment properly placed was just as effective as, and perhaps better than, a huge glob of it. Each illness or injury was a teaching moment for her. The nurse was a popular person at the seminary.

One day Inacio came to the clinic with a certain problem which Margie diagnosed and prescribed proper medication for. Taken according to instructions, this treatment would normally cure the ailment. Soon after he had received help from Margie, Inacio returned, and immediately Margie noticed that something was not right. This student was not acting as he normally did. When questioned about his medication, he quickly retorted that if this was the medication for his problem, then taking more of it would do the job quicker and better. Wrong, wrong, wrong! Margie was obliged to give Inacio a very quick lesson in following instructions and not surmising that his logic was the best solution for his cure. The lesson here was: More is not always better. Do you get the point? In spiritual matters, more of Christ, prayer, Bible reading and witnessing is better, but with medication, follow instructions and be careful. ***A wise man will hear, and will increase learning; and a man of understanding shall attain unto wise counsels.*** (Proverbs 1:5)

A DUSTY ROAD
AND THE ARMY OFFICER

From the Berean Baptist Seminary in Natal, we traveled to smaller towns in the state to help struggling churches with preaching, Sunday school classes, visiting, and other helps for the churches. The seminarians enjoyed these trips and were a big help. On one Friday morning we set out for the city of Macau in our Chevrolet Opala. The trip was challenging because of the dirt roads. With each passing vehicle, whether it was a passenger car, truck, or bus, the clouds of dust were unbelievable. The dirt impeded our vision, and at some spots it was impossible to see the road. Danger was imminent each time we passed a car. Student Zenobio yelled at me that gasoline was squirting out from the car to the side of the road. Immediately we stopped, and we discovered that the hose from the tank to the motor was split and we were losing gasoline at an alarming rate.

OUT OF GAS FAR FROM HOME

One learns to be resourceful and mechanical when under pressure. I used a vent hose from the gas tank and repaired the split hose. But now the tank was empty. We were far from our destination. What could we do? We prayed, asking God to send help. Behind us we saw a cloud of dust and soon an Army car stopped. A nicely dressed Brazilian Army officer asked us why we were stopped. When I told him, he immediately gave orders to his driver to bring the gas can from his car. The driver poured it into our tank, and the officer would take no money. We were so grateful for his kind help and never will forget God's provision for us so far from a gas station. When we read a verse like ***But my God shall supply all your need according to his riches in glory by Christ Jesus,*** we don't know how God will bless us. We found out that day, and our ministry trip was a success.

A FOUR-HOUR DUSTY BUS RIDE

———∞∞∞———

O ne privilege missionaries had as they served in the Berean Baptist Seminary was to travel to churches throughout our state and minister on weekends. The little salt-producing town of Macau, located on the coast, was one of my favorites. This church sent students to the seminary, and in turn these students served the Lord by preaching in their home churches. Most of the pastors of these interior churches were young men, and we were proud of them. The seminary provided fine young men to minister this way. I was asked to preach in Macau several times during our time on the field.

Rather than take our car and subject it to dusty, sometimes muddy roads, we took a local bus. At the station, we checked our baggage and boarded the bus. From the time I was a child, my parents had taught me good manners. As I entered the bus, I chose a place I wanted to sit during this trip. As is quite typical in this part of the world, the bus filled quickly, and to my dismay, there were more passengers than seats to accommodate them. I looked up and saw a lady standing in the aisle. My training would not allow me to sit while this lady stood. I motioned to her, and we traded places. She was grateful for a place to sit.

I spent the whole journey down this dusty dirty road standing on the bus, whose windows were all open to provide "air conditioning." The finely grained dust was red in color and plentiful. When a vehicle passed, the cloud of dust was unbelievable. Some used protection over their mouths and noses and covered their heads. When I arrived at the church, I was shown my place in a back room where a hammock was mounted. On a small table was a half gourd that I used to dip water from a huge clay jar. That was my shower. It felt good to get the heavy coating of red dust off my body.

The services were always well attended. The Lord blessed with souls being saved and believers strengthened in their Christian life. This was our reward for the hard trip. Galatians 6:9, *And let us not be weary in well doing: for in due season we shall reap, if we faint not*. When we returned, I was glad to share at chapel time on Tuesday morning, the blessings of the weekend.

NO CHURCH TONIGHT

———⁊◦◦⊰———

Hebrews 10:25 exhorts: *Do not forsake the assembling of yourselves together as the manner of some is, and so much more as you see the day approaching.* We observed in Brazil that believers and nonbelievers like to go to church. Our church was packed almost every service. It was refreshing to see such enthusiasm. We were not in the custom of canceling services.

But one night, the seminary choir was going to perform in a neighboring church that could accommodate more people, so we cancelled the Seminary Church. We thought it wise to do this. We put an appropriate sign on the church door in case someone did not know about the change of venue.

Some DID NOT know about this change. At our customary visit to our ophthalmologist, he mentioned that he had gone to the seminary church Sunday night but it was closed. When he said this, we were sick at heart. This man is without doubt the most well-known eye doctor in that part of Brazil. That is important, but even more important was the fact we wanted him to hear the gospel and get saved.

That experience settled it. We made it a point to never close the church door again at one of our regular service times. One never knows who may have come to the service if it had been open. We apologized to the doctor but do not know if he ever went there again. We learned a powerful lesson.

NEVER A DULL MOMENT

———◆◆◆———

Working at the Berean Seminary gave us wonderful opportunities to take students to churches that really needed a boost to help them out from time to time. One day in October, 1967, we had finished our weekend ministry at the Macau Baptist Church, and very early I drove our car to pick up the seminary girls and one boy, Miron, who had accompanied our son Rawlie and myself. After picking up the girls, I had the tires checked, and then we started our return trip to Natal. About an hour into the trip, we had just passed Serra Verde and were nearing the São Geraldo farm. We stopped there for a short rest, because the car had very little power.

We immediately checked the engine and noticed that the valve cover was gone. That meant we had lost all our engine oil. No wonder our car could hardly move! One of our seminary boys got us a ride to town so we could get help. We spent several hours trying to find the part for our Volkswagen engine. His brother had the spare part and then made the gasket from other material. Now the real fun began. We got another ride in a Jeep back to our Kombi bus. It was quite a ride. There were four adults and one baby in the front seat. In the back seat were our son Rawlie, myself, an old man, our seminary student Miron, three goats, dried meat, milk cans, and what nots. It was really FULL! The driver had to go off the main road several times to deliver goods and take people to their homes. While we were gone, we had left the seminary girls with the Kombi, but when we returned they were already at a nearby house and treated with such courtesy as could be expected from Brazilians. The royal treatment included dinner and the use of the household hammocks so they could rest. We finally got the valve cover replaced and new oil put in, and after our meal we left for Natal.

We had an uneventful trip back to the seminary. We did stop several times, however, to check that valve cover to see if it was staying in place. We finally arrived home, grateful to the Lord for His protection over us all the way. We often committed our trips to the Lord with Psalm 37:5: ***Commit your way to the Lord, trust also in Him, and He shall bring it to pass.*** Isn't it wonderful to be able to give your plans to the Lord for His approval, and watch Him work all things out for you? We think so, and here was a good example.

PAYING OLD DEBTS

Nelson, one of the believers, was faithful in his church attendance. He was regularly employed at a firm in Natal and participated in all our church activities, including our outings to Lake Bonfim. He was a good swimmer, and we enjoyed visiting with him.

At testimony time during one of our services, Nelson gave an amazing story of his Christian experience. After trusting Christ as his Savior, he learned that it was a biblical precept to contribute to the Lord's work with one's income. Some believe that amount should be 10 percent, but not all agree.

For years he gave 10 percent of his income to the Lord. Then something happened. Hard times hit his family, and he found it difficult to give to the Lord as he had done before. His lack of paying a tithe was a sin, he felt, and the Lord convicted him of this.

During a testimony time, he announced that he was paying all his back tithes that were not given the Lord's work. I was impressed with this man's determination to pay back all the previous times he had failed to give to the Lord's work. If all Christians had this conviction, I imagine much more could be done for missions and local church ministries. What a lesson for us. This reminds me of the Bible verse: *I will pay my vows to the LORD now in the presence of all His people.* (Psalm 116:14)

TELLING THE FAMILY ABOUT JESUS

———— ∞ ————

Maria, a lovely Christian in our Berean Baptist Church in Natal, Brazil, was a blessing to us. She was from the wealthier strata of our town but was a dedicated, humble lady. Her conversion experience was a great example of God's reaching into a family of means and transforming a life.

After her conversion, she was a faithful member of our church. She did what she could to help in whatever needed to be done. We enjoyed visiting and fellowshipping with this fine, educated lady, whose new-found faith in Christ was refreshing to witness.

Maria's driving compassion was to see her family members have what she had received through faith in Jesus Christ. It was difficult witnessing to them, because their upbringing was neither conducive to nor compatible with the Christian lifestyle. Maria prayed, talked, and lived Jesus before them, but there was no apparent agreement between what both sides believed.

Maria would ask prayer for them and do all in her means, without being offensive, to win them to the Savior. She devised a system of witnessing which was very wise and innovative. At church she would carefully select gospel tracts from those we had displayed on the literature desk. At home she laboriously copied these tracts word for word in her own handwriting. She incorporated these words into personal letters she wrote to family members around Brazil and the world as if she was the author of the contents. She felt this was the only way they would listen to her. I never asked her how many such letters she wrote, but I know she spent a great deal of time doing this, because her zeal and passion to see her family come to faith in Christ was beyond anything we had seen.

I wonder in eternity if we will know the results of this faithful servant's hand-written gospel tracts. She is now with the Lord, and we pray that many family members and friends to whom she wrote will be there also. Have you ever thought about reaching out to someone this way? Jesus healed a man possessed of a demon and encouraged him to do something that all who are believers should do: ***Return to your own house, and tell what great things God has done for you." And he went his way and proclaimed throughout the whole city what great things Jesus had done for him.*** (Luke 8:39) Dear Maria was not demon possessed, but she had a heart to win her family to Jesus, and she worked hard at it.

SMALL MAN – BIG RESULTS

—∞∞—

Now and then the Lord places people in our lives that impact us for good. In Northeast Brazil we encountered such a person, Manuel. This humble man with little formal education was a pastor in the neighboring state of Pernambuco. Eventually he came to our state of Rio Grande do Norte and was a pastor in a church about 30 miles from Natal. We watched him as he worked with people. He was kind and had a passion for people unlike anything we had seen in a long time. He may not have been a gifted preacher, but he made up for it in his day by day dealings with people on the street, in town, and in the church. He was great on visitation and had a delightful way of talking with people, especially about spiritual things.

At the seminary in Natal, we had him come to share his life with students. He was always a blessing. He was not a bragger, not "polished," not sophisticated, but a very humble man. When he spoke, folks would listen, because he was relying on the Lord for what he did and said.

We remember visiting an interior town, where we held outdoor street meetings in order to preach the gospel. On this night, I noticed how Manuel could gather the townspeople around to hear the message. Right there where we chose to have our meeting, was a "red light" district. I saw Manuel enter those houses, and talk to the women, and soon several of them were out in the crowd listening to the gospel being preached. He is the only person I ever knew who could do these kinds of things with such ease and diplomacy and get results. As the meeting progressed, he stood next to these women, and at the invitation he continued witnessing to them about the Lord. What a great man he was! He taught us so much in his simplicity that made a profound impression on our lives. Proverbs 11:30 says, *The fruit of the righteous is a tree of life, And he who wins souls is wise.*

SUNDAY AFTERNOON SAILBOATING

Hang on! Don't think this was a pleasure outing on Sunday afternoon. What we did was very pleasing, but we do not normally go sailing on the Lord's day. Again we were in the city of Macau, the salt capital of Brazil. It was a very schedule-packed day that October 15, 1967. I taught the adult Sunday School class, and our seminarians each had classes. After church we went to the salt works to take pictures, but it was closed. We had our noon meal at Mr. Raimundo's home and enjoyed our time with him, his wife, and family. After that, we walked to the waterfront and boarded a small sailboat that took us to an island. These sailboats are simple, but very valuable as transportation. Because Macau is located on the ocean shore, the wind is always blowing, and what a wonderful way to get around to those island communities. After leaving the sailboat, we walked about six kilometers, or about three and a half miles. We had a good service and then retraced our steps and sailed, reaching our host's house in time to freshen up for the evening service. What a great day that was! In the evening service two people were born again after hearing the gospel preached.

We always rejoiced to be able to preach and give people opportunity to receive Jesus Christ as their personal Saviour. In John 1:12 we have the plain word which says, *But as many as received Him [Jesus] to them He gave the right to become children of God, even to those who believe in His name.* Friend, have you made that decision? If not, do it today.

CHILDREN WHO HAVE NEVER
SEEN A CARNIVAL

❦

The Carnival of Brazil is an annual festival held 40 days before the beginning of Easter, in the days immediately before Lent. It is a very carnal time of the year. Supposedly this is a time in which a person can do all the sinning he wants before he has to "behave" at Lent time, just before Easter. This yearly festival is degrading, and millions from around the world travel to witness it and be part of this very popular event. One year, 4.9 million people were in Rio de Janeiro for Carnival. By the time it is over, hundreds or thousands of horror stories can be told about the degrading of women and the drug and alcohol consumption that have ruined many people. Millions are spent on extremely elaborate costumes, floats, etc., but what goes on "behind the scenes" is a tragic story indeed. With this backdrop of sinful practices, this carnival is something believers in Brazil should avoid.

This is one aspect of life we would rather not have to report. However, the bright side was our alternative to Carnival. When we ministered in Natal, Rio Grande do Norte, Brazil, a Carnival Retreat was planned yearly, not for Christians to have the equivalent of a holy carnival, but simply a Bible-Centered retreat where families could go for wholesome relaxation, Bible messages, studies, and plenty of good old Gospel singing. Because our camp was located on beautiful Lake Bomfin, the attraction was appealing to believers. We were so blessed to have such a place where families could go, avoiding the unbelievable sinfulness of Carnival.

It was refreshing to have families come to our camp retreat telling us their children had never witnessed a Carnival in the big city. What a testimony to the integrity of Christian families endeavoring to direct their children in the ways of the Lord. The Bible gives two dynamic verses about this. One is Ephesians 6:4: ***And you, fathers, do not provoke your children to wrath, but bring them up in the training and admonition of the Lord***. The other in Proverbs 22:6: ***Train up a child in the way he should go, and when he is old he will not depart from it***. We trust you are or have done this with your family.

DON'T STOP ON THE WAY HOME

———— ∞∞ ————

In Northeast Brazil, the waterfront is a busy place. One can look out and see the Jangadas returning from fishing trips. These frail-looking crafts are made with five logs secured as the major part of the sail boat. One wonders how these little boats can make such adventurous trips into the ocean. When fishermen return from their expeditions, the main thing is to sell the fish they caught at sea. We often observed the fishermen at the port of Natal, yelling out their appeal for people to buy their product.

One day our missionary friends in Natal were among those who purchased a choice selection of fish that provided a delicious meal. But they did not have a clue what was in store for them. Before night came, one of their children was in the emergency ward at the hospital with fish poisoning. Several members of the family suffered from this tainted food, but their small son was badly poisoned. We lived next door to them on the mission station, and we could hear their son screaming and crying with extreme pain. The trouble with this particular poisoning was that it lasted for weeks. The boy's grandparents told us that at night their grandson would use a metal comb to scrape his body and feet. His feet seemed to suffer most, and a comb would bring some relief to his aching and itching body.

In the hot sun one can imagine how fast these delicate pieces of meat decayed. About the same time as the fish poisoning incident, we were reading information from the States about preserving fresh food. Among the information were special words about fish. The article stated that when buying fish one should leave the scene where it was purchased and head directly home. It strongly urged readers not to stop anywhere but go home as soon as possible and place the meat in the freezer or refrigerator. This would slow down the deterioration greatly. We were actually amazed that we did not hear about more cases of food poisoning while in Natal. But it was a sad experience to see this family suffer so much from an innocent purchase of a very popular and much-desired variety of fish. This is a vivid reminder of how our bodies are the temple of the Holy Spirit as the Apostle Paul told us in I Corinthians 6:19-20. He went on to tell us to honor God with our bodies. He tells us in II Corinthians 4:16, ***Therefore we do not lose heart. Even though our outward man is perishing, yet the inward man is being renewed day by day.*** It behooves us to be alert and take good care of them.

SURPRISE ABOARD SHIP HOPE

―⊶⊷―

The ministry of Operation Mobilisation is known world-wide. One part of their ministry is to send out a ship called *Logos Hope* to take help and hope to the people of the world. They visit many countries to supply literature, train people for life and service, and share the message of hope in God. About a million visitors are welcomed on board every year. Teams from the ship go into communities where they are docked, to give aid and care. They also cooperate with local churches to bring hope to the people to whom they minister. We had heard of *Logos Hope* many times, and then one day it came to Natal. Our town was large with several hospitals, but the particular ministry of this ship was to give medical help to those who could not otherwise afford it. The ship was docked at the Natal port for some time, helping many with medical needs. Something quite unrelated to medical help happened on one of this ship's stops in our town. Our son, Rawlie, studying in Fortaleza, Ceara, Brazil, at the Baptist Mid-Missions Academy, lived in a home run by our mission, A.B.W.E. (Association of Baptists for World Evangelism, Inc.) Fortaleza was about a six or seven-hour trip by a Greyhound-like bus that one of the companies ran in that part of Brazil. We always told Rawlie that he could come home any weekend he wanted to. Often he did on one of these comfortable buses.

One day Rawlie mentioned in a phone call or letter that he would like to have a bicycle to help him get around better where he lived. We knew that bicycles, even though plentiful in our part of Brazil, were expensive and that the right one might not be easiy to find. I have no idea how we got the idea or who suggested it, but we are glad it happened. We went aboard the *Logos Hope*, and to our surprise they actually had a store where different things could be purchased. In looking around, we saw a display of beautiful American-made bicycles. We purchased one sold by Sears and later took it to Fortaleza for our son's use. He was thrilled, and so were we. While shopping aboard this ship, we also found other goodies which were a real treat for us foreigners living in Natal. It was almost like Christmas all over again at the wrong time of the year.

As we pondered this surprise store aboard the ship, we realized that it and the medical help given to thousands of folks was indeed a blessing. We were impressed with God's blessings. Our son's casual remark about having a bicycle and the unexpected arrival of this ship were not a coincidence. We know God directed it all. We realized in a humble manner that our God does supply our needs. ***And my God shall supply all your need according to His riches in glory by Christ Jesus.*** (Philippians 4:19)

DON'T FORGET THE GLUE

I n Natal, we had a radio program called the "Voice of the Bible." ("Voz Da Bíblia" in Portuguese.) We had a contract with Trans World Radio: they broadcast our programs, and in turn we answered the worldwide mail they received written in Portuguese. This was a good arrangement and worked well. Answering all requests required a staff of secretaries, which we had. You can imagine the time involved taking all those letters to the post office and trying to get the correct postage for each country to which it was mailed. This was quite a job, as we had listeners to this program in several parts of the world.

In Brazil in those days, envelopes were not supplied with glue, so you couldn't just lick and seal them. No, the post office had glue dispensers on a separate counter where you could use the little stiff-bristled brush, dip it in the "goop" and seal the envelope. Now this table was usually a mess, with glue smeared all over. It was a messy deal, to say the least. Some people brought their own glue or else used glue at home before mailing the letters. The stamps did not have glue on them either. After having received the correct amount of stamps for each letter, then the gluing job began. It was a chore. For personal letters this job was not so laborious, because we didn't have to send very many. But for the radio department there were scores of letters to mail. At one point in our years in Brazil, the post office started using electronic stamp machines. What a blessing that was! The operator weighed the letter, determined the price of stamps, adjusted the machine, and it actually printed the stamp on the envelope. We were told this was the safest way. Before this new machine came in, sometimes the workers would peel the stamps off the envelopes and make themselves some money by selling them, perhaps at a discounted price.

When receiving a glued letter, as you attempted to open it, often the glue would have glued the letter to the envelope. Trying to free it was a chore. This was an on-going battle. It was very aggravating, but a way in which we had to learn much patience. We did, and we're grateful also for all the mail we received. We are prone to gripe when we have to glue envelopes shut and then try to open others that are stuck tight to the envelope. Maybe we should learn to obey what the Lord tells us in Philippians 2:14: ***Do all things without complaining and disputing.*** It would be refreshing if we all obeyed this verse.

THE CIRCUS GOES TO CHURCH

———⊶⊷———

This is one of those things that "could never happen." Students from our seminary in Natal were always ready to preach in churches all over our state of Rio Grande do Norte, Brazil. On one occasion we were going to Ipanguaçu, about 133 miles interior from Natal. The team was chosen, and we soon were on our way to this little town. We took some students with us, and three others met us there. The latter were from this area and had been doing preparatory work for our arrival. When we got to the church, we showered, had a snack supper, and prepared for the meeting.

Next door to the church, a full-blown circus was in operation. The advanced team members spoke to the authorities in the city to see what could be done about the excess noise that would hinder greatly the meeting that night. To our amazement, the mayor of the city negotiated with the circus owner, and an agreement was made. The mayor kindly requested the circus owner to please suspend the operation of the amusement park for just one hour, from 7:30 to 8:30 that evening.

The circus owner's son came and talked to us. He was a kind person and very understanding. Our team was very pleased when later, after we started the service, the owner's son arrived at the church bringing many from the circus to attend the service. What a kind gesture, and one which you would have to go a long way to match. All those people heard the gospel. I preached that night on "God wants to help you." ***Believe on the Lord Jesus Christ, and you will be saved, you and your household.*** (Acts 16:31) How gracious He is. That night a girl was saved, placing her trust in Jesus Christ for personal salvation. Who knows? That may never have happened if the noise of the circus had been full volume during the service. How we praise the Lord for answered prayer in such a positive way for that service.

From the city of Ipanguaçu, we traveled a few miles to the city of Açu where we ministered on Sunday. There was plenty of excitement on these trips. Sunday afternoon, the daughter and son of the family where we were having our meals borrowed their dad's car (with his permission) for her to do some practice driving. On that practice run, she hit a tree and also an old man, which sent him to the hospital. I don't think she was ready for a driver's license yet. Oh well, we finally made it back to our home base in Natal, rejoicing in the privilege God gave us to preach the Word in churches that weekend.

FIRST OPERATION

———⊗⊗⊗———

Our seminary in Natal was surrounded by a strong and attractive wall. At the main entrance a large decorative iron gate kept everyone inside safe at night. I was usually the person who closed and locked it late at night. This particular night I was having trouble getting it shut so the pin would slide into the buried upright pipe and make it secure. As I applied extra pressure in this process, I felt a quick, sharp pain in my groin. I didn't think much about it and went on my way.

The next day or so, I realized I had strained some muscle or tendon and things were not right in my body. I contacted our doctor, who examined me and concluded I had an inguinal hernia. We scheduled surgery, and Margie and I went to the hospital where my surgery would be done.

I knew Margie was apprehensive because she would be alone. Rawlie was six hours away in high school in the city of Fortaleza. Other missionaries were in town, but I guess when you go through a situation like this, there is a sense in which you are alone. I remember when they gave me an injection to put me in "la la land" preparatory to surgery, I glanced at Margie and saw her shed a tear.

Surgery went well. I had been referred to this surgeon by our friend Dick Matthews, whose father founded the seminary. Dick knew many people in town and chose this doctor because he kept up with the latest medical technology and information. When other doctors perhaps were "out on the town" at night, this man was studying, trying to improve his abilities as a surgeon. I appreciated this greatly.

I was not the best patient. My squeamish stomach made me less than desirable in the recovery room. The nurses even told me about children who were operated on who were doing just fine, and here I was sick as a dog. In Brazil, the doctors and nurses don't like patients to exert energy after an operation by talking, so I kept quiet. This was not hard, because I felt rotten. Then while recovering I got a urinary tract infection and was one sick guy. They put me on coconut water; this God-given medicine healed me, and I soon went home.

Recovery was normal; I managed to get back into action by teaching one of my seminary classes at home instead of going to the classroom. I am so grateful for medical science that enabled me to have this operation in Brazil and not have to return to the States. God directed in it all. People were praying, and we saw the answer, because I healed quickly from this surgery. It is always a blessing to know we can call upon the Lord, as we are reminded by these words in Psalm 50:15: ***Call upon Me in the day of trouble; I will deliver you, and you shall glorify Me.*** How we thank God for answering prayer.

A HUMBLE JANITOR IS REWARDED

Macau was a town we visited several times, ministering on weekends. Sometimes we went alone, and other times seminarians went with us to our Baptist church in this salt-producing town. As you come into town you travel by huge holding areas of briny water. The wind is incessant; it whips the salty water into a foam that is swept up onto the road. The process of producing salt is very interesting, and we enjoyed visiting the plants.

In a windy coastal city such as Macau, the church janitor certainly had her hands full. It is hard to describe how wind drives sand inside the church in never-ending cycles. I used to watch her come in on Sunday afternoons and sweep the church to get it ready for our evening service. She often collected a bucket full of sand that blew in through the cracks in the door and windows, just from our morning service.

Maria, the janitor, shared with me one day her hardships. She was physically disabled and had only one arm with which to sweep and clean. Her other arm was limp and quite useless. She swept sand into a dustpan held by her feet. In those days help from the state for such a person was not a common occurrence. She was grateful for her employment at church, but it was very hard for her to live on such a pittance.

I made a bold challenge to her, asking her to think and pray about sending a letter to the president of Brazil to see if he would help her. On a subsequent visit to her church, she showed me a letter sent by the president of Brazil, stating that she would receive a disability check from that date onward. It was almost too good to be true, but the proof was in the letter. How we praise the Lord for the help this dear lady received. Maria committed this matter to the Lord, and Philippians 4:6 was special to her: ***Be anxious for nothing, but in everything by prayer and supplication, with thanksgiving, let your requests be made known to God.*** I know the Lord honored her faith and that He had given me the idea to suggest she write that important letter.

AN UNFORGETTABLE SPIDER BITE

———— ✑ ————

At Berean Baptist Seminary in Natal, male faculty members took turns monitoring the boys' dormitory. It was my night for this duty, and I went over early to fellowship with the men and stay all night. The fellows calmed down rather quickly, and I was attempting to get to sleep.

About the time I was settling down I felt a heavy mosquito bite on my left foot. I said to myself, "Boy, that was a big one!" That night I was restless, and when morning came I noticed that my left foot was discolored and sore. I left the dormitory, walked home, and showed my wife. By that time it was like the rainbow with all its colors. Margie was concerned because it was evident this was no mosquito bite. She called an army doctor friend who lived across from the seminary in the housing for Brazilian Army officers. By the time he arrived, I was really sick and ebbing quickly into some kind of "nonawareness." I do remember his asking me to squeeze (pump) my hand as he found a vein into which he gave me an IV with medicine. That was about the last thing I remembered him saying before I sort of shut down.

The doctor surmised that I had been bitten by a brown recluse spider or its Brazilian equivalent. Whatever it was, Margie and I will never forget it. This experience taught us several lessons. I was very thankful for my wife, who knew I should have immediate help. We were happy the doctor lived so close. We were glad he actually had the medication with him when he came to our home. And above all, we are thankful to the Lord for friends who pray for missionaries all the time. You *never* know what your missionaries are going through. If they come into your mind, please pray for them, because it is probably the prompting of the Holy Spirit at that moment to urge you to pray. Use the apostle Paul's admonition: **Brethren, pray for us.** (1Thessalonians 5:25)

A NIAGARA OF WATER
IN AN UNWANTED PLACE

⎯⎯⎯∽∘∾⎯⎯⎯

Our home on the seminary campus in Natal was very comfortable. It was ample for our needs, and we enjoyed the convenience of being close to our work. Living right on the coast of Brazil, we had the advantage of constant breezes, and this was delightful. We also had plenty of rain in season.

One night it was raining a lot. We had settled down for the night. Margie checked on our son Rawlie sleeping in his room. She saw water on the floor in his room. Searching with her flashlight, she suddenly noticed, to her horror, that water was coming out of the light fixture on the ceiling near his bed.

She yelled for me to come. I immediately turned off the electricity. Water was coming into the hall. We were not sure of the source, except that it was raining "cats and dogs." I noticed in the hallway that water was coming down the wall from our access door into the attic. When I opened that door a "Niagra" of water fell from the attic and kept falling. I knew we were in deep trouble but had no clue what to do.

In Brazilian houses attic floors are made of cement with plumbing placed on top. I knew if there was a leak in the plumbing, the floor of our attic would conduct water to the place of least resistance, the access door to the attic in our hall. Here's what happened. The rain was so fierce and strong that our roof tiles were not able to withstand the abnormal amount of water. Water poured down into our attic on the cement floor and then into our hallway.

In an instant, about four inches of water covered all the floor spaces of our house. It was an experience we will never forget. We are most thankful that the stream of water pouring from Rawlie's light fixture did not get electrified and charge the entire house with its deadly jolt. Thank you, Lord. The first part of Isaiah 43:2 comes to mind when I think of this incident: ***When you pass through the waters, I will be with you.***

A DOWNPOUR
WITH AMAZING RESULTS

B razilian rainstorms are monumental. Stories abound of the unbelievable amounts of rain that fall in that country. When we lived in the Amazon, we saw rains that lasted for days with lightning that was so constant one could read a book all night. In Natal, Rio Grande do Norte, on the part of Brazil that I call the "hump" (that portion closest to Africa) we witnessed a rain that was unforgettable. The Scriptures quote Jesus as saying, *He sends rain on the just and on the unjust.* (Matthew 5:45) This story takes place in front of our house in Natal. Roads are constructed of granite-like bricks. It may be that the substance from which they are formed is a laterite-type product. At any rate, these heavy rectangular shaped bricks are called in Portuguese *paralelepipedos*. They make a road very durable, and in more recent times serve as a foundation over which asphalt is placed.

When I left our house one morning, it was raining, and I noticed a small hole in the "pavement." I went to another section of town to do some shopping, and when I returned, I saw that this bucket-sized hole was now deep enough to put two

Greyhound buses inside. That is a HOLE. The pounding rains and the incline of the road had caused enough water force to wash out the road. What a mess! We know God sends the rain. We learned to respect this and realize the tremendous power of water.

A DROUGHT YOU CANNOT BELIEVE

Lack of water caused by a very sluggish rainy season can do unbelievable damage to a country's economy. When it doesn't rain, things get very difficult. In northeast Brazil, we witnessed this several times. We have seen deep holes dug in dry river beds in an attempt to get a few drops of moisture to keep cattle alive. It seems in some parts of the world, when it rains it pours, and when it stops raining, things get really DRY.

One of the hardest things we witnessed in Brazil during the dry season was when agriculture suffered so much that people became desperate. Some reached a hunger level so severe that men would band together and raid stores, seeking powdered milk and anything else for food for their children and families. Since the bandits had clubs and arms, the store owners had no choice but to give them what they wanted. Farmers placed two posts at the head of a cow and two at the rear and made slings under their bodies to support them so they would not fall over with malnutrition. You say "Why?" Well, if the animal lay down, it would die. You probably have never heard anything as sad as that. This is the most drastic measure we have ever seen. How sad to see people and animals go through such an ordeal.

In the interior of the state, the heat was unbearable during the dry season, making survival much more difficult. We heard of people eating vegetation that would not be for human consumption in a normal situation but was relied on for survival. During these difficult times, believers prayed often for God to send rain. God's grace was shown them even in the famine. *To deliver their soul from death, And to keep them alive in famine.* (Ps 33:19) Eventually rain came.

DON'T USE THAT TOWEL

—⊷⊶—

All cultures and countries have their own ways of doing things. Therefore this article is not a condemnation or criticism but only an observation of how things were when we lived in Brazil many years ago.

In the early morning, a new clean towel was placed in the public bathrooms. As the day wore on, this towel would be used a lot, and you can imagine what it looked like and what germs it held by the end of the day. In later years, paper towel dispensing machines were used, allowing a far more hygienic drying experience.

Another custom hard to adjust to was practiced mostly in outside restaurants, or sidewalk cafes. The edges of the tablecloth hung over the table about half-way to the diner's lap. In the course of the meal, because there were no napkins provided, people would help themselves to the tablecloth. This same tablecloth was used all day. As hygiene was taught in the schools, over the radio, and later on TV, you can be sure changes were made.

We committed a lot of things to the Lord when we were guests in people's homes, or for that matter, even while eating at a restaurant. Hot water and soap were not a common way to wash dishes in the early days. We prayed a lot before and during meals. I remember once having the most delicious cup of coffee served me in a porcelain cup which had hundreds of minute cracks. I have a vivid imagination and could envision what may be hiding in those micro cracks in the cup that probably hadn't seen much soap. I always knew the good Lord was watching over us as we fellowshipped with people in this way.

To show the unconcern or just plain ignorance of hygiene, one day I saw a girl at a bus stop. She had an umbrella, and for some unknown reason turned it upside down and put the end that had been in the gutter by the bus stop, in her mouth and was sucking it. What a challenge to cleanliness!

The list could go on, but in some aspects the Brazilians taught us things worth noting. When they get a cold, they will not shake hands with you. They will offer you their elbow or arm, and you just do the motions of a handshake. I think this is commendable. They are very careful not to pass their cold on to another person. I wish I had kept a specific journal of all the home remedies they used for different ailments. The Amazon jungles are full of God-given medicine, and some of the people used it to great advantage. There is so much out there in God's creation that man is using right now for medicine. When God set all in motion at Creation, how wonderful it was. ***And God said, Let the earth bring forth grass, the herb yielding seed, and the fruit tree yielding fruit after his kind, whose seed is in itself, upon the earth: and it was so. And the earth brought forth grass, and herb yielding seed after his kind, and the*** *tree yielding fruit, whose seed was in itself, after his kind: and God saw that it was good*. (Genesis 1:11,12) Science is just beginning to tap into some of the riches of the Amazon as far as medicine is concerned.

EMERGENCY TRIP HOME

⸺∞⸺

These frail bodies of ours are prone to setbacks. While ministering in Natal, Brazil, Marge had a routine checkup and discovered a problem the doctor said should be attended to as soon as possible. Because of the nature of the situation, we prayed about it and thought it best to send Margie back to our home in Washington State.

The timing of this was awkward because of my responsibilities at the seminary. I would not let Margie go alone, because leading up to this disclosure she had been getting quite weak and I knew that because of the pressure of plane changes, schedules, and everything related to flying, she was not able to handle it. About this time our dear friend, Agnes Haik, a fellow missionary, offered to accompany her home. This was such a noble and kind gesture that we never have gotten over it. All went well. Margie received the necessary treatment, and after some weeks at home, returned to Natal.

Trips such as this stretch one's faith and trust in the Lord. We were grateful to Agnes, who was willing to lay aside her personal schedule and help in this tangible way. It was comforting to know we belonged to a mission agency that was sympathetic to these emergency trips, knowing full well they were so important. Then our home church, First Baptist in Ferndale, Washington, was such a blessing. For all the years we were missionaries, they faithfully stood with us with solid financial support and prayer. It would have been hard to have made it without them.

We faced several emergency trips home during our years on the field. Each time our faith was tested to know what to do. We were grateful for many who prayed for us as we journeyed through these experiences. But we went with His peace reigning in our hearts, trusting Him for whatever the future held for us. What a comfort I Thessalonians 5:24 is: *He who calls you is faithful, who also will do it.* Each time we learned first hand the truth of Romans 8:28: *And we know that all things work together for good to those who love God, to those who are the called according to His purpose*. The Lord worked it all out. He always does.

SINGING IN THE RAIN

—◦◦◦—

Shower rooms are places where people like to sing, because the close walls make their voices resonate. On the other hand, we have experienced heavy rains in the Amazon which were so strong that singing was almost drowned out in our church. I can remember rainstorms so strong that it was almost impossible to be heard because of the roar.

In Recife, Brazil, a five hour trip from our home in Natal, lived our missionary friends Frank and Doris Jertberg. One day while we were visiting with them, it was raining "cats and dogs." Nearby we could hear a tinny-like voice singing many of the choruses we used in our churches. Soon it was evident that it was a parrot singing all these lovely songs. We were amused by the presentation. Parrots evidently enjoy rain; after all, in the jungle they get a lot of it. Evidently the Jertbergs did a lot of singing in their home, or else this bird attended church services. The parrot took bits and pieces from all our choruses and put them together in its own way. Yes, some songs were sung the way we knew them. But all of a sudden a phrase from an entirely different chorus would be interjected with its proper tune, accompanied by words.

It was quite a show as we listened to a medley of songs by this veteran bird. What a treat to hear this non-human singing songs we knew and words we understood. If rain can make a bird excited, I wonder if we can learn a lesson from this. Some people are gloomy in rainy weather; we know some. How about imitating the spirit of a parrot and learn to sing in the rain or be happy in difficult times? Paul must have been thinking this way when he wrote in Ephesians 5:19, *Speaking to one another in psalms and hymns and spiritual songs, singing and making melody in your heart to the Lord.*

WHAT TIME'S THE WEDDING

---∞∞∞---

Through the years we had many weddings. It was always a delight to talk to young people (and sometimes older ones) who were getting married. No matter where we were, in the jungles or in metropolitan areas, the ceremonies were always nicely done. It is amazing how ingenious the couple, their parents, and their friends were in making the occasion a delightful one. Most weddings were performed in churches. The décor was always beautiful, no matter where it was held. It has been my custom all my years in the ministry to counsel couples prior to marriage. I customarily required a number of sessions prior to the wedding. A biblical approach to marriage was my priority, and all those whom I counseled desired the same. In counseling sessions I gave practical help from God's Word to the couples. I also gave them "homework," and in our sessions we would hear the result of their lessons done at home. It was always revealing and helpful. Under most situations we had a good time preparing the couple for this special time in their lives.

One question I always asked was, When did you want the ceremony to start? The reason for this is based on Brazilian culture, especially in those years when we lived in their country. The common way a ceremony began in those years, was for the bride to delay a long time in getting properly dressed and ready for the service. It was not uncommon at all for the bride to hold up the proceedings by as much as 45 minutes to over an hour. All the guests were seated, waiting for the service to start. Punctuality is not as important to some, so a little waiting was okay. Because I knew weddings rarely started on time, I would seriously ask the couple when they wanted to start. I gave them the option, Brazilian time or American. I never had a couple insist on a Brazilian time for their service. They all wanted to begin on time and proceed normally. I was frankly quite amazed at this response, but I confess I was pleased they wanted to start on time.

I think the Lord is punctual when it comes to His time clock for world events and happenings. I realize this has nothing to do with wedding ceremonies, but it was fun to start on time, and the couples were always pleased I did. God is interested in time. In fact, listen to II Corinthians 6:2: *In an acceptable time I have heard you, and in the day of salvation I have helped you. Behold, now is the accepted time; behold, now is the day of salvatio*n. Friend, God wants you to be saved so you will go to Heaven when you die. You may say you have plenty of time to make that decision, but as far as time is concerned TODAY is the day of salvation. We are not promised TOMORROW. Please receive God's gift of eternal life NOW.

GET USED TO IT

In a new place there are always adjustments one must make to adapt to a new way of living. In the big city we had to get used to the fact that there was no heat in the homes. Of course, we did not have this problem in the jungle. In the jungles, we learned another alarming fact about the weather. Occasionally a strange cold spell came down from the Andes mountains during the rainy season. The Brazilians call it a friagem. Remarkably, it sickens the elderly, and some die at temperatures 70 degrees F. or below. We witnessed these in Benjamin Constant and put a Coleman lantern (which gives off quite a bit of heat with the light), under our table with a tablecloth hanging down to our knees. This was the only way we knew how to keep warm.

Riding on city buses, I had to get used to people staring at my large feet. Most Brazilians are smaller in statue than I, so they haven't seen many tall people. In the Poulson family there was a comical quip that went like this: "All policemen have big feet, but the Poulsons have them beat."

Different species and types of fruit trees were a fascination for us. We were introduced to one species of fruit that actually grows on the trunk and the limbs of the tree. It was most unusual. In the Amazon, we had to get used to "thief bananas" that were edible when green, not yellow. We learned that a certain banana is sliced and deep fried to make delicious banana chips. And we learned that delicious tropical fruit drinks were made from many of the exotic plants we had never seen. They were all very good.

We discovered an intriguing custom in public buildings like a bank. Instead of using a wastebasket, the staff would throw paper bits on the floor. Janitors made the rounds constantly to keep things orderly, but sometimes the floors were pretty well plastered with paper.

At the market it was customary for the clerk to wrap your newly purchased product in regular newspaper or plain paper. We were definitely surprised when the price of filet mignon in Brazil was the same as hamburger.

Another custom we soon discovered is the siesta time in the afternoon. Many stores closed and locked the doors at noon and did not open again until two in the afternoon. It was strange to go downtown and find everything closed with the special roll-down heavy-grated doors shut. This changed through the years as stores realized the lost sales because they were closed. No matter where we parked our car, there were always boys who wanted to watch the car. They would supposedly protect it from intruders. We wondered how much they actually guarded our car, but we gave them some pocket change each time. It was part of the custom.

On one of our first visits to a church, we noticed there were no hymn books. One by one we observed the worshippers holding a very small book like a pocket New Testament. That was the hymnbook, without any musical notes. Each brought his own. If the church provided them, it is possible people could forget and take them home. This eliminated that potential problem.

For their own health reasons, Brazilians do not drink cold water when they have a cold or sore throat. This, according to them, would aggravate the condition. They also avoid hot water on their hands from a hydrant or hose. They firmly believe this will make the recipient susceptible to a cold.

The Apostle Paul learned to adapt to all situations in his lifetime. He was quick to tell the Corinthian church members, *I have become all things to all men, that I might by all means save some.* (I Cor. 9:22) He adapted and was used to all their customs, because he wanted to win them to Christ. What a great motive, and I trust we will all follow his example.

HOW DO I FIX THAT?

———✺———

When you are in a faraway place and need material for a project or a fix-it job, what do you do? Years ago many corner stores in Brazil carried a variety of things besides groceries, gasoline, and kerosene for people's needs. But there is always something you need that the store doesn't stock. What do you do?

A squeaking door or a door handle assembly needed grease and I had none. I came up with the idea of Vaseline or shortening from the kitchen. Believe it or not, it works well. Vegetable or mineral oil takes care of a squeaky hinge when you don't have regular or motor oil. When traveling in our boat, a crucial backup item we always carried with us was sheer pins. When the propeller sheered one of these pins, we could not travel if we didn't have a pin. It was difficult sometimes to find the correct pins, so we had to make them. I used nails covered carefully with metal from a tube of toothpaste. Yes, they used to be metal tubes. It is amazing how well it worked.

Believe it or not, years ago we used fountain pens. Once in a while they would leak ink, and I learned to stop them with Scotch tape. And talking about tape, on one occasion I needed electrical friction tape but had none. To my rescue came surgical adhesive tape. It did a good job.

Walking out in the "jungle" after dark to turn off the diesel electric generator is not a fun chore. After making the trip several times and encountering "things" in the yard that were not desirable, I finally made a remote shut-off. I used nylon cord and actually had to go through a corner of the workshop. I cut a hole through both sides of the shop corner, then placed a plastic pipe in it and put the cord through. It was a long way to the generator in the dark, but I had the "switch" in our bedroom. All I had to do at night was pull it, and the lights went out. How lazy can I get?

On one occasion, working on some battery connections for a radio, I needed wire but had none. I used strips of aluminum foil instead and they did a good job. On and on it goes on the mission field. We learned to improvise. One of my favorite Bible verses is: ***The Lord preserves the simple***. (Psalm 116:6)

INTERESTING FOOD FROM BRAZIL

I have always described myself as a "chow hound." There is practically nothing in the food line that I do not like. When one lives in a different country than the United States, adjustments have to be made with the taste buds and one's general attitude about food. Each culture has its pros and cons about food choices, and I will not even begin to scratch the surface, as it were, with some of the foods we found intriguing in Brazil.

In America most people do not actually see the places where food is processed, so we would not expect them to understand some of these things. For instance, in Brazil it was not unusual to see a person carrying an entire cow's head on his head. This animal had been butchered, and the head would provide soup and other edibles for the recipients. The same applies to other inward parts of the animal that we would never think of using as food sources. But this is because it was part of their culture and it was strange to us.

At certain times of the year in the Amazon, after a heavy rain, a large flying insect invades the rain forests. There are multiplied millions of them. They are a nuisance, because they fly in your face, on your clothing, and everywhere. The amazing part of their arrival is that people knock them out of the air, twist off their abdomens and put them in their mouths. They tell me the taste is something like sweet butter. That one I never tried!

A food that can be rightfully called the national dish of Brazil is feijoada. The root of this word is "beans," and the food is a stew made of beans with beef and pork. Each cook adds to this recipe according to her wishes. It is widely eaten in Brazil and is very popular.

In Rio Grande do Norte we learned a new way to prepare corn which we considered to be very delicious. Unlike cous-cous, which is made from wheat, *cuzcuz*, as it is called in Brazil, is made of corn and steamed into the shape of an inverted soup bowl. Housewives use their own method of making this delicious corn dish. We liked it with milk and a sweetener of some kind. It is eaten along with a meal.

In our work at Benjamin Constant I was introduced to paca meat. A paca is a large burrowing rodent whose meat is very white, tender, and delicious. One of the intrigues of the Amazon area is the variety of wildlife and how some are used for food. The capybara is the largest rodent in the world. Many times we saw them. They can weigh as much as 250 pounds. That is a lot of rat meat. But just like the paca, its meat is delicious.

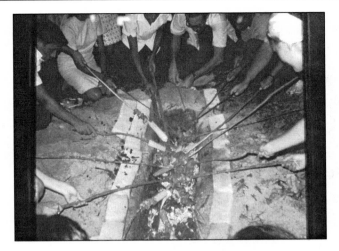

ROASTING CORN OVER THE FIRE

In Northeast Brazil we were introduced to another corn product. It was the ordinary corn cob roasted on charcoal. The difference is that the corn kernels are already pretty hard on the cob. That's when they roast them. The people love them, and eat a lot of it in season.

A vendor came to our door often, banging on a triangle bar to announce his coming. He was selling round, flat, very thin sheets of an edible product similar in taste to ice cream cones. They were very good, and we enjoyed them.

Each week a man cut down three palm trees, removing the very top part where the "unborn" (undeveloped) leaves are located. These palm hearts with a little lemon juice sprinkled on them were our salad throughout the week. Sometimes we put mayonnaise on them. We took a mayonnaise maker to Brazil with us, so we made our own (when we felt ambitious and very hungry for some).

The cassava root, which we enjoyed very much, gave several interesting and practical things for our table. Cassava meal is used at almost every meal. In fact, folks in the upper Amazon area took a half gourd filled with it to their gardens to work for the day; that's all they had to eat. I don't suppose there is much nutrition in it, but it has sustained life. A byproduct of this meal is a starch that when sprinkled into the frying pan would melt and form patties that were edible. The cassava meal, when fried with onion, garlic, and other seasonings, becomes an all-time favorite food to accompany other things on the plate. In the States we order it from Brazilian stores located in America so we could always have some for our meals. It is VERY GOOD. God is so good in supplying food around the world in many different ways. It all comes from His hand of love to us. I think of the words the Apostle Paul wrote to Timothy: ***Command those who are rich in this present age not to be haughty, nor to trust in uncertain riches but in the living God, who gives us richly all things to enjoy.*** (I Timothy 6:17)

A TREE LIKE YOU HAVE NEVER SEEN

———⊰❋⊱———

In the city of Natal in northeast Brazil, we had many marvelous sights to enjoy and treats for our tastebuds. One of those was the cashew tree. Cashews are very popular, as we all know. Some do not know that the fruit is also delicious. Eaten raw, the aromatic flavor is captivating. Wine, vinegar, jam, jellies, and a tropical refreshing drink are all made from this magic fruit. This is the only fruit that I call "the fruit with the built in handle." That's right, the nut grows on the outside of the fruit, attached to it like a handle. When cashew nuts are processed, the natural juice between the nut and fruit is caustic, and workers must use great caution. When they roast the nut, the same caution must be taken, because the smoke can injure a person's eyes. The extra caution needed to make the nuts ready for the market is why this food is expensive.

CASHEW TREE, FRUIT & NUT

Near Natal, the little city of Parnamirim boasts the largest cashew tree in the world. The accompanying picture shows the fruit and the nut. The tree from which it comes, covers an area of some 90,000 square feet. It is over 100 years old and continues to grow. The heavy branches droop to the ground and take root and keep growing. We have walked among the branches of this enormous tree. It is hard to describe with words. Many large buildings could be covered by the space this tree occupies. This one tree produces more than 2.5 tons of fruit every season. When God created things, the trees were part of it as we read in Genesis 1:29. ***And God said, "See, I have given you every herb that yields seed which is on the face of all the earth, and every tree whose fruit yields seed; to you it shall be for food.***

IN EVERYTHING GIVE THANKS

~∞~

Brazilians are outspoken in their remarks and outgoing in their personalities. A phrase from their Portuguese language is "Graças a Deus" which means "Thanks to God." We noticed their use of this phrase continually. It was good for us to hear, because it helped us remember that we too should thank God for everything.

To our surprise, we discovered that Brazilians love to have thanksgiving services in their homes on many occasions. Once we were asked to come to Pedro's house for a thanksgiving service, because he had suffered a long time with a terrific toothache but was finally over it. To show gratitude, he invited the church to his home to give thanks to the Lord for stopping the toothache. How meaningful this was! In our sophistication, I suppose we would have trouble announcing such a service to the church. But this was an ordinary thing for Brazilians, and many attended these services, even nonbelievers.

You might ask for what other reasons do they have thanksgiving services? Well you name it, and they will have a service. Birthdays rank high on the list. Finding employment would certainly qualify one for calling a meeting. If a relative had been ill but was now recovering, another service would be in order. A safe trip to visit family members demanded a word of thanks. Church-related matters were also a favorite of the folks. When the church got painted, they wanted to have a thanksgiving service. When a new addition was completed, they wanted to have a meeting. In other words, these folks did not mind having church or many home services. In America we would probably complain about so many meetings. Many churches today are doing away with prayer meetings and Sunday evening services. I guess we are not known for going to church very much. In Psalm 122:1, King David said, ***I was glad when they said unto me, Let us go into the house of the LORD.*** So whether in a church building or at home, we learn from our Brazilian believers that they enjoy going to church. They definitely are thankful for the things that happen in their lives. May we be like them!

FLEEING FROM THE FLEAS

—∞∞∞—

When we first went to Brazil, we lived for a time in the south, where we studied the Portuguese language. We attended church each Sunday in a section of town near our home. Our newborn son, Rawlie, rode in a baby buggy, which we pushed to church. It was about a thirty-five minute walk from our home to the Baptist church. We always enjoyed the walk, and on arriving at church we chose an aisle seat so the buggy would sit next to us facing the pulpit. Rawlie would sit and watch our good friend Art Cavey preach. We were learning the language, and it was good for us to mix with the folks at church and listen to a veteran missionary speak Portuguese.

After the church services, we noticed that something in our bed was bothering us when we tried to sleep. One night, after getting bitten or stung by something, I ripped open the bed covers, and to our amazement, tiny black fleas were jumping all around in the sheets and out of the bed. This was a new experience for us, and so we consulted with seasoned missionaries who lived there trying to find out what we could do to cut down this nuisance. Our colleagues were quick to tell us that in the colder weather of southern Brazil, people at church exchange these critters as they fly from one body to the next looking for a warm place to live and propagate. We really had fun with that. Finally, we found the right treatment to cut down on the flea population. Then we took other precautions both at church and at home to deal with the situation.

Later on in another part of Brazil, Margie had to learn how to handle lice in Joy's hair. These critters like to hitch-hike, and it is a process to get rid of this plague of minute creatures that invade one's body and hair. There were many other lessons we learned through the years on how to treat certain insect bites, not the least of which was mosquitoes. There were also chiggers, *pium* (a very small and irritating insect that people had to use mosquito nets to protect themselves from while eating), and many others. This is all part of missionary life, something we had to get used to. Many folks in southern states have similar challenges. All these critters are doubtless the nuisance which is part of the Fall, like thorns. We had to learn to cope with the inconveniences they gave us. The main thing is that we were in Brazil to serve the Lord, and we were grateful for that opportunity despite the uncomfortable spots along the line. ***Serve the LORD with gladness; Come before His presence with singing.*** (Psalm 100:2)

"GORJETA"

⸺∞⸺

On entering Brazil, we soon discovered the prevalence of the idea of thanking folks with a tip. It starts with the little boys who appoint themselves to watch your car when you park it anywhere. You don't have to ask them; they will invade you with the proclamation that they are going to take care of your vehicle while you are away. We did not find this obnoxious. If you give a few coins or paper money to them, they are usually quite content. We know that at the restaurant, tipping is normal in every country. In the larger city, Natal, where we lived for ten years, we learned an interesting part of tipping. At the seminary, the city garbage disposal trucks came weekly to haul away the waste. That goes on all year. But when Christmas arrives, the drivers and helpers on the garbage truck will make a determined visit to the folks in charge and ask for a tip in the Portuguese language.

Almost any money transaction where goods are purchased requires a tip. I discovered something quite interesting about this, even in America. For a certain service we receive, I decided to give a yearly Christmas gift. You cannot believe the fine service we get in return for that gesture. We read, *The*

laborer is worthy of his wages. (I Timothy 5: 18) This may be especially written about those in Christian service, but the principle applies to others as well. At least that is our opinion. It worked in Brazil, and it is working in America.

I AM JUST A HAMMOCK

—— ∞∞ ——

Of the many items a Brazilian owns, a hammock rates pretty high on the list, at least during the years we were there. I would call it a Brazilian bedroll. We were interested to see how this clever sleeping gear was made. In the Amazon, where our mission work began years ago, most of the hammocks were handmade using fiber from the chambira palm. The Ticuna Indian men harvested the leaves from this tree, and the women took over and did the rest. They stripped the tender, almost transparent underside of the leaves. After processing it, whether by letting it dry a little or whatever they did, the women took two or three strands of fiber and rolled them across their thighs. This was how twine was made. It is uniform in size, and they cleverly kept adding pieces to it and rolled them into the standard twine.

This twine was very strong. We brought some home when we returned from Brazil. I believe it is the strongest twine made. It is amazing that every inch of it is handmade. It is truly a God-given product that Ticuna Indians have perfected. The hammocks are made by forming very small squares with the twine, tied in such a way as to make them elastic-like. When a person is in the hammock, the material gives so they can actually lie crosswise in it. Many things are made from the twine, but we are talking about hammocks in this article. Hammocks are so handy because they can be set up and taken down easily. In their homes, if ample room is at a premium, which it often is, hammocks are collapsed and left hanging by one end, leaving more space in the house. When we traveled through Brazil, we were amazed at how many hammock hooks we saw in motels and hotels. I am sure there are fewer now than before, because hotels get their revenue by selling beds for the night. If you had a hammock, it would not be cost effective for the hotel owners. When you visit in a home, there always seems to be room to put up another hammock.

Many homes are constructed with hammocks in mind, and sufficient hooks are made right into the walls. Some are just regular hooks sticking out, and others are neatly embedded in the wall. When I made a survey trip by boat, it was quite a sight to see the dormitory section of the boat. Hammocks were everywhere, and sometimes they were three deep like bunk beds, in order to accommodate the passengers. These were normally tied to upright poles in the boat or sometimes horizontal ones on either side of the space.

How do you sleep in a hammock? I believe it is an art, learning how to properly place your body in one. You soon learn that you sleep crosswise or sideways in a hammock. That way it is flatter and becomes very comfortable. The hammocks made from these palm fibers are small in size but strong.

Hammocks come in different sizes for adults and children. They are easy to carry and fit in a small space. I believe the raw materials and skill to make hammocks were a wonderful gift from the Lord to people who years ago did not have the space for or money to buy beds for their families. God indeed takes care of us. ***For so He gives His beloved slee***p. (Psalm 127:2)

THAT'S A CHANGE

Paying bills in Brazil in our early days as missionaries was very interesting, to say the least. Through the years Brazil changed their currency. It happened a few times in our twenty-four years of service. Paper bills and coins were part of the change we had to get used to it. The rate of exchange differs in a country according to the American dollar. We finally learned that and got accustomed to using Brazilian money. For some reason, and perhaps because there was not a huge volume of coins available in Brazil, change was difficult at times. On many transactions we would hand them the equivalent of five dollars and get the proper change. But this was not always the case. Sometimes we felt it would be better to take our checkbook and pay for everything with a check. But then some of the store vendors did not even have a bank account, and for them to try to cash a check would be an inconvenience.

One day I was paying our electric bill and got the surprise of my life. I gave a larger denomination Brazilian bill to the clerk. I waited and waited, and finally she handed me the change. Here is the surprise. Mingled in with some Brazilian coins I saw something made of paper. I examined it and discovered several Brazilian postal stamps, used for mailing letters. They were of different denominations. The best of all was a ticket for a ride on the streetcar that ran in our city of Campinas. As I counted the amount of the coins, stamps, and street car passes, I was sure it was the correct change, but certainly in a different form than I had expected. This concept of giving stamps and tickets as change would be the rule of thumb for commerce in many places for the rest of our years in Brazil. What difference does it make, we reasoned. And I believe that is right. The main thing is honesty. ***Honest weights and scales are the LORD'S; All the weights in the bag are His work.*** (Proverbs 16:11) What a great reminder to be honest in all our dealings.

SIGN LANGUAGE

⸺◦◦◦⸺

I know what you are thinking. You think we had a ministry to the deaf in Brazil. No, we did not do this work, but we had friends who were involved in it. Our sign language title expresses another look into missionary life on the field. In Washington State, before going to Brazil, I did a lot of different things. I painted pictures on some of the business shop windows in Ferndale, Washington, at Thanksgiving and Christmas time. I have always been interested in art work and did some when we lived in Phoenix, Arizona. My distant relatives on my grandmother's side were artists in England. Maybe some of their genes got mixed up with mine and thus the interest. At any rate, we discovered in Brazil that there were multitudes of opportunities for me to use my God-given sign painting ability. I give the Lord all the credit for any gift in this line. During our years in Brazil from the Amazon to Natal, I was able to paint signs for just about everything you could imagine. In the jungles, I lettered and designed wedding certificates and made baptismal documents with special pens using different styles of lettering. When we arrived in Natal and worked in the seminary, I painted endless signs for many events.

I also taught our students to paint. There were "tricks to the trade" I taught them, such as using an overhead projector to enlarge letters to enormous sizes for special evangelistic announcements. These would be mounted on buildings. For all special occasions at the seminary: graduation, Christmas, Thanksgiving, and Easter, there were endless signs to paint. I used my lettering ability to make special graduation diplomas and a host of other items that hand printed jobs demanded. It was all very enjoyable and a part of our ministry through the years. In later years, at home in the States, my computer took the place of pen and ink, paint brush and paint. But as we go through our journals of our years in Brazil, I am amazed at how often I mentioned that I was using sign language for one thing or another. Many signs we painted were Scripture verses. We read this: ***Preach the word! Be ready in season and out of season. Convince, rebuke, exhort, with all long-suffering and teaching.*** (II Timothy 4:2) Through the medium of sign painting we were preaching God's Word. What a joy to think of those who read the signs and responded to God's message.

NICKNAMES

———∞———

I have often said that there is no one who can give a nickname like a Brazilian. All the years we lived in Brazil, I never learned what my nickname was. But this one thing I know, I had one. They just never told me. We learned this trait from them, and we had nicknames for different people, also. Nicknaming people is part of the national culture in Brazil. Any reliable history of goings-on there will tell you this. Take for instance the famous soccer player whose name was Pelé. His real name was Edison Arantes do Nascimento. If a person is small, they use the diminutive form to describe him, like Joãozinho for João (John). For children they often use the diminuitive form, as it would express endearment. They are great on shortening names like Eduardo (Edward) to Dudu. José (Joe) is often made into Zé. If a person is short he could be called Baixinho. If he is a little on the hefty side, his nickname may be Gordinho. On and on it goes.

These nicknames can be invented. For instance, one of our Seminary female teachers always wore long dresses. As she walked down the sidewalk, her dress was very close to the surface of the walk. The Brazilians nicknamed her Vassoura ("broom"). This was because as her dress swished back and forth it reminded them of a broom sweeping the walk. They are so clever.

In the Amazon we knew a man whose nickname was Perna Seca (dry leg), because he walked with a limp and it appeared the lame side of his trousers was almost empty. They also give nicknames appropriate to one's personality. A friend of ours in Santa Rita was called Camel Breath. That name may have been given by the Brazilians or missionaries, I cannot remember. Our excellent furniture maker in Natal was called Eight and a half Fingers (he lost the others due to an electric saw accident).

Brazilians are apt to name a person based on which state in Brazil he or she came from. A man from the state of Bahia would be called Baiano. Maria is a very popular girl's name in Brazil, doubtless because of the biblical Mary. A family we encountered on one of our trips had several daughters, and each was named Maria. How did their parents differentiate between them? They used numbers, by saying, "Number 1, come here and carry the wood." We knew they had at least eight Marias, because in one of our classes one was named Maria Oitava (the Eighth). In Margie's children's class, there were many girls named Maria. Most of them used their middle name, which was a good idea.

Our neighbors in Benjamin Constant had twin boys named Davi (David). They did the same thing. They identified them as Davi number 1 and Davi number 2 – the latter being the younger twin. A man who worked for us was sometimes called

Speedy even though his name was Antonio (Anthony). He was slow in his walking and talking; and thus the nickname.

Through the years we had quite a list of people with nicknames: Purple, Finger, Beanpole, Bulgy, Puffed Rice, Lupy, Sweet, Help, Gypsy, Milk, Spit Wad, Prophet, Sea Ribs, Ur, Shorty, Xote, Toothpick, Eraser. Behind each name is a story of how that name was given. I am so glad the Lord knows us by name. And for the believers in Christ, He says this: ***To him the doorkeeper opens, and the sheep hear his voice; and he calls his own sheep by name and leads them out. (John 10:3)*** Does He know YOUR name because you belong to Him?

MENSAGEM DE GRAÇA

The title of this story translated to English means "message of grace." But in Portuguese, the language of Brazil, it means something different. It still means that the message does not cost anything. But in our dealings with school children and also the seminarians, they said I gave little bits of irony, pointed lessons, or even a preaching point to people with whom I was speaking. If a person was late for something, a mensagem de graça was given them. It is also translated "free message." In other words it didn't cost them anything for me to tell them this. Therein lies the irony. They usually did not forget the lesson. One day a very dear helper of mine was late and missed a ride, which resulted in a pretty heavy headache for him and the need to find another way to get home. He got a free message.

When a student failed to label correctly all the parts of a lock he was lubricating for my desk drawer, some extra parts were left over. He got a "free message" about being more careful the next time. I caught a seminarian sleeping when he should have been awake on the job. He got a free message. One student did not attend church one Sunday and used an exaggerated excuse why he wasn't there. When this came to my attention, you can be sure he got a *mensagem de graça.* The Brazilians have a colloquial saying to describe someone like me who gives these free messages. They say he is *terrivel,* meaning "terrible." The word "terrible" here does not mean they think I am not a good person, but it is used by them to describe my particular quaint way of using sarcasm and giving them a lesson they will not forget. I often thought as I gave *mensagens de graça* that I would do well to heed the apostle Paul's command in Colossians 4:6, **Let your speech be always with grace, seasoned with salt, that you may know how you ought to answer every man.** I hope and pray that was the way I did it, and I wish the same for you.

SOME MORE BRAZILIAN HOSPITALITY

A visitor to Brazil soon learns the openness and warmth of the people. Of course there are exceptions to every rule, but it is noteworthy to see the marvelous way these folks are considerate of visitors and their own fellow countrymen. Early on we were impressed with the warm and fun-loving ways of the people we came to minister to. We understood they had much to teach us. We hoped we could communicate to them some things we brought, mainly the gospel of our Lord and Saviour Jesus Christ.

When a guest enters a Brazilian home, the hosts usually say *"A casa é nossa"* ("Our house is yours"). What a beautiful way to extend hospitality! We noticed on the Amazon River that a traveler who had motor trouble with his boat could pull up to any house and be welcomed. What a rare and special characteristic that is!

Brazilians seem to have more time to be friendly than we do. Many of their homes opened right onto the sidewalk, and any place we went, there were chairs on the sidewalk. In the cool of the evening, visitation that took place from these front door chairs was amazing. What a culture of friendliness!

Brazilians are specialists in giving greetings. We in our quick, hurry-up American styles, would meet someone and enter into a heavy-duty conversation, only to be greeted, when we finally calmed down, with *"Bom-dia"* ("good day or morning"). You see, in our American haste, we had not taken time to greet the person. I was rebuked (silently) many times until I finally learned to say "good morning" (or afternoon or evening) to a friend with whom I was speaking. I learned that if I did not greet the person first, I could talk all day, but when I finally stopped, they would give a greeting. I sometimes wondered if maybe they didn't even listen to what I said until I had acknowledged them with the proper greeting. I don't blame them for this. I should have learned my lesson. Thankfully I did, and from then on things went smoothly.

At language school in Campinas, São Paulo, we learned that the official greeting in Brazil is the handshake. In many parts of Brazil, not only do you shake hands, but you also give an *abraço*—a light embrace or just a light pat on each other's back. In many places it is proper to kiss one cheek, and then the other. In some places when people first meet, they will kiss three times, alternating right and left cheeks. This can also be done with men and women. Often, the sound (light smacking) of a kiss is used rather than an actual kiss.

Like all cultures, Brazilians do a lot of talking with their hands. A thumbs up is a common sign when things are going well. Grabbing the earlobe with the thumb and index finger indicates "delicious." Some gestures with the hands and fingers are the same as we have in America.

A visitor to Brazil needs to learn the meaning of these and many other gestures. The proper use of them is important to the Brazilians. The Apostle Paul touches on this somewhat when he said *I have become all things to all men, that I might by all means save some.* (I Corinthians 9:22) We must use wisely the customs and lessons learned from others, so we will be effective servants in bringing the good news of the gospel to them.

JUST A CRANK

———⟨∞⟩———

We were called to mission service in 1956. These were the days before copy macines and computers were standard equipment in offices. Even though there were plenty of resources available to missionaries, there was still much that had to be done by hand as we ministered in churches and schools. One of the great machines that helped us was the mimeograph. The ingenious ways people thought of to produce mass amounts of printed material were a great blessing to our work. We watched the evolution of these machines through the years and tried to keep up with the best ones so we could do our work well. The machines we used, for the most part, were hand-cranked. I was privileged to be a "crank" missionary. I trust however that I was not cranky.

RAWLIE AT THE OFFSET MACHINE

It would be impossible to list all the things we did with the mimeograph machine. For children's work, we produced picture sheets for the kids to color. We printed all sorts of Bible-oriented study guides. We sent our periodic newsletters, all reproduced on these machines. Through the years we developed methods to make all sorts of invitations, wedding certificates, baptism certificates, and a myriad of other items that helped us in the work. When we moved to the larger city of Natal, it became apparent we would use this machine even more. We printed special class material for many subjects we taught, plus a doctrinal work book. For some time we printed entire Bible courses. This happened when there were not many things in Portuguese, so we had to do them ourselves. In the large city we made yearly visits to the cemeteries on All Saints Day and on other important times. When people visited cemeteries to honor their loved ones, it was customary for the churches to conduct a gospel service right in the cemetery among the tombs. At first we printed a stack of gospel tracts on our machine, which helped so much. Then I discovered a way to put two stacks of tracts together and prepare the stencil for our mimeograph to print the address and other information on two sets at one time. That saved us hours of hand stamping, which would have been a laborious task. Before, that's the way we had to do it. Then later we used a hand-cranked machine and printed out 100,000 tracts in much less time. What a blessing to have such modern technology at our disposal. As time went on, electric powered machines took the place of hand-cranked ones. What a break! Offset took the place of the mimeograph. That was the ultimate in modern help for us, and we appreciated it so much.

We thank God for these machines that helped us in our evangelism and Bible study ministry. I often wondered if Americans realized what a wealth of material we have compared to the limited amount found in some areas of the world. We were using gospel literature to reach people with the message of the Bible. *For the word of God is living and powerful, and sharper than any two-edged sword, piercing even to the division of soul and spirit, and of joints and marrow, and is a discerner of the thoughts and intents of the heart.* (Hebrews 4:12) What a joy to be able to distribute this literature and acquaint people with God's message.

FUMIGATING

———∞∞∞———

Attending language school in Campinas, São Paulo, Brazil, was an experience long to be remembered. Along with learning how to speak Portuguese, there were other important things we learned. We lived in a home in a nice section of town. We were in this home a short time and we knew before too long we were going to move next door to a much nicer place. The house we were going to rent was occupied by a missionary nurse and her family. We were happy when we were finally able to move into it after this family had finished their language school.

The move was simple, because we just had to take our belongings next door. After getting settled into our new home, it was about time for language school to start. We soon noticed an unusual number of roaches in our new home. We had known the nurse, whose home we took over before she and her family left the language school. One day she had shown Margie around her kitchen. To Margie's dismay, she noticed that food was left uncovered in the cupboards, including butter. When we moved into this house, we soon were aware that the place was infested with roaches. All kinds of roaches, big, small, different colors, flying, etc., were living in the house. It was obvious we had to do something, or life was going to be miserable and unhealthy in this very nice house. We inquired around as to the best solution for ridding our home of this infestation. Roach bombs were the best remedy we could find. On the appropriate day, we set these bombs in all the strategic areas of our house. Any exposed food was well stored away and safe from the overwhelming smoke produced by these bombs. We three, Margie, our infant son Rawlie, and I, had to vacate the home for several hours while the killer smoke was doing its thing.

When the coast was clear, we reentered the house to see the results. Well, we were shocked to see scores of roaches dead or in the process of dying in the hallways, kitchen, and in almost every room of the house. The smoke from the bombs had penetrated every inch of the place. We had placed roach bombs in emptied cupboards, in storage areas, and in open rooms as well. They certainly did do their work. To clean every-thing again was quite a job. All the dishes and everything else had to be washed. We did not want that poisonous residue to remain on things that we would be handling. We learned the lesson that we cannot be too careful when it comes to handling food items in your home. The roaches lurk on every hand to take advantage of every place you have been careless. What a spiritual lesson this brings us, as well. ***Be sober, be vigilant; because your adversary the devil walks about like a roaring lion, seeking whom he may devour.*** (I Peter 5:8) How good it is for us to be prepared and alert.

DRIVING IN THE DARK

—⊶⊷—

B razilians do not use their headlights at night, because they think the existing light is sufficient for them. You and I would not be able to drive in that kind of light, but these folks are used to it and do it. Some would tell you that using your headlights means wearing the battery out or even ruining it. Driving this way is a personal thing that you have to experience to appreciate. You are traveling along in the dark, and the cars around you are passing without their lights on. Strangely enough, I believe that statistics would indicate that despite this unorthodox way of driving, there are not many accidents. It is a miracle.

Driving in Brazil is a challenge. Most drivers desire to be first, and they drive accordingly. On highways with more than one lane, most ignore the painted lines. Many drive over the lines to maintain the advantage of moving into one or the other lanes at an instant's notice. It is quite amazing to witness this vying for first place on the highway. Weaving in and out becomes an art, and they do it with perfection.

A little known weapon of motorists is the horn. I do believe that most motorists in Brazil think the horn is more important than the steering wheel or brake. It also seems to have preference over any traffic rules that exist. When the horn blows, the driver expects results, even though the expected result seldom comes. Driving in tense situations is like attending an opera in which the performers are car horns. Can you imagine the unbelievable cacophony of horns? Innumerable times I have witnessed a person crossing the road with busy traffic buzzing by. The horns blast away, but the person scarcely knows what is happening and walks in his own world to the other side of the busy roadway. May we use the words of the Apostle Paul and apply them to motorists today? I know that the verse means much more for the believer than this, but we will apply it here to motorists. ***See then then that you walk, (drive) circumspectly, not as fools but as wise.*** (Ephesians 5:15)

DELICIOUS BRAZILIAN FRUIT AND VEGETABLES

⎯⎯⎯ ❧❧❧ ⎯⎯⎯

To describe the fruit and vegetables of Brazil would fill a book. I wish I could remember more of them and be able to tell about each one. I chose a few to mention in this story. A favorite nut for some is the cashew. It is a tasty nut, but don't forget that the fruit from which it comes is also delicious. The process of getting the nut to stores is complicated. The cashew nut is the only one I am aware of that grows on the outside of the fruit A caustic substance between the nut and the fruit makes the process of marketing the item involved, but we enjoy the finished product very much.

Papayas are very good and are good for you. Several varieties grow, but we enjoyed most those with red meat. In southern Brazil we were fascinated with the **jabuticaba** fruit, which is about the size of a large grape and grows right on the trunk and limbs of the tree. It is quite a sight to behold. **Guava** is a well-beloved fruit in Brazil. The pulp is smooth, sweet, and extremely aromatic. God must give Brazilian children special stomachs, because they eat an amazing amount of unripe guavas without apparently suffering at all. **Pupunha**

fruit, which is bright red on the outside and brilliant yellow inside, is a tasty food either eaten as a dessert or prepared like potatoes for a regular meal. It grows on a certain variety of palm tree. **Pineapples** grow easily in Brazil, and we were intrigued with the large variety, which is certainly enough for a good-size family.

The graviola is an aromatic fruit, very delicious, and some make ice cream from the fruit pulp. It is indeed a treat. The **pitomba** is a smaller fruit about the same color as an apricot, and interestingly enough, with the same flavor. We have all heard much about the **açaí** associated with weight loss, anti-aging, and other useful purposes. This berry grows on a palm tree. The berries can be made into a refreshing drink. If left too long however, the contents ferment and can cause extreme gastronomical problems. We have had to rush people to the hospital to have their stomachs emptied. The açaí tree produces palm hearts also, which are a luxurious but necessary salad where few vegetables grew. The **chayote,** or "xuxu,"as we called in Brazil, could be cooked or eaten as a salad. It looks like a green pear. We were glad to have it. No one told us the roots and leaves of the plant could also be eaten, or we would have taken advantage of that. I believe the missionaries used this vegetable like green peppers and stuffed them.

The **maçaranduba,** a green fruit, is egg-shaped with soft white pulp. The tree produces a marvelous wood from the Brazilian redwood family. The **buriti** comes from a palm tree. The fruit and the tree produce things that are valuable: jam, juice, and ice cream are made from it, and the locals make a wine from its sap. There is much medicinal value in this tree. Even the sap can be drunk directly. The **Passion fruit** was always a welcomed "guest" in our house. This aromatic sweet fruit made delicious refreshing drinks which we appreciated in the hot weather. We called it **"maracaju."**

Guaraná may be one of the most popular fruits in Brazil. About the size of coffee, it also has a high concentration of caffeine. One of the most beloved soft drinks is made from this and is marketed in soda cans and bottles. In some parts of Brazil where they harvest and process this plant, we are told that early in the morning you can hear people grinding or grating the dried processed bars of this fruit in order to brew it into a drink. **Cacao** fruit grows directly on the trunk of trees like the jabuticaba. Chocolate is made from it. Vanilla beans grow there also, and some Indian women wear the bean pods as hair pieces. The aroma is delightful.

The **star apple** is a crisp, partly green transparent composition which makes a delightful tropical drink. **Tamarind** grew in our backyard in Natal. The fruit hangs in clusters like a pea pod. You can eat the fruit fresh, and it is used commercially to make candy, sauces, and Worcestershire sauce. **Jaca** (jackfruit) is a large fruit that grows on a very large tree. Believe it or not, its taste is similar to a tart banana and bubble gum. Another fruit that grew in our backyard was called **achiote,** known as the lipstick tree. It is used to color rice, and the Indians use it for body paint.

The **mango** fruit (which I label "the fruit with the built in dental floss") is perhaps the fruit most eaten in all Brazil. Not all varieties have this dental floss characteristic, but most of the Brazilian varieties do, I believe. It grows on huge trees, and no matter how the people mangle the branches trying to harvest some of the fruit for their empty stomachs, the tree seems to thrive. We always considered it God's special gift to many in Brazil who would go hungry without this special fruit.

Sugar apple was Margie's favorite fruit. I wish we could get it here. It tasted like sugary sweet custard. Many more fruits are available in Brazil, but we will not mention any more. We are truly impressed how God has sprinkled down on this earth so many plants that are edible. He is so good to us. Have you thanked Him for this blessing? This verse comes to mind when I think of God's goodness to us: *In the middle of its street, and on either side of the river, was the tree of life, which bore twelve fruits, each tree yielding its fruit every month. The leaves of the tree were for the healing of the nations*. (Revelation 22:2) The New Jerusalem prepared for God's people at a future time is really something to look forward to. Are you pepared for that day? You can, by trusting Jesus Christ as your personal Savior. Please do it today.

FIRST IMPRESSIONS

—◈—

V isitors to foreign countries are usually shocked, bewildered, and delighted at what they see, hear, smell, and learn. Sometimes these reactions are sudden, but some take time to etch their impressions into our lives. By no means do these first impressions cast reflections on other cultures. Each one grows up in his surroundings, and lifestyles are ingrained into us automatically. Naturally when we encounter habits and ways of life different from our own, we have a reaction. We must remember that things that may shock us are normal to the people we are visiting. They would be shocked if they visited us. Please remember that these were the customs of the folks a long time ago when we first went to Brazil. We are sure many things have changed now.

When Margie needed wax paper for a cooking project, I finally found some at the paper store. In those days it was the only place we could buy it. It came in large sheets. One day I complained to our milkman that there was sand on the inside bottom of the milk bottle. He retorted by saying, "That's okay it's pasteurized." He was right about that.

When we moved into our first house in Natal, we were wondering why so many people were in our neighborhood and why all the activity in our streets. We soon learned that *feiras* (street markets) are held in different sections of town. They close the streets to vehicles, and vendors set up stands and sell all sorts of things. It was a wonderful place to buy food for our family. Days of the week are numbered, so Monday was *Segunda-Feira* – the second day of the week street market. Each day it was in a different section of town. People knew by the day's name, in what part of town a street market would take place. The markets were very nice, and the prices were right. In Brazil, bargaining is part of the culture so merchants expect us to hassle about the price. In the end, they and we are satisfied, and that is the main thing. Life in a foreign country can be intriguing, to say the least. How interesting to think that all those wonderful people we dealt with day by day were people for whom Christ died. What a privilege we had of being there to tell them the story of Jesus. The story of Jesus is: ***For God so loved the world that He gave His only begotten Son, that whoever believes in Him should not perish but have everlasting life***. (John 3:16)

BRAZILIAN HOSPITALITY AND KIND WAYS

———— ✖✖✖ ————

T he people of Brazil taught us many powerful lessons. When it comes to hospitality, I believe they excel. If a person needed a temporary place to stay, he was welcome, even if he or she was not known by the host family. On one trip up an Amazon tributary, we were doing evangelistic-medical work, and what impressed me was how friendly the people were. Their hospitality was exemplary. In humble homes, we were always treated as guests of honor. One important part of hospitality in the upper Amazon region was serving coffee. The people in that part of Brazil offered coffee to guests on their arrival and again as they departed. Can you imagine how much coffee we drank in a two-week period? Every cup was delicious.

Brazilians love to visit. I believe this was one way the Lord opened a door for us to talk to people about the Lord. Their openness was an advantage in reaching them with the gospel.

It was refreshing to see what a giving spirit they demonstrated. Brazilians know how to share, and when someone was in need, they came forward with all kinds of innovative ways to help.

One dear retired schoolteacher who lived in an old folks home in Natal, insisted on giving part of her very meager pension to our son Rawlie when he was studying in college in Oregon. We had never seen anything like this.

A man took personal interest in my problem with arranging a quick flight back to the States when Margie was ill. He took charge, flew to the government agency to get proper papers, and then returned with the permission. Friends like this are never forgotten, and there was nothing we could do to repay his kindness. He did it out of the goodness of his heart. We were humbled. The Bible has a good word about friends: ***A man who has friends must himself be friendly, But there is a friend who sticks closer than a brother.*** (Proverbs 18:24) We thank God for the many lessons these dear people have taught us. And we are thankfulful for Jesus, who is the greatest Friend one can have.

A COLD MOTEL

────

When our son graduated from high school in Brazil, we took him on a sightseeing trip as a graduation gift. Leaving Natal, where we lived, we headed south to the state of Bahia.

In those days in Brazil, motels did not have a good reputation. They were thought of more as red-light districts than as accommodations for tourists. As our second day of travel was entering the afternoon period, we were pensive about where we would spend the night. Coming from Rio Grande Do Norte in the north and traveling southward, we also were experiencing climate changes. The temperature was much cooler, and we were not used to this.

Motels and hotels were few and far between, and when we viewed one, I stopped immediately and asked if there was a vacancy. Fortunately, there was, and there were no signs of undesirable activities around, so we decided to stay. The surprise of our lives awaited us when we entered the apartment. It was so COLD, that it is hard to believe the shock we received. These places were not equipped with heaters, and

I doubt if this luxury ever entered the minds of the owners. It was sickeningly cold. What were we going to do?

I had an idea that was so far out that I hesitate to write about it, but here it is. I sent Margie and Rawlie back to the car. I entered the apartment, went into the shower room and turned on the hot water full blast. I opened the bathroom and bedroom doors and went back out to the car. After quite a while, we reentered the motel. Now the weather had changed, and it was foggy. But it was WARM inside. I told the family to quickly get ready for bed and get in bed. And that's our story of the first night on the road in cold weather. I do not recommend this type of heating system, but we were desperate. It was very cold, and the Lord gave me wisdom how to get by that one without getting sick. ***If any of you lacks wisdom, let him ask of God, who gives to all liberally and without reproach, and it will be given to him.*** (James 1:5)

HURRY UP

———— ◦∞◦ ————

Rawlie's graduation trip took us around parts of Brazil we hadn't seen, and to one or two other countries. We purchased a used Chevrolet Opala car and had some body work done, making it more comfortable for travel. With a new paint job and a good motor, we started our 8,000-kilometer trip around Brazil. Imagine taking an active teenager, used to soccer and all the fun things kids do, and putting him in the back seat of a car. Mom and Dad were in the front seat, and the back seat was all his.

Understandably, this sort of travel can be boring to kids. It became something we laughed about for years to come. It seemed that about every minute (give or take) Rawlie would yell out "Hurry Up!" In other words, he was anxious for us to stop the driving and get out and DO something. As our son looks back on those days, he is grateful for the privilege of seeing so much of the country where he was born. (He was born in São Paulo in 1957.)

On a very rainy day on this trip, we were traveling along the highway and all of a sudden Rawlie yelled out, "Dad the rear floorboard is full of water!" We stopped, I opened the back door, and sure enough, the wells of the floorboard were filled with water. We removed the new floor mats and discovered some widely spaced very small drilled holes (for what – we do not know) on both sides of the floor wells. Water was flying from the fast-turning wheels and was driven right up through those holes into the car. We made a temporary fix until we got caulking compound and fixed the problem.

Oh the joy of traveling, but we won't forget our son's "Hurry Up!" I guess we and our son needed the scriptural advice of Hebrews 10: 36, ***For you have need of endurance (patience) so that after you have done the will of God, you may receive the promise***. We could all use another dose of this.

CHA MATE IN URUGUAY

—◦◦◦—

As we got nearer the southern border of Brazil, we planned on visiting some neighboring countries as well. Like in America, Brazil has contrasting climates, scenes, and beauties to behold. In Uruguay, we traveled across the flatlands for great distances. All we saw were distant rolling hills, and the landscape was mostly bushes along the highway.

One thing became very noticeable as we penetrated more deeply into this country. Besides the plain landscape, we began to pick up the odor of something that was quite significant. We could smell something that seemed to be the aroma of tea. But how could we smell tea so far away from any apparent town or even houses? We learned later that this whole area was known for its *cha matte*. This is a variety of tea which, according to the naturalists, contains the highest amounts of caffeine known in the plant kingdom. This product is available in health food stores in the States.

This *cha* (tea) is a favorite drink in many places of Brazil as well as in Uruguay. Even the barber shops in Natal used to serve cold *cha matte* on ice to its customers. Hot *cha matte* is served in a container made of a gourd placed in a very nice stainless steel framework.

CHIMARRÃO – GOURD AND STRAW

During a social time in homes or at the end of a meal, this gourd is passed around for each person to take a drink through a stainless steel straw which has a built-in filter at the end to strain out tea leaves. A concern for many outsiders to this custom is one of hygiene. How can I suck boiling hot water through a straw that everyone else has sucked on? Some things we just have to leave with the Lord. I figured that the tea was so hot that it would kill most germs that may be present on

414

that straw. For those who are curious, the name of this unusual Brazilian teapot is *chimarrão*. When we participated in the drinking of the cha mate, I guess the only thing we thought about that we should be courteous guests by accepting what was offered us so we would not be offensive. God's Word does give us direction about the general attitude which should be ours: ***Therefore, whether you eat or drink, or whatever you do, do all to the glory of God.*** (I Corinthians 10:31)

SUGAR LOAF MOUNTAIN

Margie and I had ridden the cable car to the top of spectacular Sugar Loaf Mountain in Rio de Janeiro several years prior to the incident I am telling now. It was an impressive trip to the top of the 1299 foot mountain. The view was awesome, though swaying hundreds of feet over the water and land is not for everyone. In those days, which was a long time ago, I could not help but notice the frayed cable and somewhat rusty looking exterior of this car to which we entrusted our lives. But at least we had fond memories of the scenery from this vantage point where we could see Rio de Janeiro in all its splendor.

When we took our trip with Rawlie before he entered college in the States, Rawlie wanted to visit Sugar Loaf Mountain. Inside I breathed heavily and nervously tried to talk our son into maybe choosing some other place to visit. But he was certain: he really wanted to visit Sugar Loaf. I decided not to put a wet blanket on his wishes. As I had visions of cables breaking under the weight of the car and its passengers, I prodded myself into practicing what I preached: Just trust the Lord. I also reasoned that the cable probably was not as bad as I had previously evaluated it. And it is certainly a fact that the authorities who own and run the operation were not expecting a major accident. Maintenance was a high priority on this run. We purchased tickets for the ascent. The first leg of the journey takes you to the top of a smaller mountain, and from there you ascend Sugar Loaf Mountain.

The breathtaking view we will never forget. I took as many pictures as I could in the time allotted us. We purchased a few slides, in case mine didn't turn out. Then we made our way to the cable car for the descent. We will never forget that excursion and the great lesson the Lord taught us of just trusting Him. Solomon outlines it so wonderfully in Proverbs 3:5-6, ***Trust in the Lord with all your heart, and lean not to your own understanding; in all your ways acknowledge Him, and He shall direct your paths.*** Yes, He will even do this for you on a cable car ride.

A NEW HOTEL

—⊶⊷—

Finding an adequate place to spend the night was one of our greatest concerns on our trip around southern Brazil and the adjoining countries. This was before the era of cell phones and GPS units, so we had to rely on "seek-and-find" opportunities.

Traveling by day was always enjoyable. We were driving in country we had never seen before and likely never would again. We were happy that our son Rawlie could have these experiences, as well.

One afternoon we started rather early looking for a place to spend the night. We located a beautiful hotel and dared go in and bargain a good price for the night's stay. The facility was brand new, the rooms were perfect, and all was appealing except the price. With reluctance and a bit of sadness we exited the building and went to our car. As we sat there in the parking lot contemplating what we should do, all of a sudden a distinguished looking gentleman came running toward our car. I feared we had left something at the check-in desk.

I rolled the car window down and was amazed to learn that it was the owner of the hotel. He was there to offer us his services at a much lower price than we had been given moments before. How could we refuse? We were welcomed with open arms and shown a wonderful room, and we made ourselves comfortable for the night.

The next morning we participated in what became to us one of the best meals of the day as we traveled. Brazilian breakfast is hard to beat. We were treated to the famous Brazilian drink called *abacatada*. This is avocado mixed with milk and sweetened to taste. It is delicious. Needless to say, Brazilian *café da manhã* (morning coffee) is beyond description. Strong, hot coffee is served in one container and hot milk in another. One pours from each to the color intensity desired, which also determines the strength of the coffee. What a treat! Then one chooses from the breads, cakes, fruit, and other goodies that accompany the meal. It all makes for a delightful way to start the day while traveling. In the New Testament, Paul told Philemon that he needed a place to stay. ***But, meanwhile, also prepare a guest room for me, for I trust that through your prayers I shall be granted to you.*** (Philemon 1:22) We prayed every day for a hotel or motel and God granted our request each time.

ARMOR MEAT COMPANY

—⊸∞⊸—

As we continued to travel with our son Rawlie, we reached the southern part of the country. The never-ending question was again about where we were going to spend the night. Somewhere, somehow, we had heard that we might check into places like the Armor Meat company. I cautiously went into the office and posed the question, thinking they would laugh at me for asking about overnight lodging. I was delightfully surprised when they said there was a place for us and that we could also eat there. Wow! We never expected a meal included with the price of lodging.

The rooms were comfortable, and there was ample room for Rawlie to have his own place. After we got settled in, we received a call for the evening meal. We sat at a nicely deco-rated table with all the appearances of fine hotel décor. The selection of food was beyond our fondest imaginations. Just about anything our hearts desired was served, it seemed. The dessert menu was scrumptious. And our very favorite finishing touch of *cafezinho* (demitasse coffee cups) made our evening a night to remember.

We wondered why or how they could supply us with such a grand meal without even knowing we were coming. We were the only ones present at this feast. The answer they gave was amazing. The hostess explained that breakfast, lunch, and dinner are always prepared. We asked why. She said they prepare the best food there is, because at any moment the owners may arrive, and they want to be prepared. Wow, what a spiritual lesson! The Bible tells us: ***Therefore you also be ready, for the Son of Man is coming at an hour you do not expect.*** **(Matthew 24:44)** We believe that some day, unannounced, Jesus is coming, and believers are ready to meet Him. I wonder if YOU are ready? Have you personally received Jesus Christ as your Savior? If not, do it now.

A TRIP WE WILL NEVER FORGET

Leaving Brazil for furlough in the United States is not without its hitches. Everything involved in packing is important because we didn't want to forget anything. We had done all that, and our flight to Miami was rather uneventful. We did have plans, however, for purchasing a car and driving across country. We wanted to visit Ralph's parents in Phoenix and then go on to Ferndale, Washington, which would be our home on furlough with Margie's parents.

In Miami we contacted a "Drive Out" company that enables people to drive to their desired vacation spot, enjoy their stay, and then fly back home. This provided transportation for us to get to our mission (ABWE) headquarters in Pennsylvania by paying only for gas.

Rawlie and I boarded a bus that took us to the general area where we were to pick up the car. First problem: the city bus on which we were traveling had quite a few passengers and two apparent gang members (rivals) began some pretty heavy-duty verbal fighting. I told Rawlie that it seemed best for us to get off the bus, which we did. Then we had to walk a long distance to our desired destination. We were to pick up the car at a very swank place with strictly guarded security. We finally made it to the posh apartment of the car owner. We gave him our credentials, he gave us instructions on where to deliver the car, and we were soon on our way.

All this happened before the cell phone age, so my dear wife Margie was at the airport waiting in the terminal, guarding all our baggage. To go to the bathroom was almost impossible. If we left our belongings for even a second, they would be taken. I wish I had thought of that before leaving the airport. But something happened which complicated this event greatly. As Rawlie and I were getting on to one of the main roads coming from Key West, I noticed a few drops of rain on the car windshield. In moments there were more, and it was a real rainstorm. You would think Floridians had never seen rain before. They all rushed to the Interstate. We were stuck in solid traffic without being able to move. It was very bad. This tied us up for hours. We arrived at the airport, parked the car, and raced to Margie, who had no clue where we were and why it had taken so long. She was sobbing heavily. I felt terrible and will never forget it. She realized, after we told our story, there was nothing we could have done to remedy the situation or get there sooner. We packed the car and headed for a more pleasant scene Walt–Disney World. Our son was delighted with that visit. From there we drove to Philadelphia to return the car. It is amazing how the Lord led us all the way when we trusted in Him. There is still much more for us to learn. ***Commit your way to the LORD, Trust also in Him, And He shall bring it to pass***. (Psalm 37:5)

DRIVING AWAY A BEAUTY

W e noticed that the drop-off point for the car was actually a car dealership in the Philadephia area. After checking in the vehicle and after we had settled everything, the manager asked us what we would be doing next. I explained to him we were missionaries and had just arrived from a term of service in Brazil. We were now on our way home to the West Coast where our families lived. I told him we were going to buy a car and head west. He said, smilingly, we sell cars here and perhaps we can help you. He stepped to the microphone and announced to his sales crew that Mr. Poulson was looking for a car to drive west. He also said to find him the best one he could and to give him a good price. "He is a missionary and we want to treat him well."

We were introduced to the salesperson and started looking at available cars in our price range. When the range was out of our possibility, he would lower it to our ability. This went on for several cars and finally we picked one that suited us. We needed a car with plenty of space for luggage and future use on deputation. He again brought the price down and we bought the car and were off for our trip home. We praised the Lord for the wonderful way He opened this door, making it possible for us to get a very good car at a wonderful price. The most thrilling part of the story is this: the man whose car we drove from Florida to Philadelphia was the owner of the company where we purchased the car. How gracious was the Lord's dealing with us. His ways are always perfect. His timing is always the best. The Lord is so good. We praise the Lord for this provision of a car to use while home in America. *As for God, His way is perfect; The word of the LORD is proven; He is a shield to all who trust in Him.* (Psalm 18:30)

NATAL BARBER SHOP

W hen we first arrived in Natal, one of my searches was for a barber shop. I actually tried several. Some were pretty sophisticated, serving ice cold cha matte to its customers. But I finally found a little "hole in the wall" shop in the old part of Natal, and for some reason it appealed to me. There was only room for a chair and the barber, plus a shelf that supported a five gallon can with a faucet soldered into it. Eduardo, the owner, used this for washing his hands and instruments from time to time. It was quite quaint. He would fill this can each day from a neighboring store's faucet.

Eduardo was a soft-spoken man. I enjoyed visiting with him as he told me about his family and friends. I was satisfied with my haircut, and Margie was also. I can remember haircuts in the Amazon where you could part your hair any place and it would somehow come out okay. I never quite figured out how they did that. As Eduardo and I became better acquainted, I invited him to our evening church services at Hope Baptist in the section of town called "City of Hope." To our delight, he started attending. He was always nicely dressed in a black suit, white shirt and black tie. He was hard of hearing, so he sat very close to the front so he could hear me. Of course not many had trouble hearing "loud mouth" (me) as I preached. My conviction was that if they came to hear me preach, I wanted to be sure that they could hear me. It was always that way. I also realized I was a foreigner and perhaps my pronunciation of Portuguese words may have been difficult for some, but I worked hard on making myself understood.

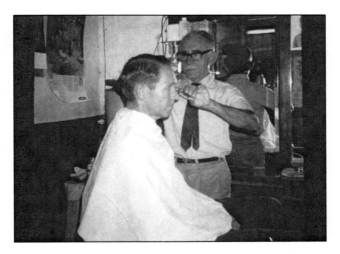

EDUARDO, THE BARBER

I would look out and see dear Eduardo, with his hand cupped behind his ear, listening intently to the gospel message. We were so happy the night he responded to the gospel invitation and received Jesus Christ as his personal Savior. What joy we had on subsequent visits to his place for haircuts, to be able to have fellowship with this dear man. He faithfully attended our church each Sunday evening. Now, years after leaving Brazil, we have flashbacks of our days there and wish we could visit that quaint little barber shop and have a chat with Eduardo.

What a joy it will be to see him in Heaven one day, all because he listened to the voice of the Lord and opened his heart and life to Jesus who said, *I am the way, the truth, and the life, no one comes to the Father except through Me.* (John 14: 6)

HAPPY EVEN ON A CROWDED BUS

---∞---

In Natal, we met a special lady, Rita, who taught us much. Rita attended the City of Hope Baptist Church where we ministered. She had lived in an interior town before she moved to Natal. One day she told about her trip moving to Natal, where the only seating available was on top of the motor housing at the front of the bus. This large encasement over the motor was hot and noisy. It was not comfortable, because there was no back rest, and it was so high that she could not even put her feet on the floor. With her suitcase at her feet, Rita sat there until the journey's end, a total of four hours. She sang most of the way on that trip.

Toward the end of her teaching years, Rita received Jesus Christ as her personal Saviour. She read the Bible avidly and learned the songs and hymns of her church. She lived in an "old folks" home (Senior home) in Natal. This home was nice and neat, and all the ladies were in one large room. Beside the beds were a dresser and lamp for each resident. We picked Rita up here each Sunday and took her to church. She sat in the back seat of our car and sang all the way to church. As we traveled along, she would ask if we were getting closer to church.

RITA, THE HAPPY CHRISTIAN

We assured her we were, and she would say, "Praise the Lord." She was the happiest person we knew. She lived on a meager pension but was very content. We are grateful for this lesson she taught us. Are you content with your lot in life as she was? ***Having food and raiment let us be therewith content.*** (I Timothy 6:8) Rita was a living example of contentment.

THE ROACH THAT GOT AWAY

———⁂———

Roaches of any species are not pleasing. We understand the roach is one of the heartiest insects on planet earth. In Brazil we had many different kinds. But this story takes a different turn than what you might expect.

Every four years we returned to the States for a furlough, a period of reporting to churches, getting physical checkups, resting, relaxing, and visiting family and friends. It was a lot to cram into a year, but that's the way it happened. Sometimes we chose to ship things home as gifts and curios to display in the churches we visited. We packed all these items in a fairly large wooden box and shipped it to Ferndale, Washington.

It was an exciting time for our family the day the box arrived. We brought it into Margie's parents' home and opened it. There on the floor, we explained some of the objects to the Monroes, as we unpacked them. Toward the end of the process, and all of a sudden, I saw a ROACH escape from his "transporting vehicle." He ran like sixty toward the living room wall and in seconds was GONE. We looked everywhere in vain for this dreaded, disgusting insect but did not find it.

With the passing of time, we forgot the roach episode. Much later, our friend Clarence Wemp, carpenter, was doing remodeling in the Monroes' kitchen. His attention was mainly on the kitchen sink and counter. When he removed the splashboard behind the sink against the wall, I stood aghast. There was the refugee roach, now about three inches long, just sitting on the moist surface. When I explained to Clarence what this was, he deftly took his hammer and sent the insect to roach heaven with one blow. Hopefully that was the end of our roach infestation. We never saw any more, so apparently only that one roach made it to America. I wonder how many insects and other creatures are transported to foreign places and survive like that roach. Even the roach has a spiritual lesson. Can you imagine how long that roach lived in that dark, dank place? It reminds me of the words of Jesus in John 3:19, *And this is the condemnation, that light has come into the world, and men loved darkness rather than light, because their deeds were evil.*

AN EVENING COLLISION

———∞∞∞———

Driving in Brazil can be hazardous, especially for a foreigner who is not yet acquainted with all the ways of a new place. Our ministry besides that of teaching at the Seminary was helping Dick Matthews at the City of Hope Regular Baptist Church in the section of town called City of Hope. Margie worked with the ladies and children, and I helped with the adults. We both had cars, because we were coming and going all the time with these two responsibilities. Margie drove a Volkswagen Beetle, or VW Bug, as we referred to them. Being small, they were easy to drive and park and were very practical in the northeastern part of Brazil. A lot of sand is in this area, and this vehicle has a plate of steel running under the motor and drive train which protects it. Another thing that makes the Volkswagen practical in that hot part of Brazil is its air-cooled engine.

One evening at twilight, Margie was making her way to church through a section of town called Alecrim. In those days in Brazil, and maybe still today, people crossed the road at any point all the time. You have to drive with caution because of this. You can sound the horn to alert pedestrians, but they seem to seldom hear the horn and just keep on walking. We laughed many times because it seems drivers use their horns a lot while driving. I think this is the reason pedestrians become insensitive to the sound and don't even hear it.

This evening, Margie was carefully moving along the principal road leading to the church, when all of a sudden, she felt a thud, a semi-violent jerk of the car. Not having a clue of what happened, but fearful a person could be involved, Margie stopped in the middle of the street, unable to move the car forward. She saw an enormous pig, probably as wide as the vehicle, get up, shake itself, and stroll to the other side of the street. Could we say this prompted the famous phrase "road hog"? Margie will never forget the power of this huge pig to stop a vehicle and yet to walk away from the scene apparently unharmed. Fortunately, Margie was also unharmed. From then on, as she drove, she was extra careful to check for animals crossing the road. You cannot be too careful as you drive in busy neighborhoods with children, adults, and animals crossing the street all the time, wherever they wish. People who drive or act with overconfidence perhaps could benefit from this encouragement and warning from God's Word: ***Therefore let him who thinks he stands take heed lest he fall.*** (I Corinthians 10:12)

A BANDIT'S RIGHT-HAND MAN

———— ∞ ————

We had a rare moment in our ministry in Natal when we worked at the City of Hope Regular Baptist Church with missionaries Dick and Joyce Matthews. Some of the details become vague in my memory, but in one of the gospel services a man named Manuel made a decision for Christ. Dick Matthews may have been preaching that night; I cannot remember. Manuel turned out to be a very colorful figure in Northeast Brazil. He told us he had been one of Lampião's right-hand men who rode into villages, and towns, terrorizing men, women and children. Lampião was a famous bandit in that part of Brazil for many years. He traveled with his small band of about 50 men on horseback, heavily armed. They often stole weapons from the police. Lampião used to attack small cities and farms in seven states, wreaking havoc. Manuel told me Lampião would go to a house and order women to prepare a meal for him and his men. He would force anyone who did not cooperate to drink a glass of water heavily mixed with salt, thus causing them to die.

What a trophy of God's grace that Manuel heard the message of Jesus Christ later in life and trusted Him as his personal

Savior! It was a joy to have him in the services, worshiping the Lord with us. People would gather around Manuel and ask him about his former life. He would tell stories that gave us chill bumps. When you pray for missionaries, you never know what contacts they will make, and who will get saved. Please do not give up. Keep praying for those out on the fields in the world preaching the gospel. In Heaven I am sure we will learn so much about millions who were saved through the faithful preaching of the Word of God. ***Brethren, pray for us.*** (I Thessalonians 5:25)

ANIMALS IN WRONG PLACES

———— ✲ ————

We had some interesting experiences in Brazil with animals in places where we definitely did not want them. One day Margie let out in a blood-curdling yell that I never will forget. I dashed to the bathroom, and there she was. She had walked by our toilet and there at the bottom of it, occupying the entire space, was a huge bat. He was flapping his wings noisily. How did a bat get into our bathroom toilet? It must have been a strange set of circumstances that allowed it to navigate the air vent pipe and somehow get into the system. But the question was this: How am I going to get rid of it? Today we have those wonderful "reachers," – a special tool to help the elderly and others fetch needed things from the floor or shelves. Well, we had none of those good things. So I got an idea. We had a flush toilet, but it was controlled entirely by a large valve which had a fairly large, round handle by which to turn the water on and off. I decided if I opened that thing full force, it may flush the bat into the septic tank. Yes, it worked and we were happy.

A very disgusting and frightening animal in a wrong place is a snake. With the exception of our son crawling under our house and getting close to a venomous snake, we have not experienced any of these in our houses in Brazil. But we heard of a family living in the Amazon who found a poisonous snake curled up on the stomach of their newborn baby. Obviously, it was seeking a warm spot. Thankfully they removed it without incident, but this is scary.

Rats and mice are a nuisance in houses. We were extremely careful to keep all doors properly shut, holes plugged up, and, in our first thatch-roofed home, all cracks in the walls and floors properly caulked.

MOTHER HEN IN BABY BED

I was amused one day while visiting a family to look across the room and see a baby bed nicely draped in a mosquito net. But instead of a baby inside the bed, there was a mother hen, sitting on her eggs. The hen had found this comfortable spot, and the family thought it was great.

Many such stories could be told of animals in wrong places, but we will suffice with these few. Please remember to pray for missionaries as they serve the Lord. The Apostle Paul implored the Thessalonians: ***Brethren, pray for us.*** (I Thessalonians 5:25) Let's do likewise.

CHOICES YOUNG PEOPLE MAKE

The young people in our youth group at City of Hope Regular Baptist Church in Natal, Brazil, were energetic and dedicated and obviously had a mind to serve the Lord. Every missionary and pastor desires to see such activity in his church.

Because of their desire to serve the Lord, they decided to do street evangelism on their own. They organized, chose the ones who would do the public speaking, and all met for prayer and planning. They chose a corner in the barrio where our church was located and gathered together and began singing choruses and hymns.

Brazilians are good at singing, and all are interested in listening. Once a lively song service had drawn people to the meeting, the chosen young people would begin to preach. Do not underestimate the power of dedicated lives. These young people meant business for God and had good results. We were always impressed. Only eternity will reveal the full results of their street ministries, and we laud them for their desire, dedication, and delivery of such a service. Our church was blessed because of these who were out announcing the good news of salvation through personal faith in Jesus Christ.

Churches that produced young people such as these were blessed. Some went on to Bible School, seminary, and higher education to become better equipped to serve the Lord in various capacities both in church and in the workplace. These teenagers who ministered in our church are now in their mid-life years, and we wonder what they are doing. It is interesting that through Facebook and related email programs, we have been able to make contact with several, and it has been a blessing.

We never cease to be amazed how God has blessed us with things we least expected. We served in Brazil for many years, and God's Word is certainly true when it says: ***Do not be deceived, God is not mocked; for whatever a man sows, that he will also reap. . . . . but he who sows to the Spirit will of the Spirit reap everlasting life.*** (Galatians 6:7 & 8b) How thankful we are to hear from seminary students and others who are serving the Lord in Brazil with very encouraging results.

FROM HAMMOCK TO HEAVEN

———⚬⚬⚬———

Brazilians are fun-loving people, very hospitable, and friendly beyond imagination. At our first church in Natal, we heard about Maria, who was ill, so we decided to visit her and get acquainted. She was cordial and listened to us but was not particularly interested in the gospel. She did want us to return and visit her again, showing us that she really might be interested in what we had to say. Many times she listened as we explained God's plan of salvation through personal faith in Jesus Christ, but her long-time roots in occult practices overpowered her and kept her from accepting God's message of hope.

MR. AND MRS. CORIOLANDO

One day when we visited her, I was compelled to repeat what I had said many times before. In a slow and prayerful way, I again explained the clear message of the gospel, how God would save her soul and give her eternal life. If she would be willing to invite Jesus into her life and ask for forgiveness of her sins, she would receive the assurance of a place in heaven when she died. After having prayer with her, I asked if she would like to make this commitment. She said, "I already did as you were praying." What joy to hear her words! Later, she improved slightly and was baptized along with her husband, who had also made that decision. Maria stayed in her hammock most of the time, because she was not well. Then one day she died and went to heaven, where she is now with the Lord. When you die, do you know where you are going? Remember Jesus said, ***I am the way, the truth, and the life. No one comes to the Father except through Me*** (John 14:6)

APRIL FOOL'S JOKE – NOT REALLY!

—◦◦◦—

When Margie became very ill, I accompanied her back to the States. We made the decision that our service in Brazil was ended and we must seek another ministry. Our son Rawlie, who was in the States already, and I then went back to Brazil to close out our missionary career in Brazil, sell off our belongings, and get back to care for Margie. Our immediate goal was to sell off all the things we did not want to ship back to the States. This was a momentous task, but Rawlie and I, and mostly the Lord, accomplished it. Conducting a two-month-long garage sale is a project in itself, and we will never forget it.

In this story I will tell about what happened the day after April Fool's Day. It must have actually started on April 1, because we heard through news reports that a dam had broken and was causing unbelievable damage along the line. Houses and people were swept away by floods. High tension power lines were washed away at their foundations, and things were a mess. By April 2, our town, Natal, was already isolated. All the roads leading to town were washed out, and we experienced a complete power outage. When things like this happen, one of our major concerns is water. It was rationed all over town. We lived in an apartment building on the top floor. We were able to draw several gallons of water before the supply was cut off. Blackout was the name of the game at night. Imagine a city of a million or more in darkness. The next great concern was spoilage. How can a city that has thousands of stores and untold numbers of refrigerators survive a power outage for so many days? When we lived in the Amazon area, we had lanterns and helps for such things because that's the way we lived. But we were not prepared for such a disruption in the big city.

Rawlie and I ate peas and canned sardines. It was not a good situation in which we found ourselves. At night I read my Bible by candlelight, and we were glad when daylight came.

Soon after coming to Natal and our work in the Seminary, Margie and I had purchased a nice chest-type freezer. We had very large containers of three kinds of delicious ice cream stored. I could not think of wasting it. I invited all seminarians who wanted ice cream to come to our apartment and enjoy a feast of something they ordinarily did not get much of. That was a festive time, to be sure.

On a serious note, the local radio and newspapers were sending alerts constantly about the dangers of walking around at night. Obviously, thievery was at a high point during this very opportune time for those in that "profession." Our apartment was less than a block away from the seminary, but our activities and classes kept us at school in the evening. How were we to get home? We decided to walk almost in the middle of the road, and jump off to the side when a vehicle passed us. It worked out well, and we had no negative results. After about six days, the lights came back on, and we were very glad. As Christians we have the Light of the Lord Jesus Christ. We were reminded of Paul's words, ***You are all sons of light and sons of the day. We are neither of the night nor of darkness.*** (1Thessalonians 5:5) What security we have in Jesus, who is the Light of the world! Are you secure in Him?

A HUGE GARAGE SALE

—∞∞∞—

I don't know if garage sales were held in Brazil at the time we had ours, but I do know that ours was a success. We were new at it, and maybe that helped. We went at it rather innocently, and it was an experience we will never forget. We lived in an apartment, off campus. Our office was at the seminary, and we had other things there that were included in the sale. I could not have done it without the help of our son Rawlie. We advertised in the paper and had good phone service, so we did fairly well. Much time was spent looking at catalogs, visiting the local stores, and getting ideas of prices. We did all this before the sale began.

We had approximately 25 years of things to dispose of before packing the essential items and going home. It was quite an undertaking. When we moved to Natal from the Amazon area, we had brought quite a bit from there as well. We had shipped many of our things to Brazil in steel barrels. People wanted to buy these, also. We saved a few for shipping our personal things back to the States. Getting everything marked with prices was an endless job. Some days the phone rang incessantly, and drop-in visitors were endless.

Because we lived in an apartment, we could not conduct the sale out on our town's sidewalk. So people wandered around in our house at will. It was impossible for us to control the traffic. We had to bite our upper lip and just let it happen. It was actually fun to have the sale this way.

One day a seminary student walked into the front room where we had our major display of items, and held up my battery operated razor. He asked me how much it cost. The razor was not for sale, but he had dug it out of a drawer in the bathroom, because he was snooping. Because of this, I put an outlandish price on the razor, and to my surprise he bought it. From then on, items they found by digging through our personal stuff had a really high price tag on them. We had quite a few Christmas ornaments and decorations, and I noticed they were not selling well at all. During our lunch break, I got several plastic bags and randomly placed a mixture of decorations in different bags. I put a price on each one as a complete unit. In the afternoon, all of them were sold, without a problem. Amazing, isn't it? I learned a lesson in marketing that day.

Finally the day came when we had sold everything, including our beds. It was time for Rawlie to stay with a Brazilian family until all our baggage had been sent to Ferndale, Washington. Then I would sleep in the men's dormitory at the seminary. Needless to say, we were filled with nostalgia as we closed the door to our lovely apartment and turned over our keys to the owner. Farewell parties were very touching for us. I dreadfully missed Margie, who was ill at home in the States. Our ministry in Brazil was finished. What a consolation for us to know that God would lead us to our next ministry. He promised it. *Commit your way to the LORD, Trust also in Him, and He shall bring it to pass. He shall bring forth your righteousness as the light, And your justice as the noonday.* (Psalm 37:5-6)

FLANNELGRAPH PICTURES

———— ∞∞∞ ————

Our first years in Brazil were spent in the Amazon jungles. We thoroughly enjoyed our ministry there with John and Paul Schlener and their families and later in Benjamin Constant. Margie prepared for her ministry before we travelled to Brazil. She purchased flannelgraph backgrounds with outline pictures accompanied by many Bible stories. The backgrounds were to be painted to make them more attractive as the Bible stories were given. I was given the task of painting these pieces. They turned out pretty well, and Margie used them for years in the Amazon. She folded them carefully after each use and protected them with moth balls to prevent damage to the cloth. Our children's work in the Amazon benefitted much from these lessons, and only the Lord knows how many boys and girls were reached with the gospel because of them. Also, I wonder how many adults were listening in and were also touched by the messages.

When the Lord called us to Natal, Rio Grande do Norte, Margie again unpacked the flannelgraph pictures and began her lessons. But something was different in northeast Brazil and that we had not planned on. The wind always blows, and it is usually quite strong. The flannelgraph pictures would not stay on the board very well. Margie and the other teachers pinned them to the board, but smaller figures would blow away in the wind. So a new approach to children's classes was adopted, that of using booklets. The teacher turned the pages and told the Bible story. That worked very well.

In 1981, when I had the famous garage sale to dispose of all our goods in Natal, the flannelgraph backgrounds were there also. I frankly wondered how we would get rid of them. I knew they would not work for outdoor Bible classes, and even inside the house, the wind often disrupted the pieces. But I put them on the table and put a price on them. I waited, and nothing happened. Then one day a very well-dressed lady purchased one, and on another day several more were purchased, and before long, they were all gone. We had many of these pictures. They were done in full color, and the one of the Garden of Gethsemane was very attractively done as a night scene. In painting them I used a technique that a painter told me was very good in that the paint did not mat the flannel but penetrated the minute fibers of the cloth. This gave a very attractive finish to the scene. As I have always said, my favorite Scripture verse is, **The LORD preserves the simple; I was brought low, and He saved me.** (Psalm 116:6)

I questioned the ladies about what they intended to do with the pictures. Each of them said they were going to frame them and hang them in their homes. I felt honored that this humble painting by an untaught missionary would someday grace the living rooms of houses in Natal, Rio Grande do Norte. Thank you, Lord, for using the simple things to keep telling Your story.

MARGIE'S MINISTRIES
AND CHALLENGES

———— ❧ ————

When your mate suffers health issues, it is very hard. Margie had plenty of setbacks during our years in Brazil. I never ceased to be amazed how she coped with each situation. I knew the burden of our daughter Joy was always heavy on her heart, mind, and body. I am sure this did not help her general health.

In Benjamin Constant, Margie taught school and helped me in the church. In school she planned the yearly September 7 programs, which commemorated Brazil's Independence Day. These were major undertakings each year, and she did them well. She had the privilege of teaching young people how to sing both solos and in groups. She turned out some beautiful trios, quartets, and duets. It was a huge advantage to our church. She also did plenty of medical work using her abilities learned in the Biola School of Missionary Medicine where she earned her LPN degree in nursing. What a blessing that training was. Her constant care of Joy for the first eight years took its toll on her health, which we are sure led to further problems along the way.

When our daughter Joy was able to move to Shepherds Home in Union Grove, Wisconsin, a huge daily load was lifted from Margie. We were asked by the mission ABWE to consider directing the Berean Baptist Seminary and Institute in Natal after the death of its founder Carl Matthews. We pondered this invitation for two years and then realized God was calling us to serve in that part of Brazil. Fortunately the medical help was more available in Natal, and we could consult with competent doctors concerning Margie's problems. One doctor suggested she have some cysts aspirated. Although this could be done in Brazil in those days, I felt more comfortable with her coming to the States to have this procedure, since she was weak and obviously in need of other medical help. We were grateful for Agnes Haik, a fellow missionary, who willingly accompanied her to a point in the States where she could safely make a connection to our home-town. We always appreciated Agnes's great gift of helps.

On one of our furloughs Margie was very ill, and we consulted with the Virginia Mason Clinic in Seattle, Washington. She went through about every test imaginable but with no clear diagnosis of what was causing her illness. We left for Brazil anyway, because she wanted to keep on serving the Lord. She actually was feeling much better before we left for Brazil, but after four months back on the field, she was back in the same rut again. Even though her days were filled with illness, she kept busy and worked much. She did the book-work for the Seminary for a long time and was zealous in that ministry. We also worked in the City of Hope Regular Baptist

Church, and as usual she was deeply involved in this, including a very active door-to-door visitation ministry besides her work with women and children.

In our pursuit of helping Margie's health concerns, we were told by our ophthalmologist (one of the best in Northeast Brazil) Dr. Raul, about food allergies. This came as a complete surprise. Could this be a possible cause of her continued downward decline?

Margie's nerves and emotions were a concern to us. I decided it best to move off campus, and we found a brand new apartment on the second floor less than a block from the seminary. That was a breath of fresh air to her. Even though we could keep busy at the seminary, she would not have the on-campus pressures that were previously wearing her down.

This continued for quite a long time, and then I noticed the downward trend again. The Lord gave us His peace about terminating our ministry in Brazil and we left in December of 1981. Our first stop was in Phoenix, Arizona, with my folks. I immediately checked all the allergy doctors in Phoenix, by using the yellow pages, and I called EACH one. I was singularly impressed by one doctor whose nurse explained carefully their routine for allergy testing. The next Friday Margie had her first appointment with Dr Herro. He turned out to be our hero under the Lord's leading. After testing and her first medications, my dad could not believe it was Margie out in the front yard raking leaves. She was getting better. This was God's will for us, and eventually we got back to Ferndale, Washington, and our home church, First Baptist. Through the providence of God, our church eventually called me to pastor this church, where we stayed for the next 18 years. And as I write this we are still members there. Because of my age, I resigned as pastor, and almost immediately Shepherds Ministries contacted us regarding the possibility of representing them in eight Western states. God wonderfully opened this door for our next 11 years of ministry, traveling in a fifth wheel trailer and moving each week to a different church where we presented the work of Shepherds Ministries. It was special for us because our daughter had been a resident there since 1967. It was rewarding for us to relate to churches our gratitude for this wonderful home that had been our daughter's for over 40 years.

The Bible tells us: *He who finds a wife finds a good thing, and obtains favor from the LORD.* (Prov.18:22) Surely this has been my heritage for these 59 years from the time of writing this piece.

ASSOCIATION OF BAPTISTS FOR WORLD EVANGELISM

———∽∾∽———

W e didn't know much about the Association of Baptists for World Evangelism, also often referred to as ABWE, until missionary John Schlener introduced us to it. He was looking for missionaries to help them in the Amazon rainforest area where he, his brother, and their wives worked. God used him to call us to that part of the world. When we were accepted we were invited to their candidate class in Philadelphia for a time of orientation. This was a wonderful experience, learning all about the history of ABWE and the fields where they minister. While in the east, our church made it possible for us to visit some of America's historic landmarks. It was a great experience for us and much appreciated. Then we started visiting churches to solicit prayer support. Eventually we saw the Lord bring in our financial support so we could begin our ministry in Brazil. Our home church, First Baptist of Ferndale, Washington, heavily supported us, which was a tremendous help. To make things more interesting, we visited the mission station, the Port of Two Brothers on the Amazon River, before going on to language school in southern Brazil.

That was a very special introduction to our time in Brazil. As I mentioned earlier, in Campinas, São Paulo, Brazil, where we learned Portuguese, was a very good school, and we are grateful for the training there. Our mission emphasized that the Brazilians would appreciate our speaking their language well, so we did our best to do that so that one day we could communicate the gospel adequately. Our son Rawlie was born in São Paulo while we were in language school.

From language school we went to The Port of Two Brothers, where the Schleners worked. It was named after John and Paul Schlener, who pioneered the work there. Our year or more there was very valuable. Then we moved to Benjamin Constant near the border with Peru, and took over the ministry so that missionary Lindsey Harrell could work with the Ticuna Indians. Our daughter Joy was born in Iquitos, Peru, while we were serving in Benjamin Constant.

Eventually we were called to direct the Berean Baptist Seminary in Natal, Rio Grande do Norte, Brazil. We were in this town for about 14 years. Throughout all these years we deeply appreciated the support of ABWE for our ministry. Their patience through the difficult ordeal with our disabled daughter Joy and later several health issues with Margie, was much appreciated. Dr. Commons was the president of the mission when we started, and our concluding years were under Dr. Wendell Kempton. These godly men taught us much, and we are so thankful we had the privilege of working under their leadership. We have only praise to the Lord for this wonderful mission and their gracious help to us in so many ways. All the staff was such a blessing, as were the host of fellow missionaries. As missionaries with this organization we became acquainted with so many others both on our field and in other places around the world. What a great family it was. Our objective with ABWE was twofold: to be engaged in church ministries and to teach in Christian schools. We did not have the privilege to plant a church but worked in organized works and taught school. Jesus' words in Mark 16:15 say it best: *And He said to them, Go into all the world and preach the gospel to every creature.* What a joy for us to have been able to go to Brazil for 25 years and proclaim this message. We pray this is your desire also: to see many people come to a personal knowledge of Jesus Christ.

RAWLIE

———◦❊❀❊◦———

Margie was several months pregnant with Rawlie when we went to Brazil. He was born in São Paulo at the Hospital Americano, while we studied the Portuguese language. Fortunately our doctor was English so we had no problem communicating. We stayed with missionaries a few days and then returned to Campinas where we lived in a rented house while attending language school. The language school was structured so the men studied mornings while the wives cared for the children. Then after lunch the women went to school while the men cared for the children. We had a very capable and talented lady who cleaned house and cooked our main meal, which was at noon. I usually made split pea soup when I made supper. Rawlie was a fussy baby at first, so we consulted with our doctor, traveling by electric train to São Paulo to see him. The doctor said Margie's milk was very weak and suggested she stop nursing and go with a formula. This made him a very happy baby, which was wonderful for him and us. Life in Campinas was great, even though we were very busy between going to school and studying.

Another couple and a single lady from our mission also studied there. We had some great times together on Friday evenings as we had supper together, prayer time, and fellowship. Language school was a very positive experience, although we and our fellow students did make some funny errors during the year of language school. We both studied very hard, and by the time we returned to the Port of Two Brothers in the Amazon, I was starting to preach and teach. We have always been very grateful for our language training and still converse and read Portuguese easily, even though our classes were over 50 years ago.

Rawlie was always a wonderful addition to our family. From a very small child, he kicked around a rag made into a ball or a small store-bought ball, as most young Brazilians did. He really didn't speak Portuguese until we returned to Brazil after a two-year stay in the States where we were getting treatment for our daughter Joy. Rawlie picked up a lot of English while we were home. When we first returned to Brazil, he spoke English to us and to the Brazilians. Then all of a sudden he started speaking Portuguese.

I taught him kindergarten in the same classroom where I was teaching first through fifth grades in Portuguese. After that, Margie took up Rawlie's education until we returned to the States on furlough, where he studied at public school with a wonderful Christian teacher.

In other stories in this book, I have related Rawlie's three narrow escapes with death. God was good to spare him. It was difficult for Rawlie being an only child, as his sister Joy, who was severely developmentally impaired, was cared for in a Christian home in Union Grove, Wisconsin, called Shepherds.

Moving to the city of Natal in Northeast Brazil was a big change for all of us. Rawlie made many new friends and enjoyed playing soccer with the seminary boys. When he finished grade school, he asked if he could go to Fortaleza, Brazil, and the Baptist Mid Missions Academy. He enjoyed classes with other students and also their sports and activities. The separation was very hard on all of us. He lived in one of the mission dorms, and there were many adjustments for him and us. However, he came home often, and he and I had projects we did together. Rawlie was very happy, but we missed him greatly during that time.

I was the graduation speaker for Rawlie's class, and I considered this a wonderful privilege. Before Rawlie graduated we took a trip around Brazil so he could see more of the country of his birth. That was a wonderful time for all. In other stories in this book we have included some of the interesting parts of that trip. While on this trip we also visited Christ the Redeemer statue and Sugar Loaf Mountain. In retrospect, he appreciated this tour around Brazil as well as some of the neighboring countries and will never forget it.

RAWLIE, GINA, BENNY, MONIQUE & NATHAN POULSON

Rawlie attended Corban University for two years when it was called Western Baptist College. We were returning to Brazil, and I had a long talk with him, explaining that he is our priority and that if he had any reservation about our returning to Brazil and leaving him alone in the States, we would seek another ministry and stay here. We would never hold it against him, and we would be completely at peace to stay here and not return to Brazil. We will never forget his answer to me. He said, "As the mother hen kicks her babies out of the nest, that's what I want you to do with me. I will not be bitter while I am at Western Baptist College about your return to Brazil." Of course we did not kick him out, but we appreciated so very much his love for missions and for us, to the point he wanted us to return to Brazil.

At college, Bob Wright, former missionary in Brazil and professor in Missions, along with his wife Rita who worked in the Admissions Office, were a great help to Rawlie. He also enjoyed their children and other missionary children because it was so natural to converse in the Portuguese language.

We have three wonderful grandchildren and a very special daughter-in-law, Gina. We thank God for a wonderful son and his wife and family. We are sure he would say his life is much richer for being raised with these wonderful people, the Brazilians. The Psalmist best expresses our love for our children: ***Behold, children are a heritage from the LORD, The fruit of the womb is a reward.*** (Psalm 127:3)

JOYBELLS

—∞∞—

When we represented Shepherds Ministries on the West Coast for a number of years, we often told our daughter Joy's story. "Joybells" was my special name for her. We sometimes referred to her as our Halloween girl, because she was born in Iquitos, Peru, on October 31, 1959. Joy was a happy baby, but not without difficulties. She would have momentary convulsion-like seizures. We began to notice another red flag signal that alerted us to the fact that we had better have her evaluated by a specialist.

We flew to Bogota, Colombia, where she was checked by a specialist who affirmed she would be developmentally disabled. The wave of emotions that rolled on us was hard to hear. I sent Margie and Joy immediately to the States from Bogota and returned to Brazil with Rawlie. We closed our mission work and soon joined them in our home town of Ferndale, Washington. This started the long process of getting help for Joy.

RAWLIE AND JOY POULSON

After a time in the States, we decided we could return to Brazil and resume our work in that Joy's health seemed to be more stable. One serious problem appeared when Joy had trouble swallowing her food. Each bite of food brought a choking spell so intense that it turned meal time into a very tense time. We even took about two tons of baby food with us for this problem, which did help her greatly. Eventually she outgrew this problem, for which we were so grateful. We were faced with the fact that she would probably never speak and her general mental condition would deteriorate.

On our next trip back to the States to give our report to churches about our ministry, we sought God's will for Joy's future. A kind lady in Phoenix, Arizona, who was a retired schoolteacher, asked me if I would like to attend the national meeting of the General Association of Regular Baptist Churches being held in Winona Lake, Indiana, in the old Billy Sunday Tabernacle. I quickly accepted her free plane ticket and thoroughly enjoyed the conference. While there I perused the display tables at the conference, and one entitled "Shepherds Home and School" caught my attention. I took some literature home with me. Margie and I read with interest that this was a school and home that ministered to children with developmental disabilities. We contacted Shepherds Baptist Ministries and filled out the application papers for Joy.

The medical part of the application followed, and it revealed that Joy tested positive for tuberculosis. By law she had to be admitted to a sanatorium for observation. This was a very definite test of our faith. Joy, young, unable to speak, was there, and we could only see her when we were fully clad with masks, gloves, and robes, in case she had a communicable disease. These were agonizing days, to be sure. One day while I was away on a ministry trip to report to churches about our work in Brazil, Margie called to say the doctors had given Joy a clean bill of health. The false reading of her x-rays was due to her inhaling particles of food during those terrible choking spells.

We praised the Lord that now perhaps she could go to Shepherds. Her care was tearing Margie down physically, and we were so concerned about what to do. Shepherds conditionally accepted her as a resident, and it was a sad but happy day. When I took her to Union Grove, Wisconsin, Dr. Andrew Wood, director, worked with us, and we were so grateful for this help for Joy. Margie physically and emotionally was not able to make the trip by air and car to Shepherds. I took Joy to Seattle, where we stayed the first night with Armond and Helen Daws, longtime friends from Ferndale.

Joy's entrance into Shepherds started a 45-year story, which we could never fully explain. Dr. Wood and his capable staff of teachers, workers, nurses, and doctors, cared for her and other residents with such wonderful, compassionate Christian care. Joy's health issues were innumerable. We figured she had a strong will to live, and she certainly did manifest this in the way she snapped back from every episode. Mastoid surgery revealed the auditory nerves were missing to her ears, resulting in complete deafness. She had two Bell's palsy episodes, which left her face badly twisted. This, along with other abdominal upsets, meant she was in the hospital many times, but each time she came out a fighter. Some of her procedures were serious enough for the staff to ask if we wanted life support for her during surgery. We opted out of that, knowing it would be far better for her, too.

In the early years of her life at Shepherds, Joy was accompanied by a staff person for visits to her grandparents' home in Ferndale, Washington. George and Frances Monroe were dedicated caregivers for her many times. Joy had a particular love for Grandpa Monroe. She adored him, and the feeling was mutual. There came a time when Shepherds made arrangements for the residents to remain on campus during the holidays, so after that, Joy did not travel out to Washington State to be with her grandparents.

When we were missionaries in Brazil, we were home for a year each four years, and we were not able to spend much time there with Joy. We always wondered if she knew us, but the staff assured us she did. Although she never spoke, she had very definite ways of getting her points across. If she wanted something, she would take my hand or arm and move it in the direction of whatever she wanted me to do. She had a way of getting us to the room where luggage was stored and getting us to take her suitcase. She wanted to travel. She had an amazing ability to get others to do what she wanted. We still joke today about it. If Margie asked me to get something, I say laughingly, "Oh you are doing a Joybell on me." Had Joy been able to function normally in doing the things that most people can accomplish, we feel she would have been a "neat-nick." She had a place for everything, and it must be in that spot. I believe in later years she was not as fussy about that detail. At Shepherds on one visit, we took her in the car for a ride, which she really enjoyed. She was in the back seat, and I was driving. Joy kept pushing my arm, and we had no idea what she wanted. Then I finally caught on. I was driving with my left hand on the wheel and my right arm relaxed across my lap. Somehow Joy in her symmetrical "hang-up" insisted that my right hand should also be on the wheel to make things even. As soon as I did this, she no longer tugged at my arm. Mystery resolved. She always amazed us.

Even though she was classified as developmentally dis-abled, and we knew she was, the staff at Shepherds who cared for her would tell me that hidden down deep in Joy was an intelligence that was amazing. We came to agree with them.

As a young child, Joy had an obsession for men's belts. We don't know how this started, but it was part of her for years. Another regular habit she had, enabled by her grandparents, was tearing up half-gallon milk cartons. She would sit by the hours and tear them into small pieces. Somehow she was able to carry the pieces around without dropping one.

To show her love of order, I watched her one day coming out of her bedroom and through her grandparents' kitchen. As she was leaving the kitchen to enter the dining room, the silverware drawer was halfway open. As she walked briskly toward the dining room, without missing a step, she reached out with her right hand and shut that drawer with one push and then kept on going. At Shepherds I was visiting her in the social area of her unit. There was a long low-level shelf on which were kept toys. Joy was on one side, and I was on the other. She put a toy on top for me to put away, because it was time to go to lunch. As I put the toy away, she reached across the shelf and grabbed my arm to indicate I had put it in the wrong place. When I repositioned it in a spot fairly close to me and her, she was content. I don't know how, but she knew where she wanted it.

At Shepherds I remember when she started having problems with walking. She would just slump to the ground and would not walk. An astute staff person, Mr. Cobb, noticed the dilemma and immediately got a walker. He gave it to Joy with a simple lesson on how to use it. Amazingly, Joy learned instantly how to use it. The back set of legs on the walker were padded with tennis balls to make it slide more easily. They told us that Joy wore a set of those out in just a short time. She was now free to walk and could do it without fear of falling. The walker was part of her for the rest of her days.

At Shepherds the residents attended chapel, and those in Unit 8, where Joy lived, also went daily for the service. We are not sure exactly why, but Joy was always the last one in the procession of residents of Unit 8 going to chapel. She was not content to have anyone behind her. Also, Joy was extremely curious. Margie says she takes after me in this. It would take a long time to get to chapel, because Joy would have to gawk into every room along the way.

In November of 2011, we received a communication from the administration at Shepherds that they were now unable to give sufficient care to Joy, so because of her present condition she would have to be discharged. We were shocked but had known this day could come someday. We had signed a special document regarding this years before.

I spent many days calling every facility I could find on the Internet near Shepherds and ALL gave a negative answer. There was no available space, and no funding. During this time, I was counseled to seek help from local agencies geared to help those with developmental disabilities. They were so kind to us, and I applied for help for Joy.

I was rebuked when I had called every facility I knew of in this area where we live and received a negative answer from each one. I finally dialed the last one I "knew" would not take Joy. When the admissions director asked me to fax her Joy's information, I did, and the next morning she called saying Joy was accepted. I cried with Margie as we received this wonderful news.

I braved the storm and asked Ruth Bose, a faithful friend and one who had cared for Joy many years at Shepherds, if she would accompany Joy to her new place in Lynden, Washington. They arrived January 15 in a snowstorm. Ruth Bose stayed extra time to help the staff at Christian Health Care Center know how to communicate better with Joy. We deeply appreciated this.

The following days were enjoyable as we visited with Joy. The nurses at Baker Landing at Christian Health Care Center were so wonderful to Joy. She was a challenge to them, because she could not hear nor speak. Joy needed special medical attention now and then, and they always asked permission from us before pursuing any treatment.

Margie had complete right shoulder replacement surgery and did her rehab at this same facility. We were so pleased with this. We were able to see Joy daily. This was a memorable time, especially when our son Rawlie and his family came on Mothers Day, 2012, and we took pictures of Margie, Rawlie, and Joy together. This was the first time they had been together in this manner in 43 years. Unforgettable! We lamented we were unable to visit Joy much after Margie's discharge from Rehab. I could not leave her alone, and she was just not up to traveling yet.

On July 20, Kara at Christian Health Care Center called and asked permission for the doctor to try some new techniques to minimize what they thought was pain in Joy's shoulder or back. Of course Joy could not indicate to them or communicate any of this information. It was all a guessing game. Kara said she was declining. We understood this. The next morning, Saturday, July 21, I stepped into my office to pick up the phone that was ringing. It was Kara, saying Joy had died during the night. There were no signs of pain, anguish, or anything out of the ordinary. She looked peaceful. All I could say was, "She just said her first word, 'Jesus.'" That was an emotional day as we contacted family and friends with the news of Joy's homegoing. Joy had suffered plenty in her 52 years. She could never tell anyone about her pains. She suffered in silence. What a glorious thought for Margie and me that she was now free from all pain. And her once beautiful face that had been twisted by Bell's palsy, was now beautiful again in the presence of Jesus.

On August 4, 2012, the Joy Poulson Memorial service was conducted at our church in Ferndale, Washington. Rawlie, our son, helped me do the service, for which I am grateful. Thus ends the chapter on our daughter Joy. Little did we know that she would precede us in death, but God's ways are perfect. The next chapter awaits us in heaven. Oh what a day that will be! We are comforted by the words of Scripture when Paul said that: ***We are confident, I say, and willing rather to be absent from the body, and to be present with the Lord.*** (II Corinthians 5:8)

GOODBYE BRAZIL

W hen we worked in Brazil, we never thought about the end of that journey. Margie had health concerns, and together we decided it was best to terminate our ministry in Brazil. This was a hard decision to make. For us it was the end of 24 years in the ministry that meant so much to us.

We advised our leaders at the mission headquarters in America and the local field council. Then we started the laborious job of phasing out. This was harder than moving within Brazil from place to place even though that too was difficult when we were doing it. Rawlie, our son, was graduating from the Fortaleza Academy. I was honored to be the commencement speaker. As we left the airport, most of his classmates flew with us back to the States. Our main concern was to get Margie's health needs cared for. We left Brazil quickly.

FLYING SAUCERS

———❦———

On August 20, 1954, Margie and I were married at First Baptist Church, Ferndale, Washington. Among the scores of gifts received was a gorgeous set of Franciscan Ware Apple dinnerware. Practically anything you could desire was included in this package. As you know, these pieces are very expensive, so we treasure them greatly. By 1957 our plans for mission work in Brazil were pretty well set in concrete. When considering what we would take to Brazil, naturally this prized set was among the items we really wanted to take. I learned from a dear friend whose daughter was a missionary, how to pack delicate items in barrels. With the clothing we were taking to Brazil and any other soft stuff on hand, we carefully got all these delicate pieces into the barrel. How in the world would this barrel survive thousands of miles without a disaster? Well, the dishes made it to Brazil and were safely trans-shipped 2,000 miles up the Amazon River to our temporary home. In that part of Brazil, we used these dishes for about 11 years.

A change in our mission work came in the 60s, and once again these breakable dishes were packed and sent thousands of kilometers to Natal, Rio Grande do Norte, Brazil. Later in this city I became the director of Berean Baptist Seminary. For the next fourteen years these Franciscan Ware dishes were used many times. They were given tender loving care and still survived all kinds of death threats. When I made the decision to terminate our ministry in Brazil, our son Rawlie helped pack all the things we wanted sent to Wahington State. So once again those dishes were packed very carefully, and Rawlie sent them to us in the States. Do you see what I mean by flying saucers? They had three major trips: America to the Amazon, Amazon to Northeast Brazil, and from there back to the place where they started: Washington. Truly they were "flying saucers."

At our home in Ferndale, Margie was unpacking these prized dishes when one slipped, fell, and broke. It was the only piece that did and at this writing we are working on our 59th year of marriage. Isn't the Lord good? He allowed this set of Franciscan Ware to bless us and many others all these years. When Margie and I took our wedding vows, a special verse was used: ***Oh magnify the Lord with me and let us exalt His name together.*** (Psalm 34:3) What a joy to follow this wisdom during our years together Are YOU magnifying the Lord with your life?

BROTHERLY LOVE

Ernest and Annetta Poulson were my parents. My older brother, Ernie, lives in Singapore with his wife, Verda. They are missionaries and have served there over 60 years. It has been a joy to fellowship with them through the years. When Margie and I were missionaries in Brazil, rarely did our furloughs match so we could be together in the States. One interesting furlough was when Rawlie, then seventeen, was introduced to Ernie for the first time. He met him in my parent's apartment in Ferndale, Washington. Imagine how special that first-time encounter was. He finally met his Uncle Ernie. In the early years, letter writing was about the only means of communication. Occasionally a phone call was a special treat. Because of our common work– missionaries—we shared many blessings and concerns related to our ministries. Later, as pastor of First Baptist Church in Ferndale, Washington, Margie and I were given the unbelievable gift of a trip to Singapore. That was a wonderful highlight for us. We saw first-hand the ministries Ernie and Verda were involved in. I was also privileged to return to Singapore for Ernie's eightieth birthday celebration. This trip was sponsored by Ernie's friends in Singapore. What a gift that was! Unfortunately, because I incorrectly read the plane ticket, I missed my flight and also the gala occasion of his celebration. But I did get there and enjoyed a week of fellowship with Ernie, Verda, and Siang, their goddaughter. We will never forget those two trips. Margie and I were privileged also to participate in a Biblical tour of Israel which Ernie had been conducting for many years. What a memorable experience that was! A kind lady in our church, Leona Vaughn, paid my fare for that trip, and Margie's was sponsored by our church and my other brother Harold.

POULSON BROTHERS: HAROLD, ERNIE, & RALPH

So my Singapore brother is 87 years old as I write these lines. What a rich ministry God has given him in that country! With the new era of email and Skype, we often chat and view one another. We have shared prayer concerns and ministry-related discussions often.

Ernie and Verda have always been interested in our ministries in Brazil, as pastor of First Baptist Church, Ferndale,

Washigton, and as Representative for Shepherds Ministries. They have been a tremendous help to us in so many ways, including special gifts to help in time of need. One of those was a truck to pull our fifth-wheel trailer with. We are thankful for Ernie and Verda's years of service to the Lord and the joy that is ours of fellowship with them even though by long-distance.

Ernie is five years older and Harold is ten years younger than me. We three were hardly ever together in our home, due to the age differences. For our adult years, however, we have had constant contact with each other. Harold has been involved in the field of electricity most of his life. He started in Phoenix, Arizona, then later got an assignment in Spokane, Washington. From there he went to Anchorage, Alaska, where he has worked for many years. One might think that it would be boring to hear stories about electricity and all the things Harold does in his work. To the contrary, his projects are fascinating. He is a prolific writer, and when he describes a job, we are all "eyes" as we read the account. When he was nearing retirement, he became part of another company that gives support to companies on special projects involving electricity. From a layman's viewpoint, I would call it very "high tech" stuff he does.

He is so good at what he does, the company brought him out of retirement to solve many of the electrical challenges they face. I know for a fact that he has been asked how he could possibly find such a solution to a serious problem. His answer would be "fifty years of experience." I believe that says it all. Ernie and I are proud of our younger brother and the

God-given gifts he possesses to do what he does. We know that our parents thought the same. They bragged much about Harold's abilities to solve challenging electrical issues. We had very dedicated parents and they were very proud of each of their sons.

Harold and his wife Marlene have been wonderful friends to us. How special have been all the times we have spoken, Skyped and emailed each other. They have been extremely solicitous of Margie's health issues, and on numerous occasions have helped us. When I needed a computer, Harold provided it. Later on, to help Margie with her vision concerns, he provided her with a beautiful iPad which has dictation-mode capabilities for sending emails. In fact, he got one for me too. What generous brothers I have! We are humbled and deeply moved by both of my brothers' kindnesses to us.

Margie and I were privileged to be in Harold and Marlene's home when we were in Anchorage representing Shepherds Home a few years ago. It was so much fun being with them and enjoying some special meals as they entertained us. To put the icing on the cake, Harold was assigned to several projects right here in Ferndale, Washington. Who would have ever imagined that Harold and I could have this time together! It has been years since we have been able to spend this much time together. The Lord is good.

I want to close this by saying how privileged I am to have two brothers that I love dearly and with whom I have fellowship. When I look around and see many dysfunctional families, I am thankful that Ernie, Harold and I are blessed and enjoy each other's fellowship. I am proud of Harold's abilities, and brag about him all the time. I also brag about Ernie's ministries in Singapore as well. We each have important work and God uses us in His own way, no matter what it is. When I think of the wonderful relationship God has given us, I am reminded of this verse in Hebrews 13:1: Let ***brotherly love continue.***

EVERY DAY IS A GIFT FROM GOD

―∞∞∞―

To the title of this chapter, I add one more thought: *"And we don't take anything for granted."* We have adopted these two clauses as our motto.

As we left Brazil, the phrase of the hymn kept reminding us, "All the way my Savior leads me." Thank you, Lord, for 25 wonderful years in that great country. *I will instruct you and teach you in the way you should go; I will guide you with My eye.*(Psalm 32:8) We never dreamed where the road ahead would take us, but the end of the story is very special too. Now at home, I would dedicate my time to getting Margie well.

The Lord graciously opened the ministry at First Baptist church in Ferndale, Washington, where He allowed us to serve for eighteen years. What a joy those years were. I had been a missionary pastor in Brazil for part of our twenty-five years, and in reality had exercised pastoral gifts even as director of the seminary in Natal. The privilege of doing this for all those years in Ferndale, was a blessing we will never forget. We thank the Lord for this gift. We did not *take it for granted* that we would pastor our home church for such a long time, but God was good and allowed us to stay there for many years.

I resigned twice, but the second time we knew it was our time to leave.

God's next gift to us was unexpected. Dr. Wood, founder and former director of the Shepherds Home in Union Grove, Wisconsin, heard we were no longer pastoring in Ferndale. He mentioned this to the president of Shepherds, Dr. William Amstutz. A meeting was arranged in Seattle to discuss the possibility of our being willing to represent Shepherds on the west coast. That was a delightful meeting and resulted in our being hired for this ministry. Again we experienced God's goodness. ***Every day is a gift from God, and we do not take anything for granted.*** We never dreamed of such a service. What a way for Margie and me to thank the Lord and Shepherds for their loving care of our daughter Joy for so many years! We were humbled, honored, and blessed by traveling for eleven years telling churches and individuals about this wonderful home that gives compassionate Christian care to those with developmental difficulties.

In many ways this ministry provided one of the richest and most rewarding phases of our many years serving the Lord. As we were returning to Ferndale from Montana to prepare for our next scheduled trip for Shepherds in California in 2010, Margie's health started to deteriorate even more. I resigned as representative for Shepherds so I could dedicate my time caring for her. The next morning's e-mail advised me that my resignation was not accepted. Shepherds requested that I cancel the California meetings, use my phone and computer to do PR work, thanking churches and individuals for their prayer and financial support. All this plus writing scores of personal letters, occupied the next year right here from our home office. What a gift from the Lord! Shepherds kept us on the payroll for another year. ***Every day is a gift from God, and we do not take anything for granted.***

At seventy-nine, I still wanted to work. I tried some Online business possibilities, but none of them solidified. Margie's health issues were mounting, and I wanted to be at home with her. I thought of helping at our local mortuary like I did when I was pastor, but to leave Margie alone at home was not an option. Her multiple trips to doctors, the calls to 911 for immediate help, and her stays in the hospital were my top priority. Through this we still knew that: ***Every day is a gift from God, and we do not take anything for granted***. Margie's falls, choking spells, and later seizures, alarmed us greatly. This, coupled with depression, and her allergy problems, and failing vision, made us realize more and more our dependence on the Lord to get us through. Because of a multitude of people praying for us, Margie's health improved. It is still fragile, but more stable. More and more our motto means much to us: ***Every day is a gift from God and we do not take anything for granted.***

With Margie's improvement, we were able to do a little more. Occasionally I was asked to preach or teach a class, which I greatly enjoyed. While I was pastor in Ferndale, I started a Bible class at the Ferndale Senior Activity Center and did this for seven years before beginning the Shepherd's ministry. In 2012 we were told the class continued, but there was very small attendance. Because Margie was some better, I offered to help if they so desired. Our first meeting had around twenty-five, and it has remained so during the months. We are grateful for this opportunity to minister.

Writing this book was a challenge. It has been sheer pleasure recounting our years in Brazil. Margie's help has been valuable, because she was the first to read each chapter and give important suggestions. Dr. Roy Zuck gave it the first professional exam. Helen Steele in Athens, Greece, also read it and gave invaluable help. Upon her suggestion we should have another reading, we asked Laurel Hicks from our church here In Ferndale, to give the manuscript some more professional scrutiny, and the final readings. We are so grateful for her years of experience in this field and the help given.

Our prayer is that the chapters of this book will help people trust Jesus Christ as personal Savior, and also give all readers a sense of what life on the mission field is all about. Margie and I are in our senior years. Every day we are reminded of our motto: ***Every day is a gift from God, and we do not take anything for granted.*** I am so thankful to God for the health He gives me to care for Margie, and I am honored to be able to do it. We are indeed grateful for the measure of health given us and the privilege of enjoying our family and friends. We pray that these words of Scripture will be true of our lives as we live for Him until Jesus comes to take us home: ***But the path of the just is like the shining sun, That shines ever brighter unto the perfect day.*** (Proverbs 4:18)

RALPH AND MARGIE POULSON

FRANCIS MONROE, MARGIE & RAWLIE

CONTACTS

**ASSOCIATION OF BAPTISTS FOR WORLD
EVANGELISM (ABWE)**
PO Box 8585, Harrisburg, PA 17105
PH:717.774.7000
www.abwe.org

-O-

SHEPHERDS HOME
1805 15th Avenue, Union Grove, WI 53182-1597
Ph: 262.878.5620
www.shepherdsministries.org

-O-

RALPH & MARGIE POULSON
6079 Summit View Pl, Ferndale, WA 98248
PH: 360.384.0937
rpoulson@Juno.com
www.ralphpoulson.com